Second Edition

Strategic Planning for Smart Leadership

Rethinking Your Organization's Collective Future through a Workbook-Based, Three-Level Model

By William J. Austin, Ed.D.

NEW FORUMS
Stillwater, Oklahoma
U.S.A.

This book may be ordered in bulk quantities at discount from New Forums Press, Inc., P.O. Box 876, Stillwater, OK 74076 [Federal I.D. No. 73 1123239]. Printed in the United States of America.

ISBN 10: 1-58107-152-3

Dedication

for
Lori, William, Miranda & Tristan

you remain the greatest inspiration of my meager life

Table of Contents

Second Edition Acknowledgements

A decade after first putting pen to paper on the original manuscript, strategic planning remains one of the most elusive challenges for most organizations. I have been fortunate in the past six years, since the book was first published, to serve in a CEO capacity where I could put all these ideas to the ultimate test.

To this end, I need to thank all of the Board and community members of Warren County Community College for allowing me the freedom and autonomy to put these ideas to work. In the end, the successes that were reaped went far beyond what I dreamed in my wildest imagination. I need to thank all the faculty and staff of the college as well for having the discipline and faith to put these ideas to the test; you are all winners I have been privileged to serve.

I would also like to thank Barbara Pratt for assisting me in authoring a new Chapter 15 for this edition that will more clearly demonstrate the need for execution in the strategic planning process. Your input, edits and revisions were invaluable. I also need to thank several colleagues from the NJ Community College sector who demonstrated real, candid, and courageous leadership that helped me to demonstrate practices that need to change in higher education. Thank you again, Dr. Robert Messina, Dr. G. Jeremiah Ryan, and Dr. Peter Contini for providing words of encouragement and wisdom to a very frustrated young man.

Thanks again to my family for all the hours lost to these endeavors. Special thanks to Dr. Doug Dollar for again supporting one of my publications and encouraging me to work on this second edition.

Special thanks and recognition is due to the greatest assistant I have ever had. Ms. Christina Kolodzieski was invaluable in re-reading the first edition and assisting me in making changes to this version. Tina, thank you so much for all your support and the time you spent away from your family to help me in my work.

Finally, I would like to offer a special thanks to Monte S. Brooks, former plant manager for M&M Mars, for chairing my college Foundation and allowing me to exit his annual Christmas party early to complete this second edition. Monte is another example of exemplary leadership in action.

First Edition Acknowledgements

This work represents a culmination of over seven years of thinking about strategic planning, the role of personnel, and the role of structure in changing the traditional operating procedures of organizations. There are many people who have contributed to the completion of this work that deserve special acknowledgement.

I must thank Dr. Robert Miller for teaching me how to plan and think strategically. It is his practiced expertise that serves as the foundation of my own thoughts on where strategic planning can evolve. I am thankful for all of the help and assistance that Dr. Anne Mulder and Dr. Jeremiah Ryan provided throughout my doctoral experience which served to enhance my understanding of organizational change, the learning organization, and strategic thinking. I would be remiss not to thank one of my most formative mentors, Dr. Peter B. Contini, who allowed me to practice these ideas at his college, and gave me the freedom to test ideas about accountability and empowerment.

I would like to make some personal acknowledgements to people who made the completion of this book possible. I would like to thank Christa Richie and Dawn Sitarski for all of their attention to detail in assisting me with the editing of this book. I offer special thanks to Dr. Doug Dollar for choosing to publish this work and for assisting me with the editing process. I should also thank all of my colleagues over the years and all of the clients that hired me as a consultant; serving all of you helped to formulate the opinions, methods, and strategies of this book.

Finally, and most importantly I want to thank my parents for a lifetime of support. For my mother who provided me with a real understanding of the worker's needs, and to my father, a small business owner, who constantly taught me about the power and responsibility of ownership. There have never been words defined that can adequately articulate my thanks to Lori, William, Miranda (and now Tristan), my wife and children; I could not have done this without your support.

Chapter 1

Introduction & Overview

If I have seen farther, it is by standing on the shoulders of giants. --Sir Isaac Newton (1642-1729)

A dwarf standing on the shoulders of giants sees farther than a giant himself. --Robert Burton (1577-1640)

Pygmies placed on the shoulders of giants see more than the giants themselves. -- Marcus Lucan (39-65)

So you want to create a strategic plan for your organization, do you? Perhaps your CEO, President, or Board has suggested that it is time to initiate a new planning process or to create an innovative strategy in your department. Perhaps you are engaged in the profession of planning, are a student of planning, or are trying to create a 'world class organization' in an ever changing and increasingly complex reality. Possibly you read a text on leadership that claimed you needed to provide a vision for your organization, your department, or your employees; yet you do not know how to envision that future, let alone inspire others to follow you toward your vision and goals.

Now you have determined that you want--and need--as much information as you can obtain to make sure that the strategic planning process you choose is a success, leads to greater profits, creates better organizational outcomes, and is enjoyable from the start so that your staff will want to participate. You do not have the time to waste on mistakes; in fact, you do not even have the time to develop such a process. You still have the normal demands of your job, and strategic planning can be a cumbersome burden. You need information immediately in order to create results for your organization or department as quickly as possible.

You might decide to go to the bookstore, a business book catalogue, the Internet, or the library to find books on strategic planning. You could read the most recent information on leadership, change, employee performance, process reengineering, corporate restructuring, or developing high performance teams. But this process will take time, and it is essential that you find an informative and useful reference as soon as possible. So, I encourage you to join me as I stand upon the shoulders of the giants in leadership and management theory. You have discovered a key resource in developing and initiating your strategic plan.

The Quest

Rather than learn these lessons myself through trial and error over the span of my career, I would have relished a practical, simple, systematic guide to strategic planning. I wish that when I was first approached ten years ago by my corporate president that there had been a practical guide that outlined what a strategic planning process really entailed; something that demonstrated the leadership and management skills that were needed and how to develop a successful plan and how this might impact the future of the organization.

I still recall the emptiness in the pit of my stomach and the sheer terror I felt when that CEO walked into my office (this unusual occurrence alone should have made me hide under my desk) and asked me to lead the organization's strategic planning process. He then handed me a stack of plans that had been developed by my predecessors. The level of anxiety within me doubled.

In reality, when that CEO walked into my office and asked me to lead this strategic planning process, I enthusiastically accepted my charge. I naively thought that strategic planning represented an established, sophisticated practice that would be easy to initiate, develop, and implement. Since I was formally trained as a researcher and I had just graduated from a research university, I initiated a formal research model (i.e., the scientific model). In retrospect, I should have just winged it.

First, I defined my problem. I did not know how to develop, implement, or evaluate a strategic plan. I wanted my process to be highly professional, and to be successful in impacting the organization in a positive way in order to promote growth and opportunity. I decided to research planning models and found the work of those giants who had defined the contemporary leadership paradigm.

I soon learned that there were lots of books on management, business practice, leadership, and one or two on strategic planning. Words like forecasting, environmental scanning, situational analysis, and *SWOT/TOWS* appeared. However, the books on strategic planning did not seem to have any relevance to contemporary books on leadership, change, or creating the successful organization. There were no contemporary sources defining a simplistic inclusive model of strategic planning based on contemporary leadership paradigms or relevant to the ideas of the new economy.

At this point, according to the scientific method, I was supposed to have a hypothesis (or in this case a model process) to help develop my company's strategic plan. I had a hypothesis all right, but I cannot repeat it here without getting a *parental advisory* warning label on the front cover of this book. Basically, still perplexed, I skipped this step and jumped right to the collection and analysis of data.

I called the person who had created the previous strategic plan for the organization (he had left the company at this point for greener pastures). He invited me to take him to lunch, where he shared the new strategic plan he had developed for his present company. I paged through the document, three pages of the company's turbulent but progressive history, a page on the magnificence of the current CEO's leadership, a page detailing the process, a page citing the company's mission and goals, fifty pages of basically meaningless organizational statistics (known as the situational analysis) that alluded to the current CEO's brilliance, and a final page of recommendations. The recommendations suggested that the company should boost employee morale, cut costs, increase market share, increase stock value for shareholders, increase the use of technology, and expand operations. Yet, it had failed to explain the plan beyond just offering the recommendations.

My search for more data produced similar results. I found committees that had been brainstorming for so long their easel pads had moved from white to yellow to brown. I found lone wolves writing plans in offices without ever talking to a fellow employee (in fact people seemed to despise these 'planners'). I found copies of plans on employee shelves that had never been read (this appeared to be the norm). I found people taking three years to develop a five-year plan. I found men and women with bags under their eyes the size of golf balls.

I could never seem to find, however, a group of people who could cite their mission, or who had implemented a plan. I heard a rumor about a certain hotel chain that revolutionized planning and employee empowerment. I paid my money, checked in, and could find no evidence of validity in the rumor. I called a corporate executive at the chain; she assured me that the rumor was indeed true (I guess she could afford a better hotel).

During the process I emailed the company's CEO, told him what a wonderful job he was doing, cited six statistical facts, and told him that increasing profits and training employees in technology were a good idea. I also suggested that we might want to increase our stock value, give good employees a raise, and weed out the bad employees to cut costs. He emailed back, nicely suggested that my email was too verbose, and suggested that I should have my planning process in place by the end of the month.

Concerned that he might take my suggestion on bad employees and start with my position, I looked on my shelf and pulled off the most basic research book. In the final chapter, I found the answer. The author suggested that the researcher should always include ideas for further research. My idea was to develop a planning process based in the theoretical frameworks I thought were most relevant. I would stand on the shoulders of giants and see further than my colleagues. I developed my first planning process. It failed miserably.

The ideas, however, kept on coming. Finally, I developed a planning process that worked better than any other I had previously encountered. I now invite you to review the development of this process, to try it, to analyze it, and to modify it. I invite you to join me on the shoulders of the giants from whom I found the answers, the methods, and the way to create a plan that achieves the recommendations we all strive to achieve.

A Summary of the Basics

I am convinced from all my research and experience as an organizational change consultant that we are in the midst of an era of great challenge and opportunity for organizations, and the individuals that comprise them. Leadership and management writings of the day suggest that organizations, which are resistant to changing their management theory, are predetermined toward failure. Simultaneously, those organizations that adopt new paradigms and new mental models, yet neglect to transform business practices such as strategic planning are merely *sugarcoated rotten apples.* It is the individuals that work within the organizations who need to transform practice, the conceptualization of work, and their ideals to match the new leadership paradigms.

Organizations should realize and confront the new realities that confound them. They should develop a strategic planning process that is designed to promote change and sensible risk taking. The process should address the competitive demands of the post-industrial world of ever increasing knowledge and technology. The process should address the emergent environments, cultures, and structures that challenge leaders. The process should focus on the current construction of the organization, addressing both short and long-term effectiveness, and finally it should embrace chaos in an attempt to create order.

This new planning process, which I call triadic heterarchical strategic planning, will suggest that all executives and staff should be given greater decision-making power and a larger sphere of influence through the planning process. It will further demonstrate that power and influence are guided by principles of trust and responsibility when the emphasis is on collaboration and "win-win" outcomes. The model will show that an emphasis on quality is paramount in the development of an organizational planning and outcomes model where measurements of success emphasize institutional, departmental, and personal outcomes over the planning process. Finally, this book will demonstrate that organizational traditions and standards should come into question and should be reviewed systematically.

This is dramatically different from traditional models of strategic planning that emphasize the conventional hierarchy, command-and-control, and the development of plans through a standard systemic process. In this sort of planning, brainstorming is key and the central decision for leaders is whether the plan should occur every year, every three years, or every five years.

Most strategies focus on developing a planning model rarely accompanied by a planning manual. The leaders then review the mission statement, add a vision if they do not have one, then decide if they want goals (or lately values). The next step includes a statistical review of data (usually known as environmental scanning, competitive analysis, fact book development, or some other form of data review). This is where many organizations stop. If the organization completes this process, they begin to analyze their data. This process is known as situational analysis, SWOT, performance review, or some other variation of the same process. This is where most organizations enter the realm of brainstorming from which there is often no progress.

Once data has been analyzed and situations have been addressed, the organization begins to set goals, objectives, and strategies. This process usually takes one of two forms: 1) the group form – where leaders sit in countless meetings (or go away on a retreat) and argue over the semantics of the terms *goal, objective, and strategy,* or 2) where a company planner enters a room with a large coffee machine and pumps out the company's new plan.

Once the plan has been written, it is published and disseminated, and employees quickly throw away their old plans and replace the space left on their shelves with the new plan; the two are often indistinguishable. The strategies used for implementing the plan, once written, are usually very vague and the outcomes are not normally assessed until the end of the official plan, when senior management goes to another retreat to review the next situational analysis. This work is designed to examine the contemporary strategic planning process, to suggest revision, to offer a real strategy for implementation, and to offer a strategy to actually involve the employees expected to implement the plan in its development and realization process.

In attempts to modernize the process, some authors suggest that employee performance is influenced by a gap between planning, budgeting, and the daily operational activities of specific departments. Closing these gaps should be of central importance to the planning design of any organization. Fundamental to this idea should be the relationship between organizational planning and individual understanding of decision-making and the goals of the organization. Most leaders and managers deal mainly in the work of daily crisis situations, and they are often inept at viewing organizational issues and "crises" as long-range institutional problems. A great deal of leadership and management theory has been written to support the notion that planning is an institutional endeavor that should be placed in the hands of decision-makers, leaders, followers, and all stakeholders of an organization. The missing element at most institutions is the ability to take these theoretical ideals and create an applied process.

There is a disparity between the individuals' values and the organization's values. In traditional strategic planning practices, even where there is a goal for the establishment of a common vision, mission, and values, there is not a process in which employees are encouraged to internalize the vision, mission, and values. The nature of the problem is the gap between individual responsibility and departmental/institutional responsibility. The current issue with the traditional planning process is that it fails to address (a) opening honest, prudent lines of cross-institutional communication, (b) building trust throughout the organization, (c) creating a system of motivation, (d) ensuring professional treatment of all employees, and (e) the creating of a system that integrates the values of all employees with the mission and plans of the company and its departments.

The goal of this work is to create a comprehensive planning process that unites individual planning projects of the organization. Planning at the level of the institution is integrated with planning at the level of the department. Planning at the department level is integrated with planning at the level of the individual. The entire process is solidified through the integration of both the budgeting process and the human resource appraisal (evaluation) method. Once the three level (triadic) process is in place, the emphasis on the top of the hierarchy is diminished by turning the entire process upside-down (i.e., the personal planning process suggests the need for departmental planning, which then identifies institutional needs and strategies). When this strategy is initiated, managing the organization evolves from a hierarchical model to an emergent heterarchy.

The Journey

This work is intended to be simple and "user friendly," yet practical. The chapter sequence is designed like a college curriculum and is likely to be appropriate for any course in leadership, management, human resources, strategic planning, or as a supplement to a mini-course or training program. The book is arranged to briefly recreate the intellectual journey I undertook to develop a contemporary, cross-institutional, cross-functional, strategic planning process based within the best practices of leadership and management theory currently conceptualized.

This book reviews relevant planning, management, and leadership literature to create a context for a strategic planning system within the theoretical framework of contemporary leadership, planning, human resource development, and heterarchical thinking. However, the general utility of the book is to act as a nuts and bolts how-to guide for contemporary strategic planning.

The book is basically designed as a "how-to" for strategic planning at all levels of the organization. The benefits of the book are that it will provide step-by-step strategies and practices to develop an institutional strategic plan, implement the plan through departmental planning, and realize the goals of the plan through the development of high performance teams and personal/professional planning. So many leaders enter the planning process with no idea of where it might take them or what the end product should look like. This book provides planners with achievable ideals of where their planning processes should lead them. Readers are presented with potential outcomes in relation to their identified goals.

Chapters Two through Four review strategic planning theory, the current nature of planning theory, its emergence as organizational practice, organizational structure schemes, and the limitations of current theoretical frameworks. These chapters demonstrate the need for strategic plans for the institution, local departments, team-based projects, and for each person employed or associated with the organization.

Chapter Five demonstrates a cross-institutional, cross-functional design that allows an organization to complete its strategic planning process for the institution, department, and each employee in less than one year. It then illustrates how the planning process becomes a dynamic expected enterprise that creates the organizational culture of success.

Chapters Six through Eight express how to use this planning process to generate a culture of empowerment, how to facilitate the use of teams, and how planning becomes the means and method of continuous improvement for the organization. These ideas are summarized within the context of heterarchy, which demonstrates how this planning process can serve as a step-by-step guide toward achieving the learning organization macro-level goal.

Chapter Nine provides a "how-to" approach to data development, to the situational analysis, and toward the constructive facilitation of the planning process across all three levels. This chapter formulates the means of quantifying and measuring the success of the organization, the progress of departments, and the activities of individual employees.

Chapters Ten through Twelve offer a series of three step-by-step workbooks for strategic planning. Each workbook (institutional, departmental, and personal) represents a unique but integrated process designed to ensure that your organization reaches its maximum potential. The workbooks suggest strategies for success, ask framing questions, suggest meeting agendas, and illustrate templates for each of the three unique plans. Finally, the concept of "owed to" is offered as the key element of integrating the three planning models into one comprehensive model of change.

Chapter Thirteen demonstrates the key leadership principles needed to implement the process as written. The ideal strategy of inspiration is defined and exemplified as the method needed to lead the successful organization of tomorrow. Chapter Fourteen discusses the need for cross-institutional, cross-functional reward systems, and a comprehensive system of employee appraisal that is integrated into the planning model. Finally, in Chapter Fifteen the goals of the planning system are summarized, implementation caveats are provided, and an argument for emergent heterarchical inspirational leadership is provided.

Leading the strategic planning process is not a project for everyone. But for those few leaders and sages with the energy, passion for change, and wisdom, strategic planning can prove to be an exciting manner of earning your living or increasing your value to the organization. I have been doing it well for over a decade and have found it to be an exhilarating profession and a life-fulfilling experience. It is, at its best, the means of change and life-fulfillment for the organization and its employees. It is, at its worst, the most confusing waste of human resources that occurs in many organizations. It is what I have chosen and will continue to choose to do with the remainder of my life because making a positive difference in the companies and people I serve is the foundation of my life work.

Remember that there are many books on strategic planning and/or leading the change process for the organization. There are also numerous books on institutional planning, departmental planning, technology planning, facilities planning, and human resource planning. This work is designed to provide a one-system integrated approach to strategic planning that affects and unites all facets of the organization. This systemic approach leverages the organization across three levels (Triadic), managed within a dynamic emergent structure (Heterarchy), that continuously examines data, culture, and leadership practice (Strategic), within a simple process for achieving goals and a successful future (Planning). Thus, I wish you a fond welcome to Triadic Heterarchical Strategic Planning.

We will either find a way, or make one. -- Hannibal

Chapter 2

Strategic Planning in the New Economy

When you get there, there isn't any there there. – Gertrude Stein

Strategic planning can be defined as a process of creating forward-directed long-term objectives for your organization (Jurinski, 1993). Drucker has suggested that strategic planning is the continual process of making entrepreneurial (risk-taking) decisions systematically and with the greatest knowledge of their futurity, organizing systematically the efforts needed to carry out these decisions, and measuring the results of these decisions against the expectations through systematic feedback (1973). Others suggest that strategic planning is best accomplished when cross-institutional plans are tied to the mission of the organization, involve a large number of the stakeholders, are data driven, and emerge from an arena of consensus that is heterarchical in leadership.

There is no single definition for strategic planning, however most processes contain at least the common elements of a predefined process, collaboration on process and outcome implementation, and a system for evaluating vision, mission, values, and goals. The process should also examine data for both the internal and external environments; it should include a situational analysis of the internal strengths and weaknesses, and the external threats and opportunities. Situational analyses can be conducted on markets, competition, technology, facility management, financial resources, human resources, as well as any other significant factors that influence the success of the organization.

Once the situation is analyzed, the organization's planners begin to discuss alternative goals that will strategically place the company into a position of competitive advantage. These actions are then evaluated and selected for implementation by examining them in light of the organizational purpose, vision, mission, and values; as well by prioritizing them according to their potential for strategic success.

Strategic planning typically results in a formal, written, structured, strategic plan that charts an organization's future. A distinction should be made between the strategic planning process and the subsequent strategic plan. The two terms are not synonymous and it is important to know that this activity traditionally has required both a formal process and written plans (Jurinski, 1993).

Plans are often implemented through the establishment of detailed accountability mechanisms. Many plans are never fully implemented because of a series of management errors or omissions in the planning process that might include a failure to develop effective communication channels, failure to use the best data for the situational analysis, or the incorrect analysis of existing data. Many companies do not understand the actual costs associated with implementing the goals that are identified, or the CEO fails to support the plan, of she creates an atmosphere where senior managers believe that involvement in and communication about the strategic planning process is privileged.

Some businesses fail at planning because they do not undertake the process; rather they borrow the plan of a competitor or another similar organization. They mistakenly believe that they have engaged in a best practice or benchmarking model; thus they never benefit from the communication, learning, or strategic decision making that proper planning would provide them. Other organizations get so caught up in the process, the data, and the reporting that they fail to develop an effective plan.

Most plans fail for one or more of the following reasons, 1) inadequate financial resources, 2) inadequate accountability system, 3) strict hierarchical structures that limit implementation, 4) unrealistic timelines, or 5) failure to empower staff and integrate planning into their worklife. These reasons emerge mainly in situations of poor leadership, inadequate management, insufficient training, and a general failure to recognize the increasing complexity of the new economy and its influence on the work and family life in our society.

The Current Status of Strategic Planning

Strategic planning is now a staple of the American business landscape, yet few organizations plan effectively. Our enterprises have passed the point of questioning the need for strategic planning and have entered an era of doubting the validity of current planning mechanisms.

Strategic planning efforts are often futile because companies are unable to produce tangible results or to realize the majority of their goals and objectives. The process is far too slow in an age of technological revolution and satisfaction-on-demand. Current leaders are unable to visualize the urgency of implementing the plans they have envisioned because of their disdain for making the tough but necessary choices that emerge as part of the planning process. Many firms are unable to realize the goals of their strategic plan because their leaders entered the process in "bad faith," and with a preconceived destination already in mind unrelated or revealed to their respective followers.

Those organizations that have been successful in the planning process have several factors in common. First, their leaders are able to envision a shared future and to inspire others to follow them in the journey to achieve this vision. Second, the senior leader is a professional change agent that has communicated her vision of organizational transformation to the entire organization, while ensuring that all of the staff have a place in its future.

The successful leaders not only have the ability to forecast the future, they posses the ability to communicate this future to others. They realize the need for an organizational paradigm shift, envision the outcome, communicate it to others, and inspire others into action by creating an atmosphere of urgency. These leaders place people, financial resources, infrastructure, and the organizational culture up for discussion and change. Transformational leaders use urgency and accountability to motivate, and they build an organization based around trust and integrity.

Most organizations currently entering the strategic planning process suffer from two related problems. First, the leader types described above do not currently head unsuccessful organizations, and second, these leaders are not aware of the transformation that our society has been going through over the past twenty years. Our society has entered a state of continuous change, continual disorder, and increasing levels of differentiation.

This continuous change and the emergently complex levels of differentiation experienced in our current society confound organizations of every type. Consider how many large corporations lost fiscal resources, invested personnel hours, and lost sleep worrying about the new internet economy that was going to replace business as usual. Think about all those colleges and universities that leaped forward into the digital asynchronous distance learning markets only to discover that these classes were full of their normal students who chose to sit in a computer lab on the campus, instead of in a classroom on the same campus. How many of these highly educated leaders raced to be at the cutting edge of the next Betamax®, buying technology, like videoconference centers, that were complicated to operate, difficult to maintain, and too costly to connect to others for the purpose of teaching in multiple locations? Finally, consider the large number of not-for-profits that turned over their funds with little to no research to operations like the New Era Foundation, a ponzi scheme that promised to double their money ("How a teacher," 1997).

How and why did so many organizations leap forward without a sound foundation of data, a well-defined plan, or a clear expectation of the outcomes expected? The answer is simple; they failed to plan strategically. Leaders did not review their plans against the organizational mission. By losing sight of the organizational mission and purpose, these organizations were unable to distinguish a sound idea from a fad, a mere educated guess, or a disaster. Finally, these organizations did not relate their plans to reality, they failed to understand the power of societal transformation on the organization, and they neglected to develop goals in reference to internal and external factors that directly influenced the long-term success of their operation.

Surviving the Postmodern World by Navigating the Challenges of the New Economy

It has become a cliché to suggest that we have entered an era of continuously interesting times with technological breakthroughs and advancements spiraling out of control. Paul Kennedy has suggested that the combination of the global population explosion and technological revolutions have created a situation where people, organizations, and nations will fall into one of two categories: winners or losers (1993). The nature of developing future predictions and forecasting appears to have become an impossible intellectual exercise.

Most people could once easily agree that our societies, businesses, and collective populace would grow and continuously differentiate, and most took comfort in the idea that there must be a finite limit to the process of change, transformation, and differentiation. The shocking reality of the new economy in the postmodern society is that the direction of the future is leading to an emergently complex growth in uncertainty.

Crook, Pakulski, and Waters have suggested that the cement that once bound our organizations together was located at the level of generalized ideas and values known as the dominant ideology (1993). This ideology consisted of the common held belief that the harder one worked the more success one might achieve in life. I believe that as growing uncertainty over the present and future increasingly diminishes the dominant ideology of our society, new ideologies and values will emerge to secure a common vision for the organization and its people. Therefore, strategic planning is better used to act as the process that creates a shared value system to protect stakeholders from the uncertainty of the postmodern world.

An era of hyperdifferentiation necessitates a culture of business that becomes emergently abstruse in reaction to ever heightening levels of specialization and complexity, which introduce new problems of value integration. If the most successful firms are those that respond rapidly to shifting markets, then the centrally controlled multilayered hierarchies of the past will by definition lead to failure in the future. The rise of technological differentiation necessitates a synonymous rise in differentiation through knowledge production and distribution, as well as an increased flow of information throughout the organization. Economic reality is experiencing an extreme level of substantive differentiation, which, paradoxically, has the effect in many instances of the reintegration of the spheres of influence known as work and home life.

We are entering a bold new economy and social macrostructure where our interdependent human relationships are more dynamic, less obvious, and emergently complex. It is a system of global social relations where every individual can interact with any other on the planet (or off it for that matter) regardless of space, time, or physical location. This emergence of diffusive asynchronous social interdependence has made distance and our existing paradigms of organizational structure obsolete. William Knoke has elegantly demonstrated how our societal transformations will influence our ability to understand and negotiate the future.

> We started at the campfire of our ancestors, as a "dot culture," where our social world was the people sitting around the campfire with us. In time, we entered the First Dimension, where we started growing crops and trading with other dots, until soon, the lines became connected in trade. In the Second Dimension, geographical areas matured into empires that spanned rivers and mountains, and later the seas. The Third Dimension gave us flight and the ascent into space. . . . we are now propelled into the Fourth, and perhaps final, Dimension --- where distance ceases to exist. (Knoke, 1996, p. 308).

As distance becomes less important, the relations of space and distance, power and structure, economy and business, the individual and the family, as well as our methods for understanding and explanation, such as religion, science, and education are entering an era of unprecedented transformation. Across the globe our societies and social relations are realigning, organizations are being continuously restructured, and governments reconstituted, causing the rigid command-and-control hierarchies to crumble as the center-based power systems of the past move toward shifting dynamic power systems (Knoke, 1996). The greatest challenge in the next century then, according to Knoke, will stem from the varying speeds at which the forces of this Fourth Dimension will transform our society as the functions of our collective institutions advance forward at differing velocities.

To better illustrate these points it would be beneficial to examine the influence of societal transformation on past business practices in light of the evolution of social functions. Table 2.1 demonstrates societal transformation in a linear display of social evolution. This table illustrates the progression of social evolution from the hunting and gathering society through the current structure of the economic macrosystem, popularly referred to as the "New Economy."

Our social formations began in a state of interdependence and dependence, where explanations were sought in the form of stories about the known past, rules and regulations, and about the meaning of life from a nature based standpoint. Technology played only a limited role in the development of human existence. As substance was abundant in the form of gathering, the knowledge of farming and horticulture was not used until the population forced its implementation (Sanderson, 1988). In the horticultural society, people were forced to bond together in tribes and kinship patterns to overcome the problem of scarcity. This bonding of people forced the development of more formal rules and leadership patterns, and the need for religions that supported positive human interaction. In this era, the material infrastructure (population and lack of food sources) caused the societal macrosystems to evolve.

As population continued to grow and the idea of private property emerged, the economic macrosystem again evolved (from horticultural to agricultural). In this era, the advancement of property and the growth of rules necessitated a strict hierarchy, that was legitimized by kingship polity and the development of a monotheistic rule based religious structure. Technology became controlled and regulated by the church in the West, and scientific advancement was discouraged. The rise of the hierarchical model of control came to dominate the notion of family, religion, the state, stratification, and the very few business practices in existence (i.e., merchants) (Pirenne, 1952).

As the population continued to grow and technological advancements were made to support mass production, the macrosystem again evolved from agricultural to industrial. The industrial model, that moved power from ascribed authority to a capitalist based meritocracy, remained structured in a hierarchy of order, and a religious system that supported personal growth, forgiveness, and a merit based life. Although the focus of social relations and

Evolutionary Stage Theoretical Framework by Economic Macrosystems*

	Hunting & Gathering	Horticultural	Agricultural	Industrial	Postmodern "New Economy"
Polity	Primitive Communism	Ancient Headed/Chiefs	Feudal Kingship	State-based Democratic Nation Capitalist	World-based/Global Diversified Free Market Capitalism
Stratification	Patriarchal Dependency	Tribal	Ascribed Caste	Meritocratic Achievement	Egalitarian Achievement
Technology	Primitive	Advanced Primitive	Controlled & Regulated	Progressive	Chaotic Hyperdiffusion
Education	Symbolic Storytelling	Purposive/Rule Storytelling	Religion Based Apprenticeship Access Controlled	Science Based Terminal Certification Access Qualified	Knowledge Based Non-Terminal Expansive Access Open
Familial	Polygynous	Unilineal Kinship	Extended Paternalistic	Nuclear Paternalistic	Hyperdiffusive Retribalization
Religion	Nature Based Symbolism	Polytheistic	Rule-Based Monotheistic	Forgiving Monotheistic Secularization	Ultratolerance Monotheistic Humanist Human Finitude
Business	Dependency	Barter Systems	Strict Hierarchy	Merit-based Hierarchy	Heterarchy
Hegemony	Inter-dependence	Materialism	Materialism	Materialism/ Ideological	Ideological

* Although illustrated as linear, these stages are often curvilinear in progression.

Table 2.1. Social Relations Predictive Workplace Practice and Ideology Matrix.

stratification evolved from birth rites to achievement, the dominant ideological framework of hierarchy remained intact.

The industrial society emerged from a need to support the growing populace (material determination), and the ability to fulfill these needs through the intelligent use of technology (ideological determination). Businesses grew exponentially in this era, were based in hierarchical models, had structures that were paternalistic and kind, and survived in a social reality that was merit based. Over the past twenty to twenty-five years, our economic macrosystem has again entered a period of transformation, from industrial to post-industrial (more commonly referred to as the "New Economy").

This society is global, diversified, and based within a free market context. This social transformation was brought about by a move toward a knowledge-based system where technological innovation is rewarded with massive wealth and prestige. For the first time in human history, a social transformation occurred through the diffusion of knowledge and ideology alone. Access to education was expanded exponentially, religious belief systems are becoming ultra-tolerant to accept an increasing number of viewpoints, and our business structures are moving from hierarchical and rule driven, to hyperdiffuse, lateral, flat, increasingly complex, or heterarchical. Planning and business relations have become more complex, more fluid, and more dynamic.

Within the phenomenological context of hyperdifferentiation, the workforce requires a vision and a strategic direction of the future. To suggest that this economic evolution will dramatically change the need for leaders and leadership in our organizations is an understatement. The issue is that dynamic leadership will be even more necessary, strategic plans will need to be more transformational, imperative, and more visionary. The problem is that the current systems of internal leadership development, strategic planning, and management are based on a social theory of structuration that no longer exists.

The workforce of the future will seek support from a variety of sources. Callincos suggests that the transformation of economic superstructures has not diminished the spread of trade unions into the service professions, to support a new generation of workers exposed to inept management (1989). The question for future leaders is whether or not they will choose to create phenomenal, influential, increasingly prosperous organizations, or they will simply overlay our past practices of unionization, command-and-control management, and limiting hierarchy over our new economy based enterprises. Let me suggest that the organizations that do the latter should begin planning for their demise.

Evidence suggests that the workforce of the future will need to change and to learn to master the changing economic and workplace landscape. Judy and D'Amico have demonstrated that five distinct forces will shape the American economy over the next twenty years: technological innovation, globalization, economic growth in developing nations, deregulation and liberalization, and shifting demographics (1997). Organizations that strategically plan within the context of these forces and develop systems to assist their employees to adapt to these factors will emerge at the forefront of their respective competitors. These forces will create a new set of challenges and opportunities for both the businesses and the workforce of the future.

Judy and D'Amico (1997) further offer insights into the future requirements of the new economy. Constant technological advancement will require an educated adaptive workforce of sophisticated and innovative approaches to problem identification and solution generation. Incessant waves of technological advancement coupled with intensifying global competition will require employees that can manage their careers to weather conditions of constant volatility. Unsafe, unpleasant, unsophisticated, and monotonous organizations will reduce in number and will fail to succeed as innovative, dynamic, and emergent enterprises rise to take their place. Finally, the workforce of the future will become more diverse, more tolerant of difference, and increasingly reflective of an aging workforce.

Strategically planning this future will require organizations to understand the evolution of the economy and all of the elements of our society. The new economy will require systems that renew current leaders and prepare prospective leaders, while increasing levels of empowerment throughout the organization. Organizations will need tactics and mechanisms that continuously advance the skills of their existing staff, while simultaneously developing workplace practices which encourage the current employees to remain with the firm. Successful companies will manage their processes and structures, leading their followers toward new mental models and paradigms. New paradigms will shift the institutional culture toward one of continual adaptation and transformational orientations.

Past systems and practices of strategic planning will become increasingly ineffective and obsolete. Managing change will require a new mechanism for organizational development and leadership practice. The successful organizations of the future will produce synergy between the three levels of the enterprise (organizational/global, departmental/local, and personal/individual). To succeed in the aspiration of synergy for the organization, leadership practice, reward systems, and the institutional culture will simultaneously require improvements in theory, practice, and process.

The final issue for the successful organization of the next century is how to efficiently structure organizations to improve effectiveness, productivity, and innovation. Just as continuously increasing levels of differentiation limit our current understanding of organizational structure, trying to manage hierarchical structures in an era of ultradifferentiation continues to prove increasingly unproductive. The best and brightest leadership scholars have come to a common consensus that structuring our organizations within a hierarchy leads to failure (Belasco, 1999; Bolman & Deal, 1997; Bridges, 1996; Handy, 1996; Helgesen, 1996; Knoke, 1996; Lawler, 1996; Lucas, 1997; Pinchot, 1996; Schein, 1996; & Senge, 1996; Wheatley, 1996). Still, contemporary practitioner leaders search for a replacement structure that will allow them to manage their organizations while effectively leading their followers.

Kontopoulos has suggested that the most robust understanding of this differentiation and societal change will come in the form of emergent heterarchy. He further posits that these heterarchies either as programs having a structure or the real structures themselves, are level structures with no ultimately distinct governing point (1993). In fact, the bodies within these structures exert determinate influence on each other due to their multiple access levels, multiple linkages, and multiple determinations. The remainder of this work will demonstrate how visionary leaders through the effective management of this new heterarchically based strategic planning model can guide the evolution to the "New Economy". Leaders will learn to dominate this societal transformation, making their respective organizations the embodiment of the postmodern successful organization.

When the rate of change outside the organization exceeds the rate of change inside, the organization dies. – Jack Welch

Chapter 3

The Importance of Organizational Structure: Why Heterarchy?

The investigation of the meaning of words is the beginning of education. – Antisthenes

Defining the Concepts

Before we begin an investigation of structure, it is essential to define the two concepts that serve as the centerpiece of the modern organization.

Hierarchy – a system of persons or things ranked one above another (Webster).

Heterarchy – a system of levels and relationships defined in terms of pragmatic criteria of scale and complexity, partial inclusion, and semi-autonomy – partial determination from below, partial determination from above, partial focal-level determination, and residual global indeterminacy, notions that admittedly are very complex (Kontopoulos).

If you have just finished reading the definition you are likely thinking to yourself that this is about as complex as an explanation of quantum physics. Next, you should be wondering if it is even worth your investment of time to read the rest of the chapter. How could a concept whose definition is so verbose and confusing lead to the management of a simpler, more successful organization? I offer you this promise: you already are intimately familiar with the idea of heterarchy, you live and breathe it every day. I also promise to explain the concept in much simpler terms that you can apply to your workplace.

Now back to that notion of the complexity of quantum physics. The term and its definition seem this complex because they are part of the explanation of the natural sciences and structured social reality. We will be stealing and amending the idea to discuss social relations (in this case the management and leadership of organizations). The idea of hierarchy is simple, traditional, and part of our everyday vernacular, so why not use it as the term to explain structure? In the simplest terms, it is too limiting, too constrictive, and fails every test of validity. It limits communication, productivity, attitude, profits, and limits the power of individuals to improve corporate performance. In essence, it is a mirage, a fantasy. Understanding heterarchy will give you the power to understand the social relations of your business enterprise at every level and within every situation present in your organization.

Unfortunately, to understand the idea of heterarchy it is essential to have a very basic understanding of the five epistemic strategies of contemporary natural and social sciences.

Epistemology is being defined here as our grasp of the origin, methods, and limitations of the everyday human awareness of reality. Were you to complete a research analysis of these sciences, noting especially the most recent work, you would uncover these five strategies. The simplest being reduction, or our belief system that says that wholes are no more than the sum of their parts. The next level being that of construction, or our belief system that we produce products from a logical order of elements (i.e., 1+2+3+4=10 or 2+5+3=10 or 5+5=10 or 1+9=10 or 8+2=10 or 2+2+2+2+2 =10, so what equals 10?). The next level is represented by the strategy of heterarchy, followed by hierarchy (both of which are defined above). Transcendence (or holism) represents the final level of epistemic understanding, which is the dominant theory of contemporary business management (i.e., systems theory without ever being named as such is a transcendent epistemic strategy). These theoretical frameworks have a common theme of attempting to illustrate the full autonomy of macrosystems (organizations) and the control of macrodetermination (management or leadership) which these systems exercise over lower levels or components (followers, staff, processes, customers, etc.).

To place these concepts into a perspective, Figure 3.1 illustrates the epistemic strategy in relation to general management principles.

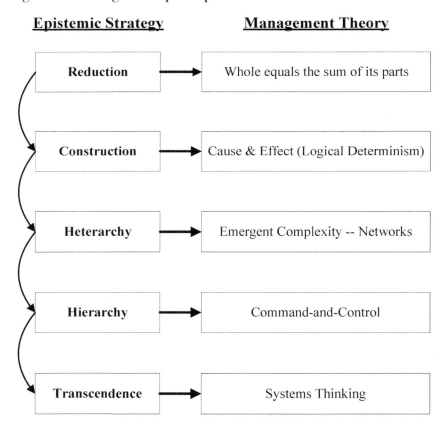

Epistemic Strategy	Management Theory
Reduction	Whole equals the sum of its parts
Construction	Cause & Effect (Logical Determinism)
Heterarchy	Emergent Complexity -- Networks
Hierarchy	Command-and-Control
Transcendence	Systems Thinking

Figure 3.1. Five Epistemic Strategies of Contemporary Science and Their Relation to Management Theory

The Simplification and Explanation of the Importance of Structure

Some have argued that understanding structure is not important in the post-modern organization. The organizations of the future may have no structure, they will be situational or project focused, and leadership will be paramount. This explanation I generally support, however all of the forecasts of future organizational structures and management composition already exist in a paradigm of structuration. Even in chaos there is order, and even in formal disarrangement there is structure, and this is known as heterarchy. To discount the notion of structure would constitute a fatal flaw in leadership and management practice.

In attempting to understand contemporary organizations and their goals for continuous improvement, change, and synergy it is beneficial to examine the role of structure and social relations within organizations in general. There is a direct formal connection between individuals and the conceptualization of the structures in which individuals live and work (Kontopoulos, 1993).

As is demonstrated in an understanding of current structure paradigms, any current theory of structures should encompass, by necessity, a theory of levels. Different levels of structural analysis imply different units of analysis, which in an ascending order become dynamically different (in scale), larger (in size), and more complex. The relation between units will not be one of complete inclusion or suppression as one would expect in a hierarchical organization – something more complex takes place here with levels interrelating to each other in an entangled way (Kontopoulos, 1993)

The epistemological theory of heterarchy demonstrates that organizational understanding should be shifted to embrace the ideas of emergence and complexity. It is this emergent complexity which should then be considered in any attempt to understand organizational change, which is related directly to organizational structure and culture. This becomes very important now that the majority of leadership theory authors are arguing that the traditional sense of hierarchy is being constantly reduced (Covey, 1999; Lawler, 1996; Senge 1994; Wheatley, 1996). It is now increasingly common for large organizations to have single-digit management levels and double- or triple-digit reporting relationships. In smaller organizations, this phenomenon has been occurring longer, since the number of positions in relation to the number of functions necessitates less hierarchy and more cross-organizational communication.

Recent work has demonstrated the emergence and formulation of these prominent functions as organigraphs as opposed to organizational charts (Mintzberg and Van der Heyden, 1999). Leaders need to view organizations and functions as a system of hubs and webs based around actual person-to-person work strategies that not only chart an organization but provide a map to its processes as well. Traditional hierarchical organizational charts largely represent the picture albums of companies, but they illustrate only that organizations are mesmerized with management. With traditional hierarchies vanishing, and newfangled — and often quite complex --- organizational forms taking their place, leaders and staff are realizing how companies actually work. This transformation of thought coupled with confusion explains why traditional organizational charts have become so irrelevant in the contemporary business enterprise.

The issue is often compounded when the traditional models of strategic planning are placed within a context of the new leadership and management paradigms. The traditional strategic planning model was designed for use within the hierarchical management system.

A new model of strategic planning emphasizes the human relationships and complexity of networks and functions that abound in the effort to plan and implement change in the modern organization. It is the realization of the limitations of hierarchical systems that suggest the need for planning across all levels of an organization to ensure that the change movement is synergistic will all components, networks, hubs, and levels of the institution.

Figure 3.2 suggests how an organigraph for strategic planning might be formulated and conceptualized. As demonstrated, management levels become less important in this formulation than in the traditional hierarchical chart. A redesigned management system is needed to represent a more flexible shared responsibility framework that better matches modern management theory. However, strategic planning even as illustrated in Figure 3.2 has yet to create synergy across the entire organization.

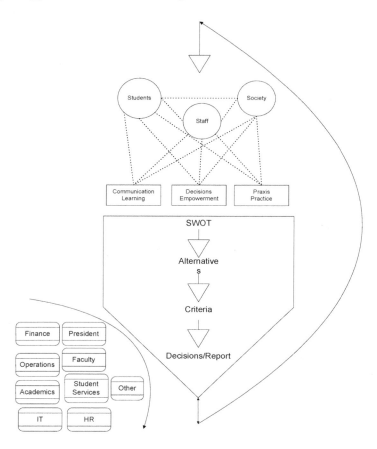

Figure 3.2. An Organigraph Demonstrating Traditional Strategic Planning (It Does Not Represent the Full Range of Social Relationships in Contemporary Organizations).

The understanding and reformulation of structures is essential to the development and change of any modern organization, notably in its planning processes. Our continued preoccupation with structure is really a representation of our preoccupation with management, that limits the level and complexity of change that can be realized. It is at the other levels of the organization where change is arguably most often necessitated and where development and local leadership are most often missing.

To create effective strategic plans we need to realize that senior leadership is just one function or process of an organization, albeit an important process. To fully understand organizational development, the process of management, its structure, and the need for greater participation, accountability systems, and processes across the organization should be realized to create the effective organization of the future. Contemporary leaders lust for order in their organizations while failing to see their true nature (Wheatley, 1996). We must welcome disorder as a partner in the search for order. Our current structures, leaders, and managers come and go, so the leaders of the moment should focus energy on the directions that emerge from deep natural processes of growth and self-renewal.

Why Heterarchy[1]?

The dominant concepts of management theory consist of either a modified version of hierarchy or the transcendence/holistic approach (known as systems theory). Neither is appropriate for conceptualizing the current state of structures from which we conduct business.

For example, I once worked with a large not-for-profit religious institution as a leader in its well-publicized restructuring efforts. In one conversation, a senior leader in this organization told me that the single biggest constraint to organizational change was the reliance on the hierarchical system. For over two thousand years, they had relied on a complex system of hierarchy that had emerged in Feudal Europe. Their local leaders (priests) had developed a series of fiefdoms (parishes) which they ruled, not too different from departments in some large corporations and universities I have served.

The Cardinal of this archdiocese wanted a system that did not violate church law yet moved them beyond this two-dimensional idea of hierarchy. The problem was that the senior religious leader ordered, his priests obeyed (actually in most cases they obeyed a modified version (another issue with hierarchy)), and his followers ceased attending religious services. This was the first time I suggested the notion of heterarchy.

---

[1] This note is for those readers who already have an understanding of the term heterarchy either from the natural sciences, social sciences, or philosophy. I am well aware that I have modified, simplified, and made minor mutations to the pure ideal type definition. This new definition is meant for application and awareness of the social relations that occur in mission driven organizations.

I demonstrated to the religious leaders that an emergent heterarchy is not very different than a hierarchy, yet it allowed for a more dynamic system of leadership and management, and turned their leaders from rulers to servants (as was their goal). I explained that a heterarchy is less like a kingdom, and more like a universe, where the Cardinal could remain at the center. This was an example that fit within their culture, and will help to illustrate the difference between the two.

Let us take this a step further and consider our Solar System as an example. We currently sit here spinning in space, rotating around a star, while the universe expands in all directions around us; where does Earth fit in the hierarchy? Do we order this hierarchy by life bearing planets, by number of thinking organisms, on the level of technology produced by intelligent life, by the circumference of planets, by the number of moons? Is there a hierarchy in the universe or is the effort pointless or merely relative in nature? What is the top or the bottom of the order?

Now someone might suggest that the universe in general or the solar system in particular is not a hierarchy, but a holistic system, thus the name solar system. Therefore, a systems approach to understanding reality makes more sense than hierarchy. In general, I agree that a systems approach is better than a hierarchy. However, the problem of anomalies persists in the solar system. Consider the problem of asteroids and comets crashing into the Earth's surface (normally the fodder of scientific movies, it illustrates the problem). Is there an order here or have we assumed order where there was chaos? Many have searched for order in chaos, tried to fit it into our understanding (or existing epistemic strategies) of the world.

Yet, a simpler explanation exists. The universe, solar system, politics, business, friendships, family, and I live within a dynamic, emergent, heterarchical structure, where succession is normal, anomalies are expected, and order is relevant to time and place. The emergent complexity of a heterarchical structure can best be described as a multifaceted set of networks that rise and fall from prominence as functions and organizational activities emerge are addressed and resolved, then vanish. Heterarchy encompasses the concepts of hierarchy, systems, and anomalies while allowing us to mentally structure and envision a successful future.

For a moment let's return to my religious leader friend. He needs his middle managers to stop ruling through command-and-control, yet at times he needs to be able to issue directives, and let's remember there is no democratic vote on sin. He needs a system where the traditions of his organization are respected and where the importance of leadership is renewed. He needs a heterarchy. In a heterarchy, he can illustrate his version of reality (his vision), demonstrating himself (or the Pope) as the center of a three-dimensional structure. The importance is that order in this structure is irrelevant since it is dynamic and emergent.

This is why in managing a strategic planning process or leading the contemporary organization, a heterarchy is the most robust form of human understanding of order, crisis, and chaos. A heterarchy allows each person, department, or function to be the center of the universe.

The problem for most of us is that we have been so indoctrinated in command-and-control hierarchical systems that over inflate the value of the leader, we fail to realize that our social relationships are better defined in terms of a heterarchy. To understand this term, one must realize the limitations of past teachings on authority, and liberate the mind toward an understanding of complexity and emergence. Consider, for instance, that you learn a new idea each week. You see yourself as a different person in a small way, yet in a larger sense you are still you, you have enriched yourself. Viewing an organization in the same way is beneficial to leading and managing change. Perhaps a series of illustrations will better emphasize the idea.

We have been taught to see our organizations in terms of a hierarchy, where the greatest influence, responsibility, and rewards are reserved for those closest to the top of the structure (i.e., the leaders). In a heterarchy, leadership is defined as the ability to manage the structure, to empower change, to react and reconstruct the system when necessary, and to envision and proactively forecast the structural needs of business. Leadership thus becomes a process rather than a position. Leadership is action rather than position, it is inspirational influence rather than authority, and its power comes from followers rather than control (see Chapter Thirteen for more details).

The opposite is true in a hierarchy, where command comes from power derived from position; where the ability to make decisions is not shared but based on jurisdiction. In a hierarchical system, the notion of "us" and "them" prevails. Figure 3.3 presents a snapshot of a simplified traditional hierarchical chart that resembles an organization in which I held a senior management position (for the purposes of this example I have removed a number of layers, but the essence remains intact). In a hierarchical system, the followers are defined, a priori, by their position beneath or below a "supervisor." The system limits the flow of information, limits team development, and empowers staff to create vindicating and mitigating circumstances for inactivity and an overall lack of productivity.

I recall once when working with a senior management team to improve organizational performance through departmental planning, I had set up an interview schedule with all senior functional leaders. I walked into a senior vice-president's office and sat down to discuss some concerns about a survey we had conducted that demonstrated no communication was taking place in his department. Before I said a word, he looked at me and said, "I am afraid this will all be a waste of your time, they do not allow us to share information here, that is why there is a communication problem." I was quite puzzled, for in this organization there was no layer between him and the CEO. I asked him to tell me who was "them." He responded, "the powers that be, you know its part of the culture and structure here." When I decided to interview the middle management layer of this hierarchy, I found similar belief system. There was this "them" that would not allow communication, and who dictated mandates that limited their ability to make the changes that middle management desperately knew their department needed to make. They told me how their VP had nearly lost his job trying to question the validity of "them." I asked if them was the CEO of the company, they told me that "them" was not the CEO, in fact, the CEO had apparently "saved the VP's job." For the record there was no layer of management above the CEO, and the staff of that department was still operating under the values, structure, and leadership of ten years ago. Apparently no one told the VP that he was "them." In essence, he limited himself and a reliance on hierarchy had limited his ability to think and reason.

Simplified Traditional Hierarchical Chart

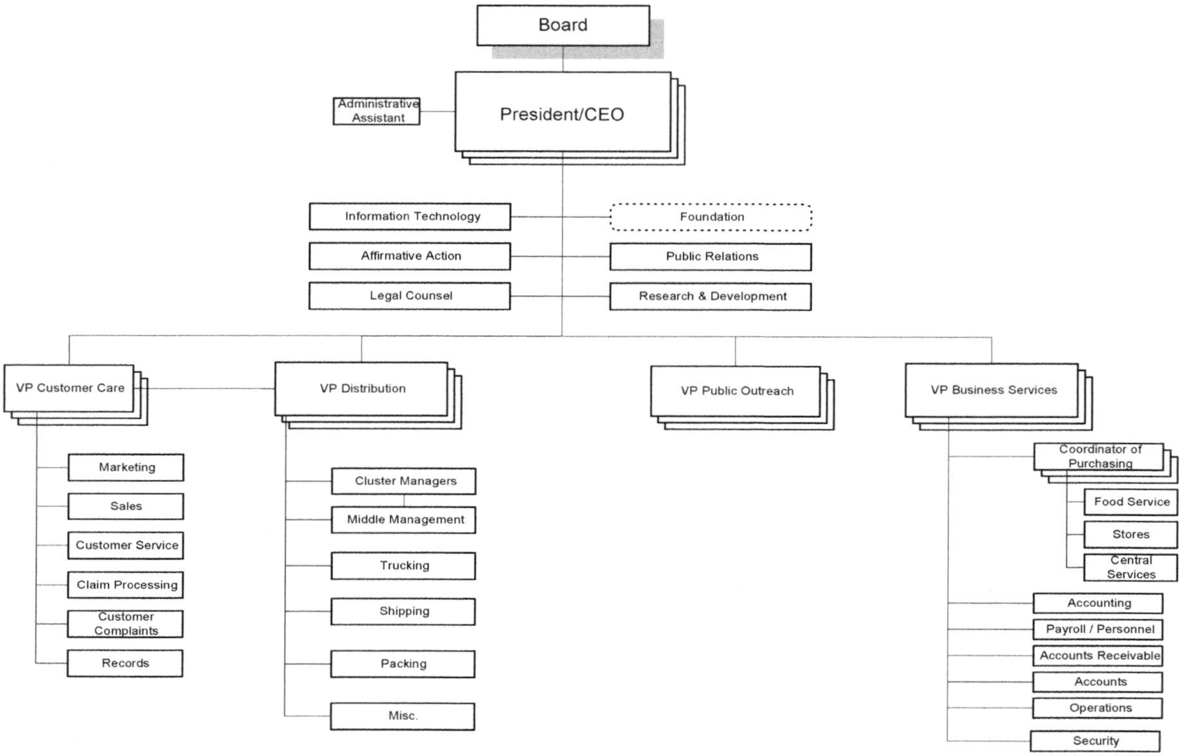

Figure 3.3. Simplified Version of a Traditional Hierarchical Chart.

First, let me admit that this is an extreme example, however it does illustrate the power of the hierarchical structure. In this organization, the structure had become a living entity that superceded the prerogatives of leaders and management. The hierarchy was able to maintain a culture that even two previous CEO's could not change or even reform.

Embedded in hierarchy is the traditional bureaucracy that is designed to maintain the status quo and designed to limit the hegemony of individual leaders. In past years, the bureaucracy was useful in that it protected us from bad leaders; however, in these times of information, technology, economic shifts, and transformation, leadership is paramount and a reliance on bureaucratic hierarchy can destroy an organization.

The time has come to realize the domination of structure over our organizations, to shift the structural paradigms, and to reconstruct the institutions, departments, and lives we have been empowered to direct. Figure 3.4 illustrates how a static heterarchy might appear in an organizational chart.

Heterarchical Organizational Example

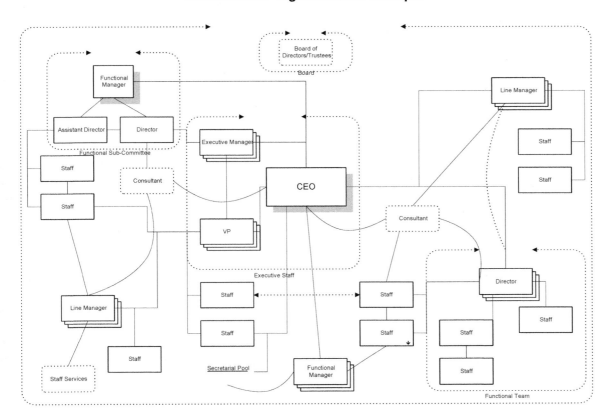

Figure 3.4. Illustration of a Static Heterarchical Chart.

I worked for a college president that wanted to leave a significant legacy to the institution before he retired. He had read so many management books that by the end of his tenure he was known around the campus as "latest and greatest." Each time he read a book or went to a conference, he would return with the latest and greatest management fad, and whomever he saw first would have the honor of initiating it. All his ideas fell short, all his experiments backfired, and all of his initiatives met with unprecedented failure. His recommendations were all top notch, but his institution was never ready to initiate them. His mandates were useless because the structure of his hierarchy was so strong that a management technique was as useless as last year's calendar.

When "latest and greatest" heard about heterarchy, he hired me to design a heterarchical chart for his institution. I explained to him that the chart was a static diagram representing only a snapshot of the organization for a certain time and place. I therefore suggested that we construct a three-dimensional model to illustrate the concept. I made the model, complete with moving elements; he hated it. My model was dynamic, it changed, there was no way to determine the top from the bottom, who was in charge; it was emergent in nature. It was not the three-dimensional hierarchical chart he had expected. As Figure 3.5 illustrates (as compared to Figure 3.4) , a heterarchy is complex, emergent, and dynamic.

Heterarchical Organizational Example (Time 2)

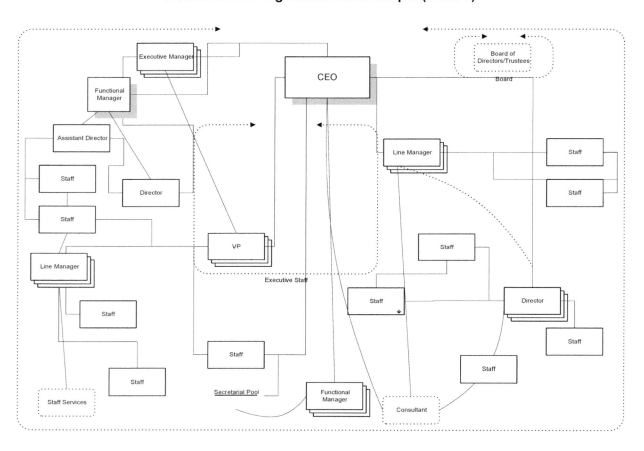

Figure 3.5. A Two-Dimensional Illustration of a Dynamic Heterarchical Chart.

Figure 3.5 is a replica of Figure 3.4 at a different time and place, and under different circumstances. Heterarchy is not an organizational chart that is concerned with showing off management. Heterarchies are not even really charted, rather they are visual representations of action, problem solving, teamwork, and leadership. The emphasis of the heterarchy is not the structure but the action that takes place within an emergent reality of social relations (in this case of organizational management).

The same phenomenon of heterarchy versus hierarchy applies to the department (and actually the individual) as well. For example, in Figure 3.6 a traditional department is illustrated as a hierarchical chart. While in Figure 3.7, the same department is shown in its heterarchical form. Again, the heterarchy is illustrated to demonstrate functions that are dynamic and emergent. Different functions and positions will work together to accomplish organizational goals and projects. Leaders will emerge within teams and within substructures of the heterarchy. This does not mean that the department will not function in terms of its traditional hierarchical form; it may operate that way frequently.

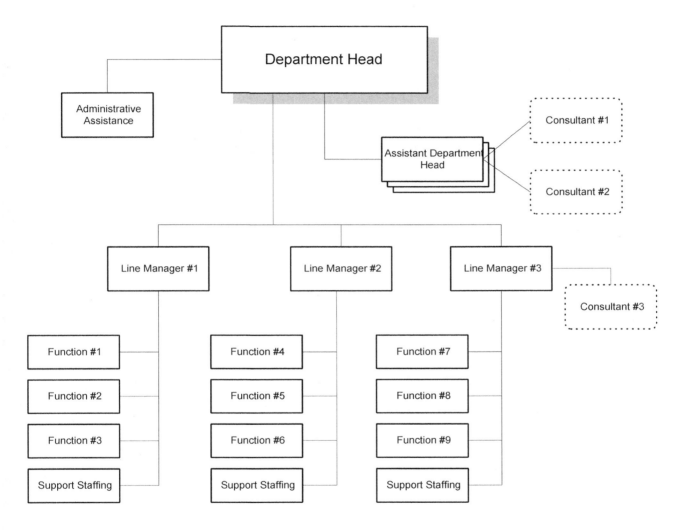

Figure 3.6. A Traditional Departmental Hierarchical Chart.

However, to constrict its operations to that model would influence communication patterns, productivity, and operational effectiveness. The traditional reporting relationships rise and fall from prominence based on activity and need (they exist but do not control the system).

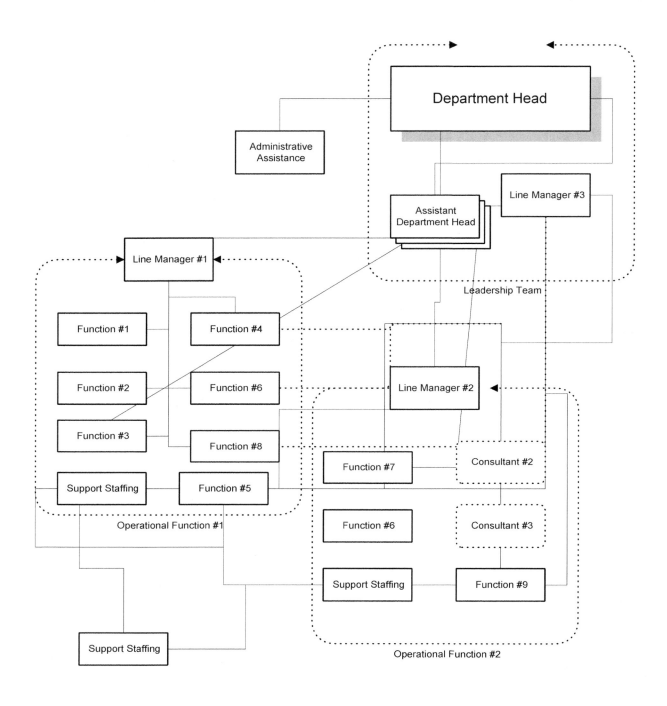

Figure 3.7. A Heterarchical Illustration of the Department in Figure 3.6.
Figure 3.8 again illustrates the department (now at a different time and under different circumstances). In this illustration, the importance of teams is highlighted. Teaming and cross-functionalism are essential to the organization.

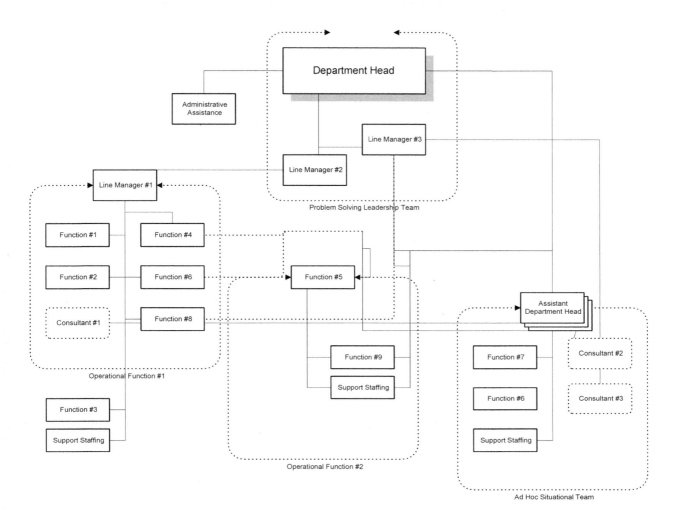

<u>Figure 3.8</u>. The Heterarchical Illustration of the Department in Figure 3.6. at Time 2, with Emphasis on Team Empowerment.

The time and money spent on team development and teamwork training in contemporary organizations suggests that this idea of management has made an important impact. The problem is that just as hierarchy has limited the role of management, it also limits the current effectiveness of teams.

I was invited by a college vice-president to assess her organization to find out why the teams she had initiated did not significantly increase productivity or revenues for her operation. First, she spent three hours explaining to me why her method of teamwork was an example of best practices, and how she had won an award for her innovative team strategies. As my partner examined market share and market demographics, I began to ask questions about the nature of the teams she had created. She explained how she wanted to improve communication and how the president had asked her to diminish the command-and-control model he inherited. She demonstrated how she had used a systems thinking approach to initiate teams to reach her goal of creating the elusive learning organization.

Once my partner had determined that by all demographic and statistical accounts her market share should have naturally increased, I asked her to draw her vision of teams for her operation. Figure 3.9 illustrates a representation of her team development framework.

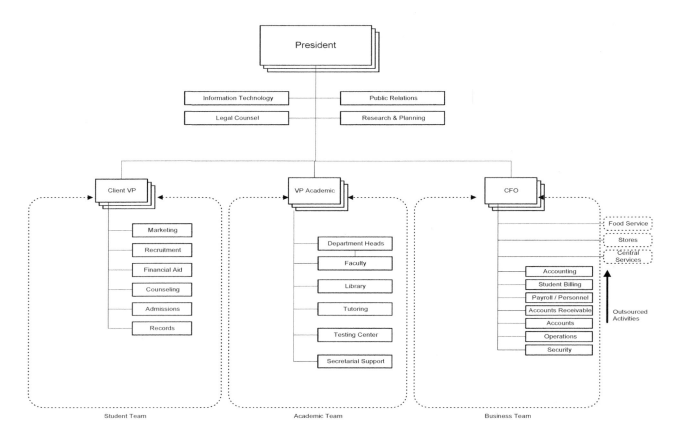

Figure 3.9[2]. Illustration of a Teaming Model within a Traditional Hierarchical Structure.

She had used a large amount of institutional resources to develop teams that overlapped her existing organizational structure. Her teams were nothing more that an extension of the organization's command-and-control system. Communication systems had not expanded, integrated servicing of students (customers) did not occur, and the process of teaming had done little more than remove staff from their daily activity to take part in team development training. I conducted a great deal of research and determined that her staff's involvement in team development training created a situation where they lost students due to poor customer service practices (i.e., people were taken away from their primary duties and responsibilities to engage in an ineffective management fad).

---

[2] For the reader's benefit, I have intentionally simplified the drawing but left the essence of it intact.

Teamwork can be one of the best practices for any contemporary organization if it is conducted within an environment of open communication and is cross-institutional and cross-functional in nature. Central to the need for understanding structure as an emergently complex heterarchy of purposes is the requisite to create a feeling of ownership across all organizational processes in an institution. The teamwork strategy that leads to ownership is often referred to as empowerment. Empowerment through team development requires a system that replaces the old hierarchy and creates autonomy in the staff by making the employees feel and behave like owners.

Through empowering everyday employees, organizations and/or departments can learn to cooperate as teams that address functions, processes, and challenges to unleash new opportunities. This team development concept involves the systematic coordination of the performance of individuals who work together to achieve individual as well as common goals. Recognized theory suggests that team building and training assists in the elimination of managerial "command-and-control" positions and their "carrot-and-stick" motivational strategies that work to retard empowerment (Katzenbach & Smith, 1999).

However, many institutions are unwilling to allow the open and frank cross-institutional communication systems that allow organizations to reach excellence through team development. The leadership of these organizations truly desires teams and communications, but the limitations of their conceptualization of structure eliminates any chance for true teamwork to occur. Teamwork will not naturally occur and emerge in either a hierarchy or a systems based approach.

For example, I was hired by a large non-profit to review the implementation of their team development strategy. I met with leader after leader and determined that they were working within intradepartmental teams instead of the interdepartmental teams necessary to address the issues and strategies their plans were trying to achieve. I asked why the teams had not been developed across departments. I was told that this was the duty of the central leadership team. I suggested that they had removed all decision making power from the problem and had placed it almost six levels away in their hierarchy. To my amazement, I was told that this practice was constructed by design. When I dared asked why, the response was a three-word answer from every senior manager, "to avoid jaywalking." This one concept negated all of their team goals, but was essential in their attempt to apply a systems approach.

Although I was certain the phenomena would not be a surprise, I knew I was either too old or too young to have heard this term. "Jaywalking" was apparently no mere misdemeanor in this firm, and it went well beyond the "end-run" concept I initially thought it might represent. It was the practice of any member of one functional unit speaking to a member of another functional unit about a business practice, process, or decision. Over the years, I have never again uncovered this term, but I have uncovered the practice of squashing jaywalking practices in many "well led" organizations.

The move to a heterarchically led organization will require a bit of positive and productive 'jaywalking." In Figure 3.10, the problems of hierarchy and negative "jaywalking" are illustrated. The problem with my "jaywalking" client and the traditional

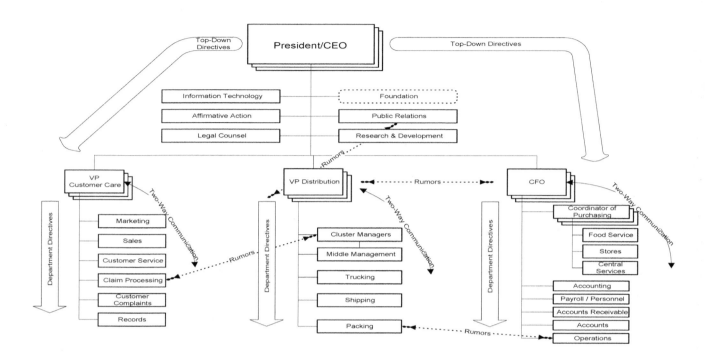

Figure 3.10. A Hierarchical Organization Embedded with Communication Questions.

hierarchical structure is that both suffered from a limited system of open communication that their systems based management approach did not address. The traditional strategy calls for a series of top-down directives from the senior leader, which are then reiterated, but slightly amended in content, as departmental directives (both usually in the form of a memorandum, or maybe an email). In a well-led hierarchy, a system of two-way communication might be initiated (usually in the form of a staff meeting). Now "jaywalking," regardless of policy will begin (normally in the form of rumors). Every organization has a form of well-structured rumor based communication, however rarely do the senior leaders seem to have access to that highly effective communication stream. In a heterarchy the leadership role is changed, as is the management style, to realize this phenomena and to change the informal communication system from a negative influence to a positive means of organizational transformation.

Figure 3.11 illustrates the communication system of a well-led heterarchy. Given the emphasis of emergence, structural dynamics, and empowerment through teamwork, open communication is necessitated in the form of dialogue over monologue. The emphasis is on cross-functional cross-institutional communication that places decision-making power in where it can be used to increase revenue, market share, employee morale, and organizational effectiveness.

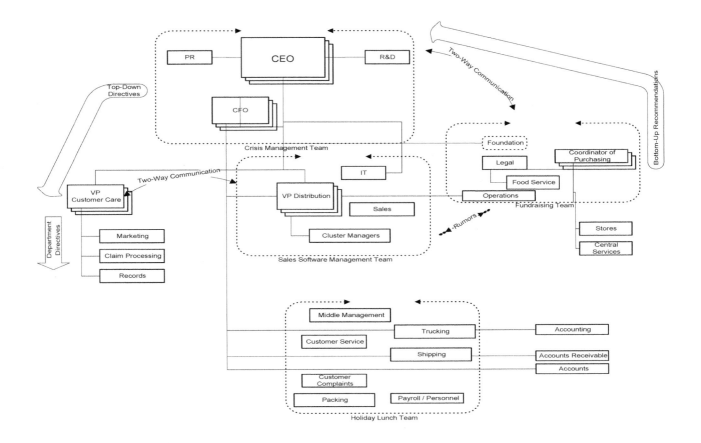

Figure 3.11. An Open Communication System Illustrated in a Heterarchy.

Teams communicate with other teams, and reporting relationships rise and fall from prominence based on the need for action and activity. Leaders do not concern themselves with "jaywalking" or putting out the fires created by rumors; rather they work to ensure open lines of communication, that barriers to effectiveness and productivity are diminished, and that the best possible data and decisions are guiding the mission and goal achievement of the organization. This does not mean that rumors will cease to exist, or that unproductive "end-runs" will not be initiated. It means that leaders are prepared to discourage this activity by proactively addressing rumors, and by not engaging in destructive "end-runs" on colleagues.

The point of this chapter and of sharing the concept of heterarchy is not to suggest another design for organizational charting; rather it is to suggest that managing any company by means of the traditional hierarchy is a problematic exercise. The point of heterarchy is not a means for charting your organization, not a means of illustrating the placement of formal positions within the corporate structure, nor is it even meant as a means of illustrating the structure of your organization. As leaders we are asked to lead dynamic organizations that exist in a constant state of change. Our institutions are emergent and growth oriented. The level of complexity in organizations is so great that a reliance on the knowledge strategies of hierarchy or systems thinking is inefficient and often counters productivity.

Our organizations are composed of independent actors engaged in leading, managing, or doing the good work of our company. If we do not realize that our organizations emerge from a complex set of social relations, that are dynamic in nature, then our leadership practices will not realize the goals of success. Therefore, we should be prepared to change leadership practices, strategic planning practices, human performance enhancement practices, performance reward systems, and all other activities associated with management. This chapter was designed to begin this conversation, to suggest in a very basic way how our understanding of internal structure will influence the performance of our organizations. These issues on management practice as well as understanding this structure both internally and externally will be covered in more detail in subsequent chapters.

The power of transforming your conceptualization of management from either hierarchy or systems to heterarchy is the ability to lead your organization toward the end goals of the contemporary leadership paradigm. These goals can be summed as open multilevel communication channels, the realization of high performing teams, the development of a learning organization, and the realization that all of the leadership goals you set can be achieved. This chapter is meant to serve as a brief introduction to the naturally occurring phenomenon of heterarchy (which we have been wrongly taught was to be understood through other epistemic strategies). The remaining chapters will explain how to lead a heterarchy, and how to use a new form of strategic planning to renew your organization from within a heterarchical understanding of human relations.

The creation of a cross-institutional cross-functional three level planning process that is embedded within a heterarchical conceptualization of structure will allow leaders to simultaneously and systemically initiate individual level human performance and productivity improvements, departmental and functional process enhancements, and organizationally oriented mission achievement and goal realization strategies. This triadic heterarchical approach is a combination of planning and performance enhancement for continuous improvement in the institution, its departments, and for employees. It creates a unified system of multilevel relationships that materialize and redevelop into a managed, complex, emergent heterarchy.

> *The knowledge of the world is only to be acquired in the world, and not in a closet.*
> -- Lord Chesterfield, Letters to his son.

Chapter 4

The Art of Triadic Strategic Planning (Institutional, Departmental, & Personal)

Unto whomsoever much is given, of him shall much be required. – Luke 12:48

As senior level managers represented the majority of the participants attending my strategic planning seminars, I discovered that they often wanted direct control over the planning process, goals, and objectives. Yet, as I attempted to explain, all members of an organization need to be involved in developing the strategic plan if there really is a desire to execute it.

When a leader in an institution initially contacted me for assistance with strategic planning, I explained that my process has been designed and developed for implementation across the entire organization. Leaders, managers, and staff need to know that hierarchical structures limit the role of leadership. This approach to planning is designed as a catalyst of empowerment for continued growth and change.

The model of yesterday was restructuring; the model of the future, notably in light of the 2008 economic meltdown must become emergent heterarchy, which implies no set uniform structure but rather a multilevel, multidimensional, fluid structure of continual adaptation. This system is best created through a practice of triadic heterarchical strategic planning (institutional, departmental (unit), and personal (individual)).

As the three level planning process is implemented, leaders are asked to implement a system of personal goal development and evaluation that unites the focus of institutional and departmental values with those of the staff. This creates a system that is more heterarchical and more likely to generate a shared vision as well as a system of shared responsibility that is often publicly expressed and sought.

Strategic planning is a means of creating organizational change and increased effectiveness; however, unless individuals are incorporated into the strategic change movement, unrealistic personal illusions emerge. These illusions influence the outcomes of organizational change. It is the local empowered individual that must incorporate the visions of leadership into everyday practice. It is important for management to realize the necessity of integrating the ideas of employees into a long-range planning model.

The Triadic Planning Model

Writers and theorists often suggest models for strategic planning that focus either on the organizational or institutional level, the departmental, unit, or team levels, or in rare circumstances at the individual level (sometimes as part of a larger institutional human resources plan); all from a command-and control standpoint. The triadic model of strategic planning is designed to represent one plan divided into three separate but closely aligned and integrated levels developed from a collaborative standpoint. Figure 4.1 illustrates the need for this three level model.

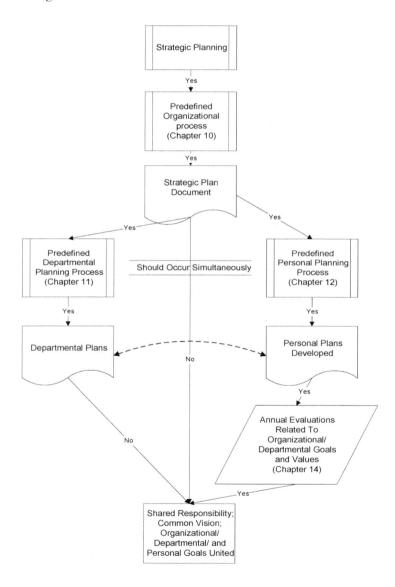

Figure 4.1. Common Vision Reached Via Triadic Planning Model.

The first step in initiating the triadic planning model is the development of an initial strategic plan for the organization. This plan should be developed through the use of cross-institutional, cross-functional planning teams that embody the vast majority of the stakeholders of the organization. The initial strategic plan should be developed with a comprehensive execution plan designed for completion within a timeframe of no more than three years. The strategic planning process is designed to incorporate up to 100% of the staff directly into the planning process of the organization. The process is completely described and detailed in Chapter 10 of this book.

Once the strategic plan has been written and approved by the governing body or senior management of the organization, all department leaders (depending on your organization this might include vice-presidents, directors, deans, coordinators, or other management based titles) or functional leaders should initiate the departmental planning process. This process is again designed to be a comprehensive and inclusive process that incorporates 100% of the management and staff working in each functional area of the organization. The process is intended to lead to the development of departmental plans that are designed to implement the plans, strategies, goals, and objectives of the organizational strategic plan. These plans can be thought of as the action plans needed for executing the larger organizational strategic plan. This process is completely described and detailed in Chapter 11 of this book.

At this point in the initiation of the model, you have reached the point where most organizations that plan well have completed their respective process. The problem for organizations at this point of the planning process is that there is no real "buy-in" from the staff; and no sense of "ownership" over the respective departmental plans. The employee is not connected with the larger planning process, so the vision is never fully realized.

In an ideal environment, senior management has invited input from all levels of the hierarchy into the creation of the organizational plan, and department managers have involved staff members in the development of departmental plans. In reality, the organizational plan is often developed at a retreat held away from the organization. This plan is then shared with the department heads, who often are instructed to develop departmental objectives. The departmental plans (or objectives) are usually written over a weekend and subsequently shared with the department's staff. Occasionally, the staff is invited to provide some feedback; but mainly the whole process is viewed from the bottom-up as the usual command-and-control, top-down mandates that are normal operating procedure for the organization.

Organizational leaders now suggest that the shared vision process is being implemented. The shared vision for the employee here is simple: "they tell us the vision and goals and we tell them we share it." This is a shared vision; the managers have now had the decency to share their vision with the staff, who if they wish to remain employed must agree to share it as well.

This may be better illustrated by an example. I once interviewed for the chief planning officer position at a large private university. The interview took place over two days and I was able to meet with a large number of staff members, including the president, senior VPs, middle managers, and members of the staff. After going through the normal routines of the Human Resources office and the roundtable search committee (this is the norm for higher education), I began my series of one-on-one interviews starting with the university's president.

In each interview, I answered the typical questions about my experience, qualifications, and goals. Then I asked a series of questions about planning, vision, and goals of the institution. In sum, I asked the president to share with me his vision for the university and for higher education. He looked at me as if puzzled and said that his vision for the university was that of a shared vision. I asked him what that vision was and he responded that it was the one shared by members of the organization. I asked if he was looking for someone to develop that sense of shared vision. He responded that they already had a vision.

When I asked his VPs about the shared vision, they told me that the president was a dynamic man that had shared his vision with the rest of the college. I again pressed for what that vision might be; one VP shook her head and said, "education." Middle managers all stated that they thought that the planning position I was applying for was created to help develop this vision. Support staff members alluded that the shared vision was outlined in individual job descriptions, and one stated that, "having one of those senior people just acknowledge our existence might be a good start."

Although this example appears extreme, it illustrates the point that the notion of shared vision cannot be realized in the traditional planning processes currently in place at most institutions. Sharing requires a dialogue and a realization of equality that is not present in the hierarchical mental model in place at most contemporary organizations. This is why the learning organization, which appears so desirable on paper, is so elusive in reality.

Most managers and staff view strategic planning as an add-on to the daily work activity, a leadership responsibility that should be hidden from most employees so as not to overburden them with another workplace activity. Many managers have come to view the planning process as a waste of time that they are required to complete. This dominant ideology remains well deserved, since most strategic plans fail to ever be fully realized. This becomes a vicious cycle, since managers often view the planning process as positive when completed; while most staff view it as a means for management to justify mandates and greater workloads while the planned outcomes never become part of the reality of the everyday employee.

The point of the three level model is to force management and staff to reach an ongoing dialog on the purpose of the planning enterprise, the mission of the organization, the values of departments, and the goals each member of the organization is working to achieve. Triadic planning synergizes the institution with the departments and synthesizes the missions of the organization, departments, and personnel into a single unit.

The final step of the model is the development of personal plans for each employee of the organization. Everyone is asked to construct a personal mission which is connected to the departmental mission and the organization as a whole. Each person is asked to develop a personal professional plan designed to realize and execute the goals of the departmental plans, which were developed with the purpose of implementing the organizational strategic plan. This process is completely described and detailed in Chapter 12 of this book.

Figure 4.2 illustrates the three levels of the planning process and the associated outcomes expected as a result of the successful implementation of the planning process. The organizational planning process is closely related to the traditional strategic planning model that renews the vision and mission, analyzes institutional level data (i.e., conducts a situational SWOT analysis), identifies alternative actions (goals and objectives), creates criteria for goal prioritization (strategic change to increase productivity), and moves the organization toward a common vision (culture).

The departmental process is designed as the implementation mechanism for the organizational plan; it articulates a departmental mission that is integrated with the institutional mission. The departmental planning process analyzes local data (SWOT), distinguishes alternative actions (action steps designed to implement organizational objectives), produces a sense of action prioritization (strategic change to increase productivity), and unites the department under a common vision (realized in the development of a culture of effectiveness, execution and efficiency).

The personal planning process is designed as the implementation mechanism for both the organizational and departmental plans; it necessitates the development of a personal mission and accountability that is integrated with the organizational and departmental visions, missions, and values. The personal planning process analyzes the realization of personal and professional life goals and accomplishments. It creates an opportunity for the development of new and renewed personal and professional goals (which the process attempts to focus within the context of departmental actions and organizational goals). This process intends to create a culture of expanding personal and professional success (strategic changes that increase productivity), while uniting the individual, department, and organization under a shared vision (realized in the development of an ever increasing sense of positive attitude and productivity).

The triadic model is designed to be implemented in the following order: organizational strategic planning process and formal plan articulation, then the simultaneous development of departmental and personal plans. Departmental plans are fully developed first while the development of personal plans assists the departmental planning process as the final step in the triadic planning process. The implementation strategy is illustrated in Figure 4.3.

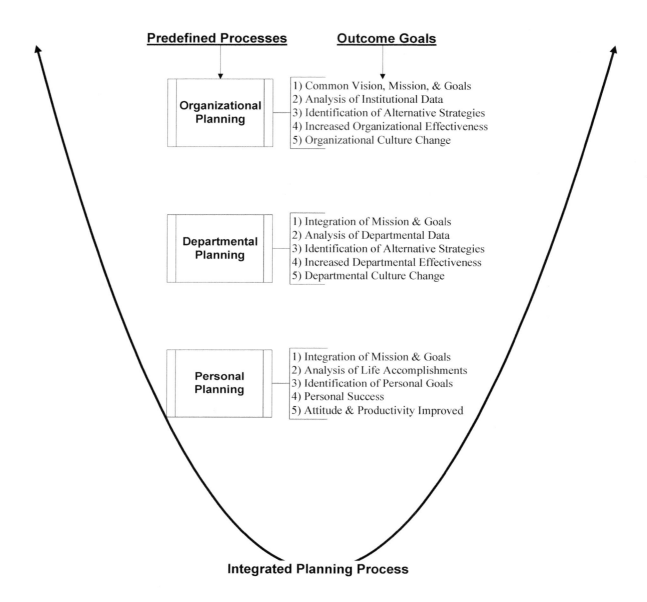

Figure 4.2. The Integrated Outcomes of the Triadic Planning Model.

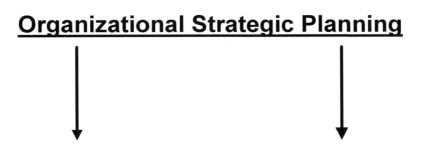

Time One

Organizational Strategic Planning

Departmental Planning ⟷ Personal Planning

Figure 4.3. Moving the Planning Process from the Global to the Personal.

The execution strategy, which starts with organizational planning moves to departmental planning and then proceeds to personal planning, only represents year one of the process. Once the entire process is in place, the model is designed to become an ongoing comprehensive strategy of strategic planning. The ongoing model of planning is illustrated in Figure 4.4. In the realization of the triadic planning process, the organization will move away from a process of static time defined strategic plans toward a culture of continual adaptation linked to the emergent heterarchical structure.

Once the system is in place, each year (as part of the personnel evaluation system of the organization) personal plans will be renewed, rearticulated, and revised to ensure ongoing personal success and goal accomplishment. When the personal plans are evaluated and revised, the context of the departmental plan realization and success is used to the assist in the evaluation of the individual. This process of evaluation will force each employee and their supervisor to examine the current departmental plan in relation to individual accomplishments and goals. Once the departmental plan becomes directly related to the success of the individual, it will become real as opposed to a document of wishes or elusive unrealistic goals.

Eventual Goal (Time 2 & Beyond)

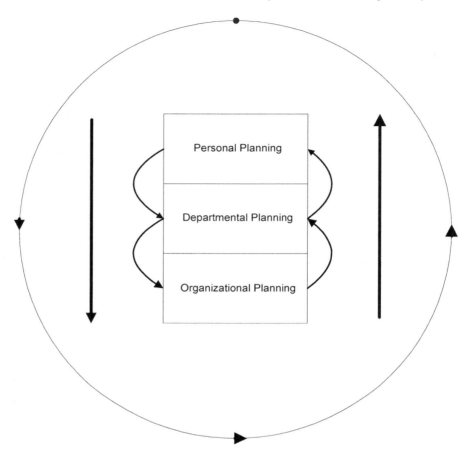

Figure 4.4. Triadic Planning within the Culture of Continual Adaptation.

As the examination of departmental plans becomes more intense and systemic, it will influence the annual evaluation of departmental success. The purpose and realization of departmental actions will influence the goals and strategies of the organization, thus influencing the organizational planning process. The organizational culture will move toward one of continual adaptation that begins with the annual appraisal of personal plans, directly related to the evaluation and the effectiveness of departmental plans, which will in turn influence the articulation of organizational planning.

Figure 4.5 demonstrates that the final steps in the implementation of triadic planning are the processes of aligning personal evaluation with the effectiveness of the institution and the local departments; and unity in the development of budgets that are designed to implement the organizational, departmental, and personal plans. The strategic planning process can only be truly realized in full, when the goals of the institution, departments, and the employees are directly related and meaningful to one another.

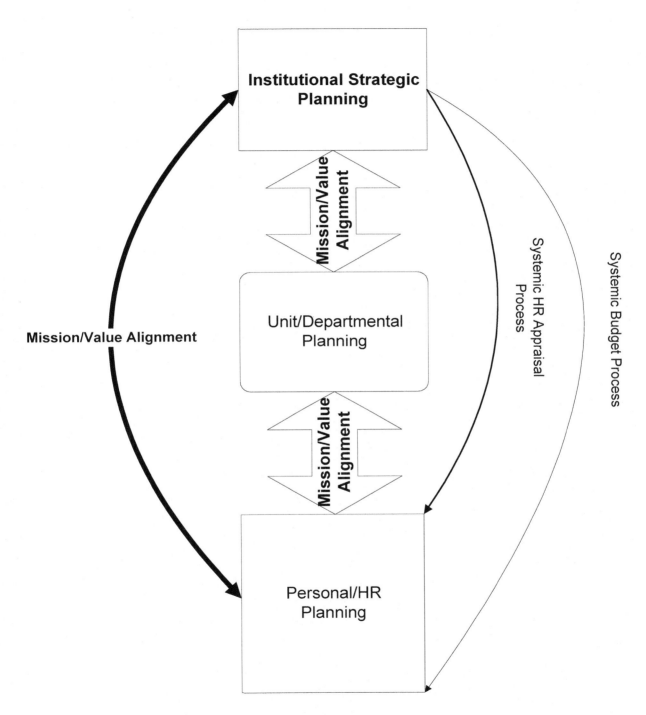

Figure 4.5. Key Cross-Institutional Alignment Components.

The Value of Adding the Personal Level
to Traditional Strategic Planning

Individual planning and appraisal structures should enhance human resources and move the leaders of the organization to a management style of coaching and teamwork that allows for the realization of the structure of heterarchy. Through a participatory management and planning development process, the organization merges the conceptualization of human resources management, structure, and teamwork into a dynamic environment of success and motivation at the institutional, department, and personal levels (i.e., across the three levels).

The development of the personal planning step in overall planning efforts creates a management system where the individual's values are integrated with the organization's values (where the spheres of influence (home-life and work-life) no longer compete for the individual's most scarce resource, time). Personal planning appraisal in the context of departmental effectiveness and organizational goal achievement allows for managers and leaders to realize that the most effective employees are ones who view their career and families as non-competing interests. The successful organization of the future continuously changes to become a non-competing enterprise. Personal planning, if produced within an emergent heterarchical model, can produce a systematic culture change within an organization (across all levels, and beyond the traditional leadership retreats).

A unified triadic planning process ensures that as individuals strive to implement the goals of the institutions they serve, their values and goals are not contrary to those they are attempting to reach for their organization. The establishment of a common value paradigm becomes paramount in the structures and systems designed to increase institutional effectiveness. The process of triadic planning in an emergent heterarchy provides the impetus for change; it is the condition that will lead to culture change and success. As the results of the department and the organization become relevant to the personal success of the individual, the idea of ownership becomes embedded within a culture of continual adaptation and success for the company.

As the values of the organization, the department, and the individual become interrelated and interdependent, each employee comes to view the organization as an extension of their life. Employees realize that the success of their professional careers is directly related to the success and goals they possess in their personal lives. Furthermore, they realize that their professional and personal successes are integrated with the success of their respective departments and the organizations that they serve. Simultaneously, the organization should recognize the value that each individual employee adds to the organization, creating strategic goals that remove competitive interests between people and the company. In this way, the individual realizes this "sense" of ownership that leads to the development of a shared vision of success for the organization.

The Power of the Three Levels: Communication, Empowerment, & Ownership

Traditionally, companies have viewed work and personal life as competing priorities in a zero-sum game, in which a success in one arena means a loss in another arena. Friedman, Christensen, and DeGroot (1998) argued that a new era of leadership was emerging where managers and employees collaborate to achieve mutually beneficial work and personal objectives. A decade later these are becoming more apparent as the new generation of workers enters the workforce. They further contended that the strategies and systems of priority unification had largely been informal, but as this approach becomes better appreciated through its demonstrated success, more companies are coming to view leaders that unite values as the agents of change. The triadic planning process is designed to allow all leaders at your organization to become the agents of change, and to formalize the process of creating mutually beneficial objectives.

Forty years ago, Paul, Robertson, and Herzberg (1969) argued that for employees to take on more responsibility there would need to be a constant feedback loop where managers continuously evaluated subordinates. Belasco and Snead (1999) reasoned that in the contemporary learning organization and workplace these loops were also necessary but rather than as a command-and-control mechanism, as a means to creating ownership throughout the organization's workforce. Ten years later, this ideal of increased ownership is best accomplished through a synergy of values, mission, and goals throughout the organization. The triadic planning process was designed to create a formal process of transformation that is initiated heterarchically to ensure that a synergy of mission and vision becomes an authentic reality.

Covey (1992) further demonstrated this point by illustrating that the creation of mission driven organizations leads to the development of organizations which embody the ideals of change, empowerment, and transformation. This exciting literature on change and personal transformation suggested the need for a process of personal enrichment that complemented the existing processes of organizational enrichment already in place at many contemporary organizations. It further suggested that the duty of personal development is not only a supervisor or human resource department activity, but that it is a global organizational priority that deserves the same level of attention to detail that strategic and departmental planning have experienced in the past twenty years.

Figure 4.6 illustrates the heterarchical process that occurs when the missions of the organization, department, and individual are integrated into a common mission through a formal process of planning and organizational development. This development ensures that the leadership of the company will begin to examine policies and procedures that ensure a continual synergy of values and goals. The establishment of this synergy coupled with an appraisal system that unites the success of the organization, department, and employees allows the leadership of the organization to concentrate on the articulation of heterarchy and the formation of high-powered teams designed to improve institutional performance.

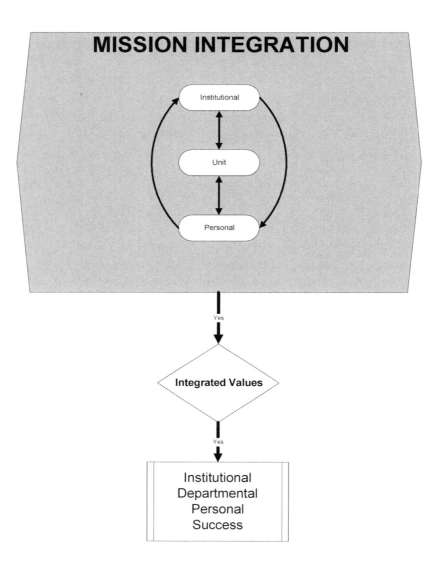

Figure 4.6. The Cross-institutional, Cross-functional Heterarchical Triadic Planning Success Flowchart.

The entire triadic model can be measured for effectiveness, in reaching the goal of becoming a learning organization, both quantitatively and qualitatively. The framework of the strategic planning process (institutional, departmental, or personal) is best accomplished within a framework of heterarchical-based systems thinking that leads to the emergence of the high performance organization. To create an organization that acquires, and transfers new knowledge in a continuous fashion it is necessary to ensure that all levels of the organization (global, departmental, and personal) have systems in place that are change oriented, forward forecasting, and designed to create organizational synergy (Garvin, 1993).

We must indeed all hang together, or most assuredly we shall all hang separately. — Benjamin Franklin

Chapter 5

Completing the Entire Process in Less than One Year

Out of intense complexities intense simplicities emerge. – Winston Churchill

Strategic plans should not take such a long time to develop. The time devoted to planning varies: many businesses have reached the point of making six month plans, hospital strategic plans average three years, college and university plans still average five years, Wall Street barely planned at all, most non-profits still seem to plan once every ten years, and the 'Big Three' automakers seem to have abandoned long-term planning altogether. Currently, the three-year strategic organizational plan appears to represent the average and most effective means of planning (if one remembers that plans should be dynamic).

Why do businesses, colleges, and not-for-profits make plans for differing lengths? These differences are due to various factors. Businesses strategic plans are in a state of continuous renewal reflective of the market; they tend to mirror departmental plans more than larger macro-corporate plans. Colleges and universities often live within the luxury of public funding, which limits their subordination to market forces; not to mention they tend to overindulge in committees over execution. Not-for-profits and hospitals also rely on public generosity and governmental funds which allows them to move less swiftly as well. It should be noted though that hospitals have been forced in the past decade to move more swiftly as they are more reliant on market forces and insurance carrier payouts.

Evidence suggests that longer planning cycles do not seem to lead to more successful plans. In fact, it can be argued that planning outcomes are actually diminished. Business planning is often more effective as the sense of urgency and the seriousness of the effects are heightened by their need to generate increasing profit margins. These plans are not successful because they are developed more quickly; rather they are successful because the plan's outcomes have some effect over the leaders trying to implement them. This assumes some level of integrity in leadership which abounds in business enterprises (Enron, Tyco, Wall Street bankers and hedgefund brokers are the exception not the rule).

Does this mean that all organizations should rely on the model of high-powered corporate enterprises? The notion of continuously developing six-month plans is problematic for several reasons. First, long-term plans allow organizations to minimize the phenomenon of surprise while allowing for a mechanism to adapt to change (this lesson is clear in the example of Detroit automakers). Also, short-term plans concentrate on the present, while not ensuring a successful vision of the future, its opportunities, its challenges, or its management. Long-term vision, mission, and planning development ensures that the organization has a culture and life that extends past the leadership style, investment, or fads of present management. Finally, long range planning allows for a better approach to the competitive environment, internal problem identification, and a better chance for long-term success over immediate gratification. A lesson we could all do well to remember in the coming decade.

We are left with a final question, what is the appropriate timeframe for the strategic planning process? The answer is that strategic planning has no end, it might originate in many forms, but it should be continuous, dynamic, and comprehensive. Successful organizations, like successful people, should have strategic long-range goals, short-term goals, and an ability to transform and rise to the occasion in a time of crisis or in the event of a windfall. Consider the ability of individuals to come together and succeed in the face of great challenges, in times of chaos, or in any time of need. Consider the majestic story of any everyday hero or heroine. Now ask how your organization can possess this very ability.

I once presented at a conference where the chief planning officer for a state college in New Jersey described the ongoing process detailing the development of their strategic plan. He described the one-year process of mission renewal, and the two-year process of data gathering and analysis. He then suggested that the finalization of their five-year plan would be completed within the next year. To my amazement, many of the attendees applauded the college's ability to move through the planning process quickly.

This put the final completion of their organizational strategic plan at about nine years. The average term of a college president falls short of this timeframe, suggesting that at nine to ten years no plan in higher education is likely to be fully executed or evaluated for effectiveness. How any plan over nine years is expected to be successful is mystifying, just considering the implications of finance or technology alone.

The planning process of the institution I represented was initiated differently. We had developed a new vision, mission, and values within three months, had finalized the plan within six months, had departmental plans within three additional months, and had initiated a system of personal planning in less time then that state college had taken to come to consensus on its mission. Additionally, the planning system of the institution I represented had included 100% of the staff at the organization. The state college had only included a special team of senior administrators and faculty leaders.

From the immediacy of the business planning process to the 'life-of-its-own' model of higher education institutions to a failure to plan realistically by Wall Street and the automakers; strategic plans fail because there is no connection between them and the people asked to do the work of implementation. Plans fail because they have no basis in reality. They are developed because organizations of all types feel an obligation to their existence. The feeling that strategic planning will really influence the outcomes of any institution's success has been lost. It has become a mundane exercise that companies initiate with the same energy and enthusiasm they approach the annual personnel performance evaluation mechanism. The fact is that strategic planning in its current form has not improved communication, staffing, resources, technological advancement, or the bottom line of most organizations developing them.

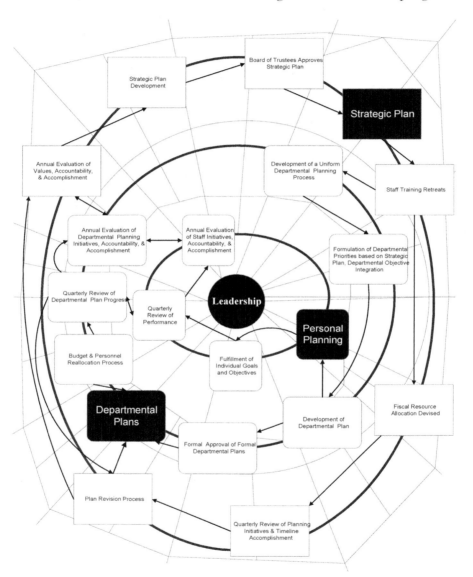

Figure 5.1. Sample Triadic Heterarchical Strategic Planning Model[1].

---

[1]This version of the triadic planning model represents a revised adaptation of Fogg's Corporate Accountability Cycle. For more information on corporate accountability, quarterly reviews, performance reviews and implementing your strategic plan see Fogg, C. D. (1999). Implementing Your Strategic Plan. New York, NY: AMACOM.

Strategic planning should be designed as an ongoing process that has no timeline directly related to plan completion. Rather it should be a process that is simultaneously forward directed, continuous, and contingent. The planning process should be dynamic in nature to ensure that leaders can generate data and strategies to address both internal and external conditions. It should serve as the communication mechanism for the organization, the process for resource allocation, and the process for the evaluation of success at the organizational, departmental, team, and individual levels. The triadic heterarchical strategic planning model illustrated in Figure 5.1 meets these criteria.

In the background of the triadic planning model is the web of leadership and communication. Although the planning process is designed to cycle and interrelate levels of the institution at specific times and under preconceived conditions, the reality of heterarchical organizations are that the practice of leadership (under the best conditions) and top-down management (under the worst conditions) influence the sequential nature of the process. Simultaneously, the informal communication systems and networks will influence the execution of the planning process and the development of goals, strategies, and objectives. The web represents discussions in the hallway, over the email, texts, blogs from external forces, and from interoffice communiqués. The triadic heterarchical model illustrates leadership over the internal communication system, a process for managing change, and the means for ensuring long-term cross-institutional success.

The actuality of any company is that employees feel a relationship between the organization and themselves, between their departments and their lives, and between leaders and their personal ability to be successful. The triadic heterarchical model moves this backstage reality to the frontstage, ensuring that the leadership and staff are continuously and proactively transforming the organizational culture. Leaders are asked to directly lead both the formal and informal communication systems by inspiring employees to develop the workplace of the future.

The traditional models of planning regard the corporate plan as the overarching strategic plan, departmental plans or task assignments as the implementation mechanism, and individual performance standards as the ultimate uniform accountability vehicle. For the past thirty years there have been numerous resources that suggest that planning should occur throughout the organization (Baldridge & Okimi, 1982; Bradford & Cohen, 1998; Chair Academy of Leadership Training for Chairs, Deans, and Other Organizational Leaders, 2000; Fogg, 1999; Heskett & Schlesinger, 1996; Howell, 2000; Juranski, 1993; Lawler, 1996; Lippitt, 1981; Portillo, 1997; Rothwell, 1996; & Varcoe, 1993 to name just a few). This part of the concept is not a novel idea.

The triadic heterarchical strategic planning model suggests that the strategic planning process is composed of three distinct but interrelated levels: organizational (global), departmental/unit (local), and personal (individual)). In this model, strategic planning is continuous, adaptive, dependent, interdependent, and independent. Successful planning emerges from inspirational leadership within a culture of adaptation based on the need for each employee to move toward a mental state of ownership, personal accountability, and shared responsibility.

Unlike traditional models that are based within the command-and-control leadership paradigm (which emphasizes hierarchy, control, negotiated performance accountability, reengineering, regular personnel removal, and top to bottom plan alignment), this systemic approach is designed around the new leadership paradigms (heterarchy, empowerment, ownership, inspirational performance accountability, continuous improvement, work/life balance, emergent leadership, and bottom-up grassroots organizational change).

The model in Figure 5.1 demonstrates an ability to implement the triadic planning process within one year. The process begins with organizational planning, moves to departmental planning, and is fully executed through personal planning. The three planning processes are fully integrated to ensure a cross-functional, cross-institutional process that is universal for the firm. The model can be fully clarified by examining each path of the continuous process. The nature of managing a heterarchical organization requires a planning system that leads to a culture of continual adaptation to modify the leadership practice toward an inspirational agenda.

Organizational Planning Process Path

The first step of the triadic planning model is the implementation of the organizational strategic planning process (Chapter 10). Figure 5.2 demonstrates the organizational planning annual path (the outer circle of the triadic model). Once the planning process is initiated, cross-institutional planning teams meet, perform the SWOT analysis, develop strategies, choose the goals that will be most beneficial to the business, and then formulate the final plan.

Once the plan is formalized, the organization's Board or senior management team should ceremoniously approve it. Next, a series of retreats should be offered to educate the entire organization in the expected planning process outcomes, the formal plan, and the departmental planning process that will be subsequently initiated. The organization's fiscal resources should be examined and re-prioritized to ensure that the goals and values of the plan are funded for full implementation.

The implementation of objectives should be evaluated on a quarterly basis in a public forum by a special team of senior management leaders and department heads. If plan goals and objectives are deemed unachievable or have been fully realized the plan should then be revised or renewed as part of this quarterly process. Each goal should be evaluated at the conclusion of each year, and a summary report should be disseminated throughout the organization. While the organizational plan begins the implementation stage, the departmental and personal planning processes are being developed and initiated.

The tangible outcomes of the organizational planning process should consist of a review, revision, rearticulation, or confirmation of the firm's vision and mission. The

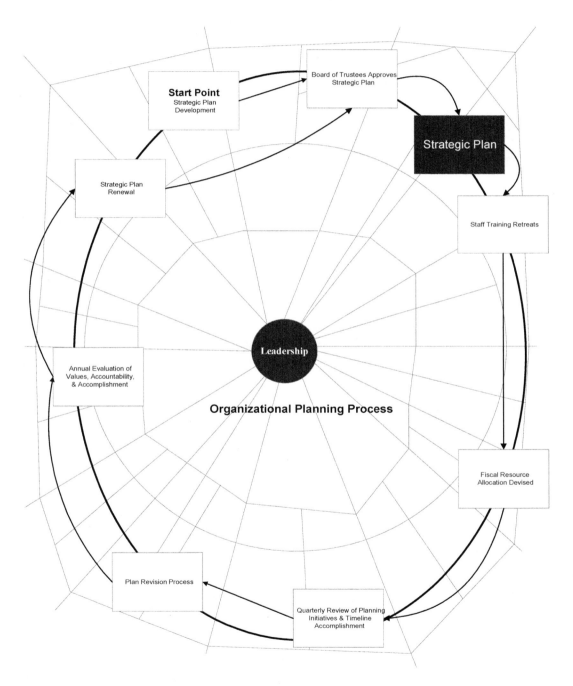

Figure 5.2. Triadic Heterarchical Strategic Planning Model (Organizational Level).

organization may choose to establish a set of unachievable abstract values that publicly express those ideals tangible and intangible that embody the true essence of the business or operation. Traditionally, these values have been expressed as an abstract set of goals. I would suggest that all goals of the organization should be achievable, thus those macro ideals that are not realistically achievable should be expressed as values. Otherwise, members of the organization believe that there is no real accountability in the planning process, since the goals cannot really ever be achieved.

Once the organization has developed a public vision, mission, and value set, it should then begin a comprehensive examination of available information and data. The planning teams will perform the situational analysis, examining internal strengths and weaknesses and external threats and opportunities. Data should be developed by a central office or by a specially developed ad hoc team. The gathering and synthesis of data should not become so cumbersome that the planning teams expend all useful energy on this part of the process. I suggest that the system be developed where planning teams ask for the data, and that the research office or an ad hoc team to provide data with an executive summary. From the situational analysis, the planning teams will then develop a list of long-, short-term, and contingency based alternatives for action.

Using the vision, mission, and values as a guide, this list of alternatives should be prioritized, synthesized, and reduced to a set of achievable goals. The goals should then be balanced within the context of one of the organization's values. Once consensus is reached on each of the goals, a set of practical objectives should be compiled for each of the identified goals. Timelines for objective execution and goal achievement should then be developed. Finally, a formal proposal should be developed and presented to the organization's Board or senior management team. Once approved, the formal written strategic plan should be assembled and disseminated throughout the company (including timelines, key responsibility assignments, and strategic outcome performance measures).

Formal plan dissemination should be coupled with an understanding that it is the responsibility of every employee to ensure the successful implementation of the organizational plan. Each department manager should be prepared to meet with staff, discuss the implication of the plan on departmental operating objectives, and to promote the importance of the planning goals to the success and appraisal of personal initiatives. Far too many businesses fail to make the organizational plan relevant to the personal success of each employee, or to develop the appropriate accountability mechanisms.

Departmental Planning Process Path

The second step of the triadic planning process is the implementation of the departmental strategic planning process (Chapter 11). Figure 5.3 demonstrates the departmental planning annual path (the center circle of the triadic model). Once the planning process is initiated, department heads are empowered and trained to involve all members of the staff as active participants in the planning process.

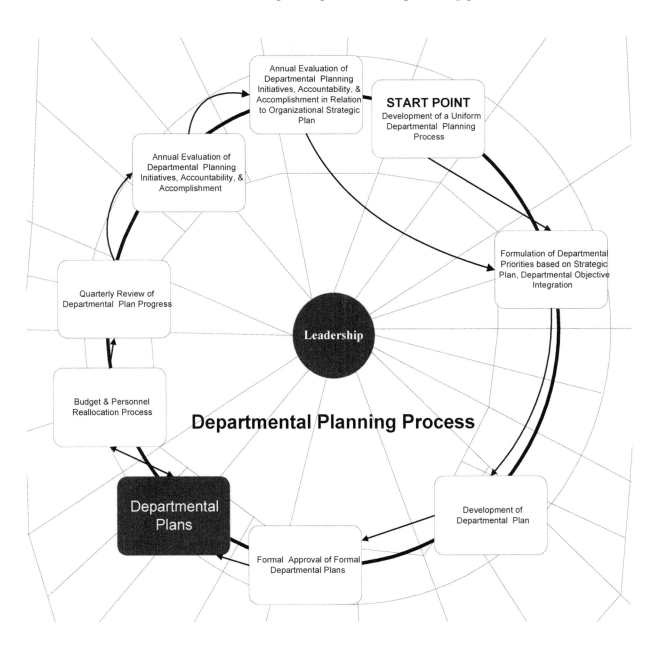

Figure 5.3. Triadic Heterarchical Strategic Planning Model (Departmental Level).

The departmental planning process should be an outgrowth of the organizational planning process, and should be integrated and related to the overall planning system of the institution.

Using the organization's vision, mission, values, goals, and plan as the contextual framework, the department should formulate its objectives for discussion with its staff. Next the development of the plan should be completed, approved by senior management, and formally written and disseminated to all stakeholders interested in the function of the department. The department's budget should then be reexamined in light of the plan and in relation to the organizational budgetary priorities. Once the plan is being implemented, the department leader should evaluate the effectiveness of execution on a quarterly basis, ensuring cross-institutional accountability (see Chapter 11 for more details).

After a year of implementation, the departmental plan should be reviewed and revised to reflect success and setbacks. Each departmental objective should be evaluated at the conclusion of each year, and a summary report should be disseminated throughout the department and to the organizational planning evaluation team. While the departmental plan is being implemented the personal planning processes is assisting in the development of the department's plan.

The departmental planning process should include the education of staff on the need for empowerment, emergent heterarchy, and the diminishment of ineffective hierarchical structures and top-down mandates. Department heads should explain the new system of personal planning and departmental accountability. The process should look to use data and other information to evaluate the current departmental culture and values in relation to the organizational goals.

The new accountability system will require that all employees are empowered to meet the goals of the department, the organization, and their respective personal plans. The achievement of departmental goals and increasing accountability will require that each employee understand their respective positions and relate the position to the organizational, departmental, and personal plans. This operation of process mapping will begin the phenomena of integrating the goals and values of the organization, department, and the individual within the institution.

The real integration of the goals and values will begin when the department and personal planning process necessitate each employee to publicly express their commitment to the department, the organization, and to one another. This process referred to as the "pledge" system of responsibility, assists leaders in harmonizing the mission, goals, and values of the three levels of the organization. Again, the nature of leading the heterarchy removes the command-and-control mechanisms, the organization moves from a culture of mandated change to one of continual adaptation, from evaluation to appraisal, and from management direction to leadership inspiration.

When this shift in the leadership paradigm is completed within a framework of cross-functional, cross-institutional triadic strategic planning, the progressive realization of the professional goals of employees becomes the guiding force of organizational change and continuous improvement for the organization. The organization moves from a reactive enterprise to a proactive success oriented model of business.

Personal Planning Process Path

The final step of the triadic planning process is the implementation of the personal strategic planning process (Chapter 12). Figure 5.4 demonstrates the personal planning annual path (the inner circle of the triadic model).

Once the planning process is initiated, department heads meet with each employee that they directly supervise to begin addressing the mission of the institution, the goals of the department, and the long- and short-range goals of the individual employee. Individual supervisors then meet with the employees they lead and begin the same process of mission and value integration, coupled with an emphasis on achieving a practice of work and life balance throughout the organization.

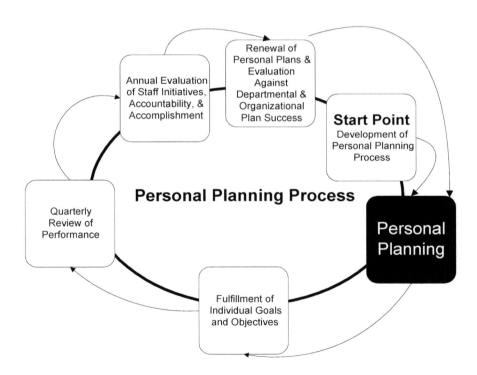

Figure 5.4. Triadic Heterarchical Strategic Planning Model (Personal Level).

The paramount objective of this process is to achieve an environment of organizational synergy for the total organization across and between each of the levels (i.e., organization, department, and personal). The values of the organization should begin to change to reflect the values of the staff, and likewise the counterproductive values of the staff will begin to change to reflect the vision, mission, values, and goals of the firm.

As planning discussions around the process begin, employees are asked to assess their life goals and then to create a plan that rearticulates personal goals. The development of new, revised, or remembered personal goals will be placed within a context of their respective professional life. As the value of cross-institutional synergy is communicated throughout the organization, staff members will begin to view their worklife as the realization of their personal and professional goals. The role of leadership is to establish a core sense of values and a set of standards identifying the high potential employee. The role of the staff is to productively react to these values and standards, through the formula of becoming constructively discontent with their level of success in attaining their life objectives.

Each individual in the firm will then develop a set of short- and long-term professional goals that the organization is prepared to assist them in reaching. The realization of personal goals should allow each employee to proactively develop a better attitude that leads to enhanced productivity throughout the collective enterprise of the organization. Simultaneously, the realization of personal and professional goals should lead to a culture of continual adaptation at the local level, and a sense of proper life/work balance throughout the company.

Finally, individuals will assess the legacy they plan to leave their families, their social relationships, and to the organization they serve. This assessment of goals and legacy will be formally articulated in the development of personal mission statements (that are associated with the departmental and organizational missions). Once the mission is formalized the individual develops a personal plan that identifies strategies for reaching their personal goals, for implementing their department's plan, and for assisting the organization in strengthening the organizational strategic values.

The personal planning process causes each person to fully understand the positive role they have in the success of the company. Each staff member realizes that their relationship with the organization is important, that their contributions are essential, and that their actions can affect all other employees at the organization. The relationship between the individual and the department, the department and the organization, and the individual and the organization is examined and revealed.

The Purpose of the Triadic Model

Unlike the typical planning model that emphasizes the hierarchical command-and-control directive of change, the triadic heterarchical model emphasizes the ability of staff to envision the future, to assume leadership roles, and to plan the successful destiny of the organization. The heterarchical model reveals to each staff member, regardless of position in the organization, that his or her contributions are valuable and appreciated. This model emphasizes the talents of each employee, matching the organization's strategic goals and the departmental business functions with employee talent. When leaders begin to better understand the goals, talents, and dreams of their followers, they begin to act as agents of change in the lives of their staff. The staff begins to fully comprehend their ability to influence the direction of their fellow employees, their department, and the organization.

The process is effective because it empowers employees to begin to create the ideal workplace, and to work to enhance their existing talents rather than having them waste energy overcoming a perceived weakness or talent gap. Leaders ask each staff member to envision the environment in which they can provide the greatest level of service. Then through a constructive and proactive dialog, the leaders and staff develop sets of mutually beneficial objectives that create an environment of accomplishment for the individual, the department, and the organization. For a business this may represent the best means to higher profits, for a not-for-profit it may be enhanced service, for higher education it might mean actually achieving the elusive goal of shared governance.

The need for leadership qualified to manage an organization heterarchically cannot be adequately stressed. The leaders of the future realize that they are there to manage the planning process, to manage the communication systems, the organizational structure, to match employee talent with business functions and organizational goals, and to establish highly effective work teams. They further realize that leadership is not a management function, but rather the ability to inspire and guide their followers (staff) toward the successful realization of their personal and professional ideals. As these ideals are reached, employees begin the practice of increasing their value to the organization.

If we again examine the complexity of a triadic heterarchical planning system, as in Figure 5.5, consider the model as one that moves from the inside outward, rather than from the outside inward. Our first impression is that the model goes from the global to the level of the individual (as is the case with any of the traditional hierarchically based strategic planning models). However, once the system is developed and fully implemented, the triadic heterarchical model continuously adapts from the level of the individual to the global level. The role of the leader is to manage the process, to aid in resource allocation, and to make decisions about direction. Leaders learn that rather than to compose directives designed to hamper innovation and empowerment, organizations are more successful when people lead the change process.

We have been taught to expect direction from the level of the organization. We have become a system of actors without original thought, without questions, without challenges to business as usual. From the time we enter school, we are taught to listen and obey (Bowles and Gintis, 1976). We expect authority to reign down from above and we anticipate that our ideas and values will go unappreciated. The power of hierarchical thought and perspective limits our individual ability to change, to venture, and to innovate; and it limits our company's ability to be successful.

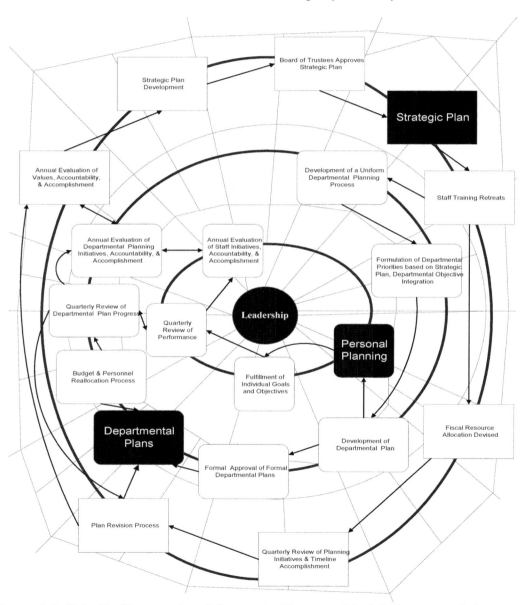

Figure 5.5. Triadic Heterarchical Strategic Planning Model (Integrated Across Levels).

To illustrate my point, consider this example expressed to me during a personal planning session. A long-term staff member approached me during a break extremely excited about the process. She said that for twenty years she had walked the halls and attempted to greet senior managers with a 'good morning' or a simple 'hello.' For twenty years they had ignored her gestures, and had failed to acknowledge her existence unless they were issuing a command. She then suggested that she did not know if personal planning would work, but at least for her final year before retirement, those in authority might now publicly recognize her worth as a human being. Not only did they acknowledge her, she was named employee of the year, and her firm quickly became the highest performing organization in its region. The process gave her greater personal value, greater value within the organization, and influenced her ability to succeed in all levels of her life, while simultaneously motivating all employees achieve and excel.

Consider also how life might be different for so many Wall Street executives, automakers, plant workers, investors, fund managers, and home buyers if more members of the workforce had their eyes on the ball. When power becomes overly unregulated without any input from those doing the work, senior managers can become blinded by their positions and entitlements. It takes input from all levels of any organization for long-term stability and success to be achieved.

The illustrations of this chapter are designed to demonstrate that the entire strategic planning system can be developed, initiated, and at least partially executed in under one year's time. It takes less than one year to affect the productivity of employees, departments, and the organization. Figure 5.6 illustrates a timeline where the process can begin at the level of the organization, move to the department and individual in less than a year[2], and reverse itself to a bottom-up change structure in less than two years.

The implementation of strategic planning within this timeframe permits the organization to complete its organizational planning process in a three-month period. Firms can execute the organizational plan and fully develop both departmental and personal plans by no later than seven months into the process. By the seventh month, the organization should have established fully interrelated synergistic missions for the organization, departments, and for each individual. Once the missions are integrated, the evaluation and assessment of planning implementation and outcomes can begin by the end of the first year. The entire cycle can begin again by the twentieth month, this time moving from the level of the individual to the level of the organization, ensuring a full and accurate assessment of the planning process by the conclusion of the strategic plan implementation timeframe.

---

[2] Some organizations may elect to take a longer time period to complete the process due to local traditions or current cultural constraints. I suggest that this process should be completed in no longer than eighteen months to ensure complete implementation and cultural transformation.

At the point that the process has moved from the global level to the individual level and entered the grass roots bottom-up framework, each employee has three years of planning experience allowing for the development of the most effective planning process possible for the organization. Rather than taking years to develop a mission and situational analysis, the company has learned to plan, assess and evaluate plan outcomes, revise plans, and to plan the organizational future across all three levels. In less time than most organizations complete a single strategic planning process for the institutional level alone, the organization has created a common shared mission, integrated value systems, and built unprecedented levels of trust throughout the corporate culture and the company. This will result in unprecedented accomplishment and goal achievement. This will also ensure that senior management is highly rewarded for the execution of the plan and its related successes. Ideally, those in senior management should ensure that all levels of the organization are subsequently rewarded for the process to continue to reach higher levels of achievement.

The workbooks presented in Chapters 10-12 of this book will take you step-by-simple-step through this one-year process. They will guide you through the entire process, ensuring your organization's ability to move from one level of planning to the next. They will allow you to share the purpose of the planning process with your staff from start to finish, thus lessening questions and the unpredictability of traditional strategic planning models. Ensuring a uniform predictable process with clear expectations and outcomes,
permits the organization to complete the procedure in the most expedient manner (with the suggested cycle of less than one year).

Prior to implementing the process, leaders should understand the power of planning in teams. They should ensure that the process permits the organization to develop a culture of change and continual adaptation. Leaders will develop learning systems to enhance the initial execution of the planning process, and create mechanisms for essential data development and reporting, which occur prior to the initiation of the planning process. These activities will enhance the strength of the web of leadership, assisting the organization in the positive progress through the planning process within the demonstrated timeframe.

This planning system permits all organizational types to act quickly and strategically (as in the normative patterns of the business models), while simultaneously engaging in profound reflective practice (as in the normative patterns of the not-for-profit and higher education models). Through the combination of the strengths of business and higher education planning practice, the organization can create a culture of continual adaptation that leads to greater levels of success. The process captures the traditional ideal of planning strategically for short-term, long-range, and contingent conditions. It will give organizations of any type the competitive advantage over their market, as institutions will become focused, visionary, and flexible.

What is actual is actual for only one time.
And only for one place.
  -- T.S. Eliot

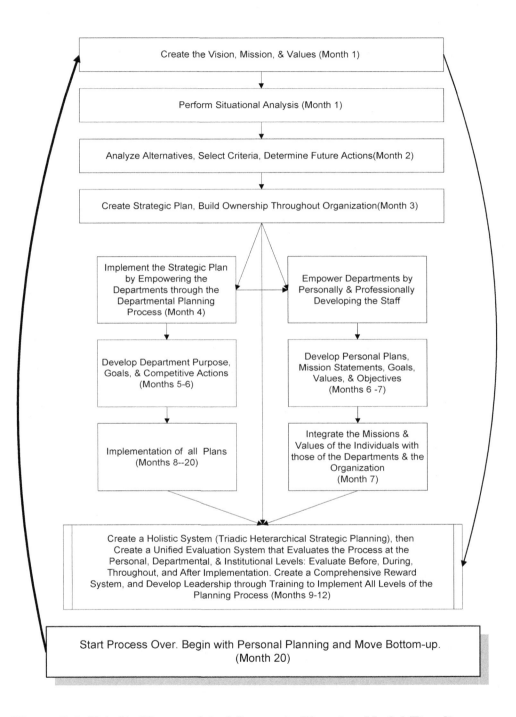

Figure 5.6. Triadic Heterarchical Strategic Planning Model Timeline.

Chapter 6

Achieving Empowerment: The Essential Nature of Teams & the Culture of Shared Responsibility

Loneliness and the feeling of being unwanted is the most terrible poverty. —Mother Teresa

The use of teams to implement strategic planning, special project implementation, and organizational development is a popular mechanism to ensure employee empowerment. Organizations have begun to develop a fundamental understanding of the value of teams in the realization of strategic goals across all levels of the company. The teaming movement continues to grow each year, as do the number of "teams" addressing issues in organizations throughout the business enterprise. The problem is not that "teams" are not continuously being developed and used; the problem is that the majority of teams developed range from ineffective to outright useless.

High performance teams are the rarity rather than a norm. This chapter posits that there is a current lack of significant accomplishment among most teams, and suggests a means for reviving your organization's teams through the triadic heterarchical strategic planning process. Most teams currently in effect are mere representations of the current command-and-control hierarchy (as illustrated in Figure 6.1 below).

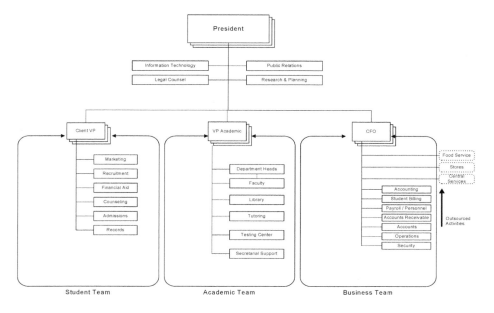

Figure 6.1. Traditional Hierarchical Team Model (Higher Education Example).

Teamwork can be a best practice for any modern organization, if it is conducted within an environment of open communication and is cross-institutional and cross-functional in nature. Central to the need for understanding organizational structure as an emergently complex heterarchy of purposes is the requisite to create a "sense of ownership" across all organizational processes. The teamwork strategy that leads to a "sense of ownership" is often referred to as empowerment. Empowerment through team development requires a system that replaces the old hierarchy and creates autonomy in the staff by making the employees feel and behave like "owners" of the organization or department.

By empowering everyday employees, organizations and/or departments learn to cooperate as teams that address functions, processes, and challenges to unleash new opportunities. The team development concept involves the systematic coordination of the performance of individuals who work together to achieve individual as well as common goals. Recognized theory suggests that team building and training assists in the elimination of managerial "command-and-control" positions and "carrot-and-stick" motivational strategies that work to retard empowerment (Katzenbach & Smith, 1999). The most effective means to renew existing teams, develop new teams, and to abolish ineffective teams is the triadic heterarchical strategic planning process.

The Role of Teams in the Triadic Strategic Planning Process

One of the greatest challenges facing an organization entering the strategic planning process is the ability to assemble diverse groups of people (staff, leaders, community members, customers, and perhaps even board members) and persuade them to work together in high performance teams. The organizational planning process (Chapter 10) calls for the development of cross-functional, cross-institutional planning teams to emerge and proceed through the process.

Teams are required throughout the planning process (see Figure 6.2). At the level of organizational planning, the firm's leadership will need to identify and assemble a series of unique ad hoc planning teams to fulfill the planning process requirements detailed in Chapter 10. For organizational planning to be both an effective and affective process the planning teams should move from the level of work groups to that of high performance decision-making groups capable of identifying the strategic initiatives that will allow the organization to determine its short- and long-term priorities.

In departmental planning, both work groups for task specific activities, and high performance planning teams should be used to fulfill the planning process activities.

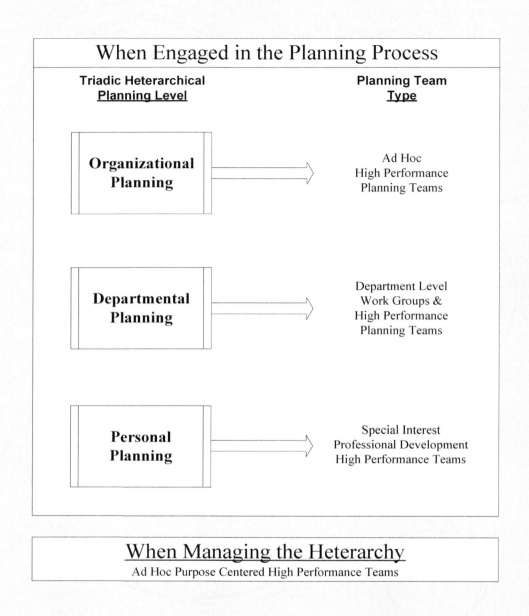

When Engaged in the Planning Process

Triadic Heterarchical Planning Level	Planning Team Type
Organizational Planning	Ad Hoc High Performance Planning Teams
Departmental Planning	Department Level Work Groups & High Performance Planning Teams
Personal Planning	Special Interest Professional Development High Performance Teams

When Managing the Heterarchy
Ad Hoc Purpose Centered High Performance Teams

Figure 6.2. Types of Teams Needed in Triadic Heterarchical Strategic Planning & Beyond.

Work groups can serve the department in data development, SWOT brainstorming, and developing a process map of functions. However, a high performance team is necessitated to discover the key business functions, to match staffing talents to work, and in the establishment of departmental objectives. Many departmental objectives require the development of the high performance teams to fulfill a department's strategic activities.

The personal planning process is most effective when organizational leaders assist in the development special interest professional development teams to support staff in the realization of their personal and professional goals. When the triadic heterarchical strategic planning process is completed, the strategic goals are likely to require the development of purpose centered high performance teams. Depending on the nature of the purpose, the team's intentions might include both ad hoc and universal functions. To ensure the initiation and implementation of high performance teams, the organizational leadership should develop a culture and environment where high performance teams prosper.

Heterarchical System Environments That Produce Effective Teams

Leaders should initiate a heterarchically based systems approach to the development of high performance teams. They should work to establish an environment where effective teams can be developed and can flourish. Prior to the initiation of a strategy of empowerment through teamwork, leaders should establish a heterarchical structure and responsibility culture that ensures the emergence of effective empowered teams.

First, leaders must develop a vision for the organization coupled with a set purpose for each team chartered. A purpose for the team is essential to the performance of the team. Team members will need a purpose to rally around, to work toward achieving, and to accomplish as a means to rewards and earned celebration. Figure 6.3 demonstrates the seven heterarchical system components needed to produce high performance teams.

Once the senior leadership has established the purpose of the team, a team leader should be identified to engage the team, assign appropriate responsibilities, and to lead the team toward the achievement of its purpose (which should be synergized with the organizational vision). The team leader should identify the key team roles required to accomplish the team's purpose (i.e., team mission). Once the roles are identified, the team leader in an atmosphere of open cooperation and communication with the team collective, works to align each team member's talents with the essential roles of the team.

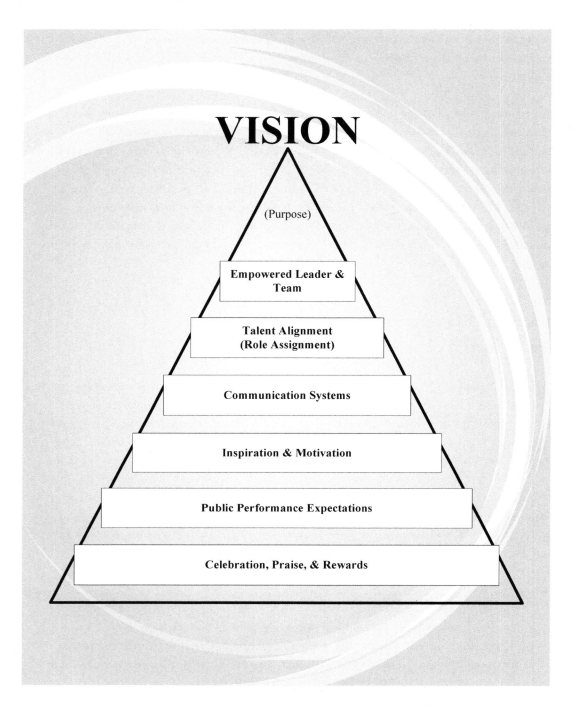

VISION

(Purpose)

Empowered Leader & Team

Talent Alignment (Role Assignment)

Communication Systems

Inspiration & Motivation

Public Performance Expectations

Celebration, Praise, & Rewards

<u>Figure 6.3</u>. Systems that Ensure High Performance Team Development.

To illustrate this point consider the annual professional football team's quest for the Super Bowl. The leader (coach) attempts to motivate the team toward engagement, choose appropriate players, and then to align the skills of the players with the roles needed to produce a Super Bowl champion. Rarely does a coach suggest to an offensive lineman that he would be better suited as a quarterback or a running back.

Yet, most organizations assign the roles on teams in terms of traditional hierarchical positions (or length of service) rather than in terms of team member talents. The effective high performance team will be led by an inspirational leader who not only engages the followership but also matches the talents of team members with the functional needs of the team.

Senior organizational leadership and team leaders should also develop a process of open communication. Information sharing should be used to empower all team members to perform their respective roles toward achieving the team's purpose. The team leader will act as the team's coach using motivation and inspiration (see Chapter 13) as the best means to ensure team participation and "buy-in." Team members should feel as if they are participating in a process that transcends personal interests, or they will fail to fully contribute to achieving the goals of the team. Open communication coupled with an inspirational agenda will produce an environment where team members develop feelings of "ownership" and appreciation for the respective responsibility of fellow team members or the firm.

Senior organizational leaders and the team's leader should publicly acknowledge the existence and importance of the team. The organization's senior leadership should publicly emphasize the need for the team, the importance of their charge, and the overall expectations that leaders and the organization have for the respective team. The team should be expected to publicly report the results of their efforts on regular intervals, and to review feedback from the entire organization (or department if the purpose is on a more micro level).

Feedback from the organization can be both positive and negative in nature, as long as the input is used as a positive motivational force for team success. Avoid the desire to destroy the team with typical 'constructive' criticism. There is not now, nor shall there ever be any criticism that leads to the development of enhanced creativity or the construction of any meaningful outcome.

Considering the example of professional football, how important is the role of the fans in the motivation and accomplishment of the team? In organizational development models of teaming, far too often the fan role is absent. Through open and public communication between the team members and the organization, coupled with the acknowledgement by senior leaders of the team's importance, the development of a cross-organizational fan base is possible. The team leader can use the organizational fans as both an inspiration and as a motivational force to better engage the team in its work.

Finally, when the team's purpose has been accomplished, the team should be celebrated in a public and positive fashion. Too many organizations fail to recognize the need for celebration. I have served as a consultant for many organizations where teams accomplished goals that many felt were not possible; only to be met with questions on why more wasn't achieved, or where the team was informed that external circumstances had changed (i.e., their collective hard work was not a real factor). Too often when team members succeed they fail to be adequately rewarded and organizational jealousy diminishes their collective sense of accomplishment. It is the role of leadership to ensure that successful teams are celebrated, publicly praised, and adequately rewarded for hard work, dedication, and shared accomplishment.

I have come to believe that this should become one of the primary focus of a company Board. The board should hire the CEO, advocate for the organization, maintain fiscal oversight, and become the cheerleaders of organizational success.

Measuring Team Effectiveness

The problem with many teams is that they are not teams at all, rather they are complex work groups or departments where roles are hierarchically defined, where command-and-control mechanisms limit the overall level of empowerment and the ability of members to learn and grow. These work groups are committees where tasks are assigned and people perform their respective hierarchical functions, taking no "sense of ownership" in the collective purpose. Members of these work groups become quick to describe how their role was not supported or acknowledged by other members or the organization. These committees become the place where ideas are sent to die a long painful death.

Most organizations are comprised of teams that have no set purpose, no sense of common identity, and no sense of shared responsibility. Figure 6.4 illustrates the steps that should occur in the development of a high performance team. As a consultant, college administrator, and CEO; I have witnessed the establishment of teams where the purpose is often never clearly defined, where the team's level of authority (i.e., empowerment) is never established, and where there is no clear expectation of achievement beyond the traditional "make recommendations to senior leadership." In fact, people often like this model as they then have no accountability for their work or recommendations.

Organizations are filled with groups of people working diligently toward no set finite purpose other than reviewing the current situation. These groups (I refuse to acknowledge them as teams) serve as a place to complain about the ineffectiveness of leadership, other departments, or the organization as a whole. The discussions are often filled with destructive levels of pointless debate. If these groups are left intact for a significant period of time, most members will mature to a point of not remembering why they began meeting in the first place.

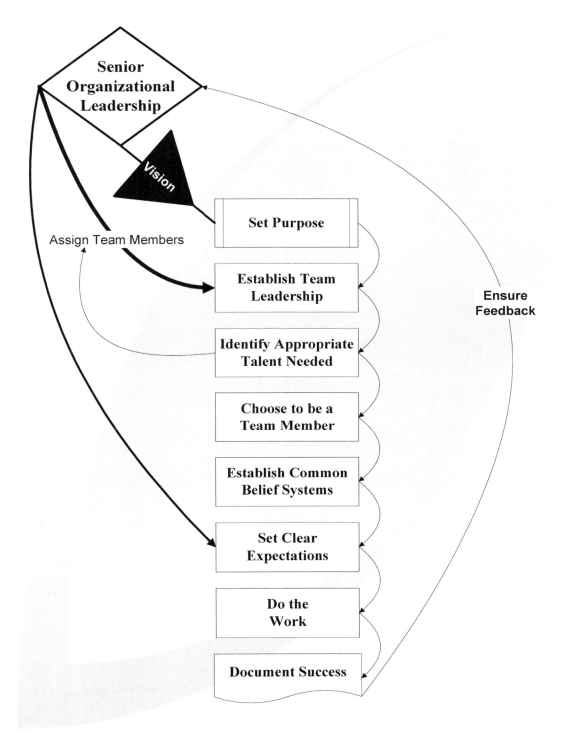

Figure 6.4. Paradigm of High Performance Team Establishment.

If organizational leaders desire high performance teams, they should establish a clear process of team formation where expectations are stated. Using the vision as a framing model, leaders should only establish teams where there exists a set purpose. Additionally, organizational leaders should assign team members based on a diverse set of qualifications, perspectives, and abilities. Once team membership is determined, a team leader role should be identified and assigned.

The final input from organizational leaders should be the public statement of team expectations, clearly identifying the anticipated results and outcomes that the team should produce. Senior level organizational or departmental leaders/managers should then remove themselves from the process. Team members, under the direction of the team leader, should evaluate the composition of the team. If they determine missing talents, the team should request the assignment of additional members to address the talent gaps within the team.

Once the team is fully established, the team development process should begin. The first step is for team members to fully realize and acknowledge their role in the fulfillment of the team's purpose. Teams that fail to reach their respective goals are often plagued with no sense of shared purpose, where team members do not realize their role on the team, nor do they actively engage in teamwork. Low performance teams are comprised of people who do not realize their ability to influence the performance of others. For teams to reach levels of high performance, team members must choose to actively partake in teamwork, they should publicly acknowledge their roles, and they need to realize the talents and value they offer their teammates in fulfilling the purpose of the team's mission.

Team members that choose to actively engage the teaming process will come to see their ability to make group decisions through consensus. The organization should support the team by empowering it to make decisions and then by supporting the decisions that teams make as a collective enterprise. Team members should also reflect on the expectations of their purpose and should develop a set of common beliefs and values that will guide them toward the fulfillment of senior leadership expectations. Before beliefs can become cohesive standards or before most members can choose to actively engage the teaming process, the expectations should be understood and constantly evaluated against the work expected.

The essential step in the establishment of functioning high performance teams is the active participation in the work by all team members. Most teams fail to reach their goals because some members choose not to engage the process; they allow others to carry the majority of the workload. Far too many teams are successful because of the work of only a few members, while the remainder of the team waits and watches. The team leader must ensure that all members view their role as significant to team success, and the team leader should set team expectations and accountability mechanisms. Team members that do not engage the process should be addressed by informal and formal sanctions as deemed necessary by the team leader.

The final step in the development of the high performance team is to document the success of the team throughout the process of achieving its purpose. The achievement of success (i.e., the reaching of preset milestones) should be shared publicly with organizational (or departmental) leaders to ensure ongoing communication loops and necessary feedback that will ensure team success through organizational support. Continuous feedback will allow the organizational leadership to establish formal goal setting and performance appraisal systems to reward team success (see Chapter 14).

The high performance team, like all teams, will progress through a series of stages of team development (forming, storming, norming, performing (Sholtes, 1988)). During these stages, team members will experience successes and setbacks, excitement and malaise, as well as feelings of cohesion and disruption. The role of the team leader is to inspire the team and keep members focused on the purpose. The role of organizational leaders is to set the purpose and expectations, review overall performance, support decision-making, and reward the successes.

Teaming in the Heterarchical Structure

To effectively manage a heterarchically based structural system, organizational leaders need to empower staff members to make decisions, change processes, and form the teams necessary to accomplish the goals established as part of the triadic strategic planning process. Through empowerment, organizational leaders can use teams and teamwork to actively create participation by greater numbers of staff members in decision-making.

By empowering the staff, organizational leaders can create a "sense of ownership" among staff members, managers, and all stakeholders of the firm. When people are fully engaged in the team process, they feel a true sense of control over their work lives, their workplace, and the process of continuous organizational development. Engaged teams give employees a sense of freedom over their destiny, and a feeling of participation in the achievement of organizational and departmental goals.

Empowered teams are not micromanaged; they are provided the freedom to succeed, and to make decisions about the fulfillment and achievement of the company's mission. Once freedom in the decision making process is provided, members begin to feel a sense of responsibility to one another to fulfill the team's purpose. Like the owner of a business, team members have a vested stake in the realization of the team's mission. This shared responsibility and a "sense of ownership" allows teams to succeed. The heterarchical structure gives organizational leaders the ability and freedom to empower teams to fulfill the organization's mission.

The leadership of the heterarchical organization desires teams to thrive in an environment of open communication. The heterarchy's limitless conceptualization of structure allows for true teamwork to emerge. Teamwork will not naturally occur and emerge in either a hierarchy or a systems based approach. However, within a non-nested emergent heterarchy, team establishment and creativity is controlled not by management but by leadership, peer responsibility, and heterarchical accountability systems.

Figure 6.5 illustrates the practice of a heterarchical team based structural system. Traditional reporting relationships become less important as the results and outcomes of clearly defined and publicly acknowledged team expectations become the driving forces of leadership, empowerment, responsibility, and accountability.

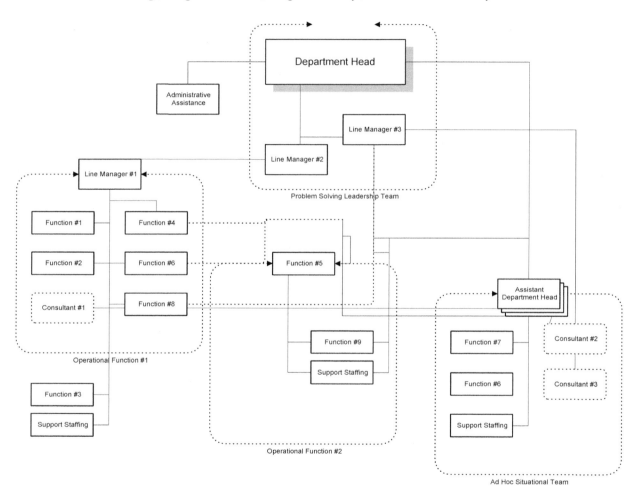

Figure 6.5. Team Structure in the Heterarchical Organization.

Teams and the Future

Organizations initiating heterarchical systems that work to ensure the development of high performance teams should have a greater likelihood of reaching their goals and achieving their mission. Heterarchical team based organizations use the heterogeneity of their staff as a resource of diversity in thought and perspective. Leaders that value diversity see the power of the high performance team in developing diverse opinions and perspectives into action plans created through group consensus.

Those organizations that rely on team development will possess an empowered staff of decision makers that reach goals through consensus and open communication. Team members improve the performance of their organization as they are expected to improve and to grow through the realization of their combined ability and talents. Through working together in an environment of learning and continuous improvement, collective individuals can fulfill the purpose of the team, while simultaneously improving the ability of individual team members.

High performance teams do not create a culture of "group think" and group mediocrity based on group consensus, they create an atmosphere of free and open dialog. Open communication systems demand creativity and individuality as opposed to diminishing them. Committee based decisions of the old hierarchical systems tend to diminish the ability of teams to develop into a high performance model where individual members are encouraged (in fact required) to share opinions and to intellectually debate their merit. The high performance team of the emergent heterarchy requires each team member to fulfill the team's purpose through the full engagement of their creative ability and their individual talents.

When organizations develop the ability for groups to share a common goal in the context of a culture of shared responsibility, individual freedom, and empowerment within a structure of clear accountability; then success through goal achievement can be fully realized. Teams require a common purpose coupled with group "buy-in." Once these two components are achieved the role of the inspirational leader will be to coach the team to success, to set clear expectations, and to keep the team focused on the realization of its purpose.

The role of the heterarchical system based high performance team is to match the talents of the individual to the team's (i.e., organization's) needs. The high performance teams of the future will have a set vision (purpose), with poignant leaders, open communication structures, and clear expectations. The leaders of the heterarchical organization realize the power of talent alignment, vision/mission synergy, and the contributions of individuals working within the context of high performance teams.

The best things and the best people rise out of their separateness; I'm against a homogenized society because I want the cream to rise. – Robert Frost

Chapter 7

Strategic Planning as a Means of Continuous Improvement

> *Turbulence is life force. It is opportunity. Let's love turbulence and use it for change.*
> -- Ramsay Clark

Successful organizations that excel create and enter an era of continuous strategic planning where improvement and change are viewed as a natural ongoing process of renewal. Organizations engage in strategic planning for a variety of reasons and with a diverse set of outcome expectations. Most organizations enter the planning process with the hope of achieving tangible results or changes that will affect the future of their business. However, it is neither the plan nor the outcomes that offer the greatest degree of success; rather, it is the *experience* of the planning process that often leads to an organizational culture of continuous improvement.

The best organizations use a continuous process of strategic planning at the institutional, departmental, and personal levels (Bossidy & Charan, 2002). These organizations creatively develop cultures that engage the planning enterprise from all levels of the organization, which fosters long-term leadership development across the enterprise. The act of planning differs from strategic planning because the exercise of planning is not beneficial to an industry if it does not engage the organizational collective. If planning becomes the responsibility of an office, or of only senior management, then planning becomes merely a series of institutional management mandates that are readily ignored and/or ridiculed by the staff. Strategic planning is a form of continuous improvement, organizational change, cross-institutional growth, and intra-, inter- and external communication.

Thinking Strategically

As leaders decide to enter the strategic planning process, they need to ask themselves a myriad of imperative questions:

- ☐ "What type of organization are we trying to build?
- ☐ Will it join the overwhelming majority of organizations that exist and simply watch things happen, reacting to issues and concerns one after another only as they arise?

☐ Will the business reach an unfortunate conclusion of failure, and will these employees be forced to look back on their glory days wondering what went wrong?

☐ Will it be an elite business enterprise that makes things happen, where leaders and staff working together decide the destiny of the firm?

☐ Will the organization enter an era of unprecedented proactivity where it no longer benchmarks, but is benchmarked for its best practices?"

The companies and businesses that learn to think strategically will evolve to experience continuous improvement and progress exemplified by the innovative institutions in the latter part of the aforementioned illustration. Those that do not employ a strategic thinking model will remain reactive decision-making enterprises, which use change processes only to address particular problems (see Figure 7.1).

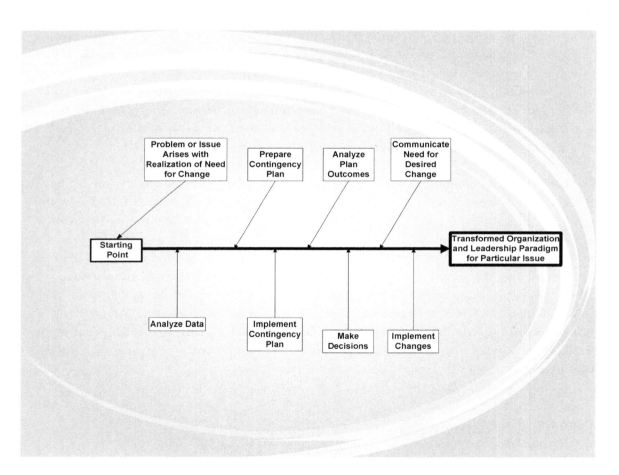

Figure 7.1. The Typical Reactive Change Organization

Leaders should educate their respective staff on how to be productive in planning for the future rather than how to be passive actors and responders to the future circumstances and issues created by outside forces, whether internal or external.

Covey (1990) has demonstrated that effective planning should be used to provide the compass by which leaders steer their departments and the institution through the increasingly complex and challenging environments in which they find themselves. The act or engagement of planning creates this compass. The initial outcome (i.e., the plan) is the roadmap to the future. Once the roadmap (the plan) is in place, the act of planning or engaging the compass must be continuous, or the organization and its respective departments quickly and easily become lost. Organizations should learn to think and plan strategically, as strategic planning is synonymous with continual ongoing and effective progress.

To think strategically, a number of essential elements should be considered:

1. The organization should examine the external environment (items might include: demographics, communication systems, technological advancement, competitors, customer bases and market potentials, partnerships and collaborative opportunities, economic forces, political forces, social forces, etc.) and dichotomize these external forces into opportunities for exploitation and threats to be addressed and overcome.

2. The organization should examine the internal culture and circumstances (which might include: the captured customer base, lost customers, internal data, sales, human resources, fiscal resources, internal political forces, economies of scale, cooperation, prevalence of internal fiefdoms or 'warring factions,' intellectual capital, facilities, growth potential, best practices, worst practices, customer service, customer satisfaction, needs assessments, technological capability, communication systems, structures, process functionality, etc.).

3. The internal factors are then dichotomized into internal strengths or internal weaknesses, and external opportunities or external threats . Once these four lists (i.e., strengths, weaknesses, threats, and opportunities) can be paralleled to match internal strengths with external opportunities or threats, and internal weaknesses to external opportunities and threats.

This exercise, commonly referred to as SWOT, begins the process of strategic thinking by placing all organizational issues within a matrix of strategic actions that can be easily understood, communicated, and addressed by the company. The exercise will illustrate where change is needed, where resources should be placed, and where the next issue that the company will need to react to is likely to arise. Once this matrix is developed and communicated, the firm can move from reaction to proactive operations.

Although SWOT can serve as a bridge between reactivity and proactivity, it is merely a method of beginning the strategic thinking process. Once the issues have been identified and plotted, the organization should examine alternative courses of action through the development of essential criteria that illustrate those factors, which will make the organization successful. Criteria should be developed to illustrate those things that the firm is generally capable of achieving. The criteria are then used to narrow the list of strategic actions to a number that can be addressed by the organization. Once this list is determined, the organization establishes a strategic timeline that places actions in the most appropriate and strategic sequence to ensure implementation and success. As the sequence is determined and agreed upon, an appropriate timeframe can be established and enacted.

The last phase of strategic thinking is the continuous improvement follow-up strategy. In this strategy the organization uses its timeline and plan to determine both a macro level expected outcome and micro level sequential outcomes (in the form of departmental or personal planning) that lead to the larger macro level result desired. Quantifiable measurements should be identified to assess the achievement of the outcomes specified. Once the implementation process begins, a subsequent process of outcome measurement and evaluation should commence to ensure continuous improvement and progression toward the goals developed as part of the strategic thinking and planning process.

The comprehensive institutional strategic planning process initiated in total is normally required at least every three years. The organization should not repeat the entire course of action sooner as it would not yield the level of results necessary to justify the time and expense used to complete the process. However, the use of a systemic yearly evaluation and revision process will allow the organization to act more strategically to yield better outcomes. It is necessary to annually examine the key operational objectives and actions in order to make pertinent corrective revisions to goals to meet the larger more macro aims of the institutional strategic plan.

Creating Change

As the process of organizational change is reviewed, a discussion to address the overwhelming level of emphasis currently placed on changing culture and structure without regard for the need to change leadership is warranted. I have counseled countless clients that desired a change in structure, or set goals for changes in organizational culture without realizing that neither was practical or advantageous. Many organizations that continuously change their internal structures hoping to create better results, in actuality need to change senior leadership. Many organizations with destructive cultures, political divisiveness, and socially demeaning workplaces are reflective of the senior leadership team and prevailing management styles of the organization.

I served as a consultant to one organization that changed structures seven times while we proceeded through one planning cycle. The president of the company would attend a conference or read a new piece of organizational development literature, and come to believe that the success he sought could be achieved if the hierarchy was adjusted.

The problem of course was that the people, who were expected to do the work, found themselves in a constant state of reconstructing. Anarchy became normal, and few people understood the reporting relationships or accountability systems established. His culture became one of mistrust and coercion. The irony was that he felt trust was vital and coercion was counterproductive, yet he trusted no staff member, and used manipulation as his motivational technique. This organization was a mirror reflection of its leader.

Organizational change, when it is warranted, should be accomplished within a comprehensive strategic planning process where the costs and benefits are carefully considered. Change can be a great success generator for an organization if it is used as a proactive means to achieve greater success and results. Walker (1992) has demonstrated that strategic planning can occur across three distinct levels of an organization: institutional, departmental, and/or human resources (personal). In fact, he suggests that the most important tool that management has for implementing long-term change is in the strategies themselves that the organization chooses to implement (p. 104). Belasco (1990) and Covey (1992) called these strategies the identification and implementation of vision. Lineberry and Carleton (1992) expanded this idea further by suggesting that a change in the organization is experienced by a change in culture, which emerges from the values/beliefs/behavior systems that local leadership creates (p. 233). These systems can be transformed within the strategic planning processes implemented by an organization (as described in Chapter 10).

The strategic planning process can empower an organization to reflect on the past, present, and future of the institution and to discuss its vision, mission, and goals (Brinckerhoff, 1997). The company can work by using a collaborative process to evaluate the current vision, mission, goals, strategies, and values; as well as institutional effectiveness, current programs, sales strategies, marketing, technology, facilities, and financial considerations (or any other major functional area of process management). In light of a strategic plan, planners often work to evaluate the structures currently in place and recommend necessary changes, improvements, developments, and enhancements.

Developing a systematized cross-institutional planning structure represents a fundamental paradigm shift in the way the managers have traditionally approached leadership and decision-making. The key to implementing such structural changes and making a substantive cultural paradigm shift is leadership within a complementary structure. "The leader of the future, realizing that vision and implementation are both leadership roles, will learn to care little about defending the traditional hierarchy" (Blanchard, 1996, p. 85). The culture of an organization is not emergent from any one individual; rather, culture emerges from groups of people. Yet, the degree of cultural change possible will emerge from the vision and trust embodied by the current leaders of the organization.

Although creating a cultural change depends on the will of leadership, it does not automatically emerge from a change in leaders or leadership patterns. Rather, the culture of the organization should be addressed both from the grassroots (i.e., at the level of the individual) and from the leadership (i.e., from the vision). "I sometimes hear managers say they want to change because 'a learning organization should have a more open culture,' or because 'it came back in the benchmarks; everybody else is doing it, so we'd better do it too'" (Senge, Kleiner, Roberts, Ross, Roth, & Smith, 1999, p. 335). The real reason for change is that it is in the best strategic interest of an institution, department, or individual.

A vision of leadership will be paramount in organizational change and the development of a new paradigm to empower all constituents through the development of lateral processes of leadership, decision-making, planning, and change. As a result of being the leader of this type of project, a willingness to turn the current pyramid upside down through the implementation of a vision of accomplishment is necessitated (Blanchard, 1996, p. 85). If leadership in the cross-institutional planning process is effective, change can emerge from all levels of the organization, and this change will be progressively strategic rather than stagnantly reactive.

As Lucas demonstrates in his classic work on organizational change, truth is the key to effectiveness and to change. "You hear it all the time. The main thing we need is more [information/resources/training/education/experience/innovation/teamwork], baloney. The main thing we need is truth" (Lucas, 1997, p. 1). He illustrates that truth can be achieved through the shedding of personal and organizational illusions, through the sharing of information, and through the discovery of how the organizational mission is best aligned with the goals and values of individuals within the organization. This is the essence of the effective strategic planning process. Goold and Campbell (1998) argue that in the end it appears to be synergy that managers and leaders are seeking to create and promote within their organizations. For an organization to be successful, they suggest that executives need to subject all synergistic strategies to a clear-eyed analysis that plainly demonstrates the costs and benefits prior to implementation (p. 143). This principle suggests that the structure of an organization as well as its long-term goals should be fully understood prior to the implementation of a synergistic process such as triadic heterachical strategic planning. The realization of synergy can transform an organization from the reactive change style (Figure 7.1) to a continuous change culture within a heterarchical structuration (Figure 7.2).

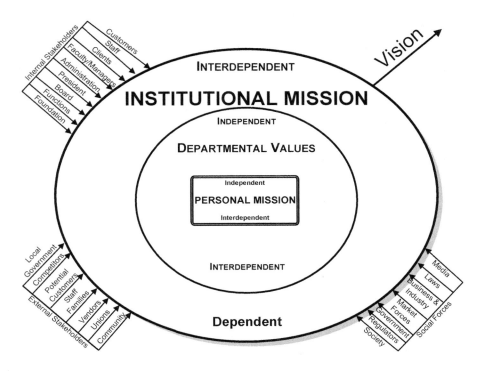

Figure 7.2. An Organigraph of Synergistic Culture & Heterarchy.

Improving Practice & Processes

To reach a level of effective planning, a managed process should be developed from within the existing successful traditions of the organization to ensure lasting and meaningful change. Holistically, contemporary literature on organizational development suggests that planning is a managed process of strategic change. It is the mechanism and process that organizations can effectively use to transform culture (symbols), structure (interaction), politics (justification), and human potential (Bolman & Deal, 1997, p. 243). The key to organizational change and effective planning is in neither the process nor the formal plan; rather, it emerges from a shift in focus, structures, mental models, and paradigms. Planning becomes effective when leaders empower staff to succeed and to develop a shared vision of the future.

To transform an institution, each stakeholder will need to see the necessity for change and be asked to lead the organization through some part of the evolution. Leaders currently are compelled to focus their attention on the people more than the process, for it is the people that will make the process and the institution successful. The key to the success of the process will ultimately depend on the ability of the organization to transform its structure and culture, and most importantly, for the current leadership to have the courage to empower their staff to work beyond the command-

and-control systems previously negotiated. No process without the support of the current staff will create positive change.

The culture of the new successful organization will transform to one of service, excellence, and quality. To meet the needs and wants of this century, we have been told that organizations will need to partner effectively, live up to their commitments, develop new paradigms, think "out of the box," etc. To do this, management and staff will need to share a common vision and mission that celebrates innovation, ingenuity, flexibility, and shared leadership. What is often missing from these discussions is how to accomplish these abstract goals (i.e., the goal of chapters 10-12 of this work).

Human Resource Improvement

To assist in the creation of a paradigm shift across systems, a strategic unified personal planning system that empowers employees to create a shared vision, synergistic missions, and common values should be coupled with a proactive, positive evaluation system that is designed to assist employees in reaching their complete potential. Rothwell (1996) illustrated that the main purpose of human performance enhancement (personal planning) is to identify the gaps that exist in the organizational systems devoted to human potential. As staff grow in potential, so too does the potential for organizational excellence and growth.

As individuals strive to implement the goals of the institutions they serve, it is essential that their values and goals are not contrary to those that they are attempting to reach for the organization. The establishment of a common value paradigm becomes as important as the structures and systems designed to increase institutional effectiveness. The key to achieving a culture of continuous improvement lies in the firm's ability to engage individual employees in the planning process to affect a larger change on institutional culture.

Much of the work on organizational development and leadership has struggled to determine the best means of incorporating the individual employee into the decision-making and long-term planning processes of the organization. Belasco (1990) has argued for the development of a common vision that is understood across the organization. Belasco and Snead argue that value alignment does not mean the establishment of a KGB-style monitoring system; rather, the system should strive to discover the common values of all those who serve the organization, and then align those values with the vision and mission of the organization (1999, p. 302). Rothwell (1996) demonstrates that the key to strategic plan implementation lies in the development of human performance enhancement (HPE) strategies, and the integration of these strategies with the grand strategy of the organization.

Traditionally, companies had viewed work and personal life as competing priorities in a zero-sum game, in which a success in one arena means a loss in the other. Friedman, Christensen, and DeGroot (1998) argue for a new era of leadership, where managers and employees collaborate to achieve mutually beneficial work and personal objectives. They further contend that the strategies and systems of priority unification have largely been informal, but as this approach becomes better appreciated through its demonstrated success, more companies will come to view leaders that unite values as the epitome of agents of change (Friedman, Christensen, & DeGroot, 1998). The goal of continuous improvement should be realized through the continuous professional development of the staff and leadership expected to improve the company.

Ken Blanchard, D. W. Edington, and Marjorie Blanchard (1999) suggested that the best workers (in this case managers) are those that can balance their work and life. They argue that physical and mental health are not only in the interest of the individual, but are in the best interest of the company as well. Stephen Covey (1990) has contended that achieving oneness with ourselves, our family, our working associates, and our work leads to the highest and most productive outcomes for highly effective people (p. 318). Covey demonstrates through his work that each individual should have a vision and mission that demonstrates what is deeply important to her or him that leads each individual to manage each day to do what matters most (1990, p. 98).

This exciting literature of change and personal transformation suggests the need for a process of personal enrichment that complements the existing processes of organizational enrichment already in place at many contemporary organizations. It further suggests that the duty of personal development is not only a supervisory or human resource department's activity, but that it is a global organizational activity that deserves the same level of attention to detail that strategic and departmental planning have experienced over the past thirty years. Without stating it directly, this literature suggests that human resource development should be a strategic focus of all organizational development activities.

The essential key element of individual planning is that it occurs within a well-structured heterarchical system based strategic planning process designed to create a learning organization. The learning organization should strive to teach people how to be productive rather then telling them how or when to be productive. Belasco and Snead (1999) argue that great organizations are the ones that open up the systems of learning by realizing that people want to grow.

Portillo (1997) has demonstrated that strategic personal planning should contain elements of self-discovery, expectation development, value integration, validation and feedback, and lifetime exploration designed to overcome barriers and reach personal goals. Moses (1999) has demonstrated that a personal plan should help an individual think globally, communicate powerfully, ensure long-term learning, develop competence, be future oriented, manage time, and be true and kind. Knowdell (1998) illustrates that a personal plan for the future will allow an individual to take charge of her/his work and career, develop interpersonal relationship skills, sharpen communication skills, be a discoverer of change, increase personal flexibility, embrace technology, keep learning, and continuously develop new capacities. When the level of the individual is united with the levels of departments and the institution within the framework of organizational strategic planning, contemporary organizations will reach even greater levels of success.

Forty years ago, Paul, Robertson, and Herzberg (1969) argued that for employees to take on more responsibility there would need to be a constant feedback loop where managers continuously evaluated subordinates. Belasco and Snead (1999) have reasoned that in the contemporary learning organization and workplace these loops are also necessary but rather than as a command and control mechanism, as a means to create an ownership perspective throughout the organization's workforce. This ideal of increased ownership is best accomplished through a synergy of values, mission, and goals throughout the organization. Covey (1992) has further demonstrated this point by illustrating that the alignment and creation of mission driven organizations leads to the development of organizations that embody the ideals of change, empowerment, and transformation.

In summation, a strategic planning process should contain elements of vision alignment, mission synergy, value integration, systems that foster interpersonal relations, continuous learning and capacity development, a method of personal and institutional self-discovery, and an emphasis on seeing the global organizational perspective and communication in the achievement of realistic goals. For the planning process to be effective, it should be situated within a clear heterarchical accountability system that has a clearly communicated evaluation methodology. The development of such a planning system and subsequent evaluation method depends on the ability of the organization's leaders to embrace the concepts of empowerment and vision.

Strategic Budgeting

Strategic budgeting incorporates the control and management of all organizational resources including fiscal, personnel, facilities, equipment, technology, intellectual capital, and time. Strategic budgeting does not merely extend to the distribution of these resources but includes the acquisition for, management of, allocation to, and responsibility for all forms of institutional resources. When strategic budgeting is in effect, planners work to budget among all initiatives, projects, activities, and units of the organization and its stakeholders.

Far too many organizations fix budgeting in the arena of fiscal resources distributed annually at a percentage increase (for most not-for-profits), in a game of zero based (for most for profits), or in an activity based model (for progressive organizations). Rarely does the firm suggest that budgeting is in line with the strategic plan, encompassing all resources (financial, facilities, personnel, equipment, etc.).

The budgeting of resources in the organization should be designed to meet three major purposes. The first purpose is the accomplishment of the specific goals and objectives of the strategic planning enterprises (i.e., organizational, departmental, and personal). The second purpose of allocating all resources is the implementation and accomplishment of the prioritized initiatives, objectives, and actions identified as part of the strategic planning process. The final purpose of strategic budgeting is to respond to goal outcomes and evaluations on an annual basis, and thus to reallocate necessary resources to ensure that the macro level goals of the company's strategic plans are met. The budget requests within the organization that are not directly or indirectly related to the strategic goals of the company are not likely to produce the desired outcomes identified in the strategic planning process, so the budgeting of these requests should be placed under a greater level of scrutiny.

The strategic budgeting process should naturally emerge from the strategic thinking and planning processes, yet many organizational leaders identify plans and desired outcomes without then reallocating the necessary resources to implement the plans. At times the political and social ramifications of the reallocation of budgets limit the perceived ability of leadership to make such revisions. However, if the strategic thinking process has really been engaged, then the leaders should not hesitate to reallocate fiscal resources, personnel, facility usage, equipment, technological resources, or intellectual capital. If a level of hesitation remains, then arguably the organization is not thinking or planning strategically since these political and social forces should have been addressed as part of the SWOT analysis and the overall global strategic planning process.

Continuous Improvement through Strategic Planning: A Worthy Goal

It has been said that nothing can stand in the way of a well-developed plan established to achieve a worthy goal. In the turbulent times that organizations currently find themselves, it is important that organizations view change, turbulence, and even disaster as an opportunity for growth and accomplishment. Those organizations that plan effectively across all levels of the organization will have the best opportunity to achieve a worthy goal.

Institutions that become more emergently effective through the development and understanding of complex systems of social and structural relationships (i.e., through accepting and managing the heterarchies that naturally occur within the institution) will transform into learning cultures of success. All business enterprises can become learning organizations by understanding the limitations of command-and-control mechanisms, the limitations of their current hierarchical structures, and the problems associated with traditional institutional level strategic planning models. Until leaders realize that living, transformational, social organisms implement their best-laid plans, they will not construct purposeful systems to initiate and manage change to realize these plans, and there cannot be real change or growth within those institutions.

To develop an organization that creates, acquires, and transfers new knowledge in a continuous fashion, it is necessary to ensure that all levels of the organization (global, departmental, and personal) have systems in place that are change oriented, forward forecasting, and designed to create organizational synergy. The learning organization will be the adaptive firm that realizes the interconnectivity of the global, local, and personal levels of human social and business relations (as demonstrated in Figure 7.3).

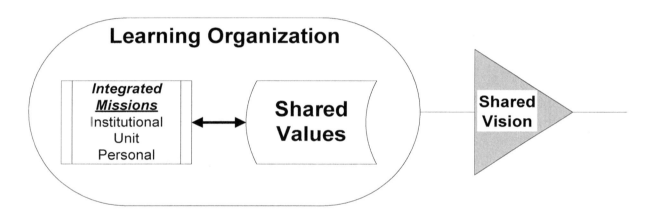

Figure 7.3. Mission Synergy: The Realization of a Worthy Goal, The Learning Organization

The basis of measuring the overall effectiveness in each of these levels will be the realization of the heterarchical structure and organizational synergy based on the triadic planning organigraph (illustrated in Figure 7.2). It demonstrates the relationships between the three independent planning processes and their respective dependent, interdependent, and independent relationships; as well as the influences of external constituencies (pressures), and the desire for a common vision. The organization of the future will realize the intricacies of this organism, its ability to change, transform, and merge, as well as the unique and emergent complexity that emanates from its existence.

Through the integrated triadic heterarchical planning system, an organization's leadership should be capable of turning the intent of strategic planning into the actions for change desired. The united processes help set the vision-focused direction for the firm and allow for a change in culture, structure, and the general leadership perspective. These patterned changes will move the business in the direction of the common vision established as the learning organization emerges.

> *... if one advances confidently in the direction of his dreams, and endeavors to live the life which he has imagined, he will meet with a success unexpected in common hours.*
> -- Henry David Thoreau

Chapter 8

Creating the Learning Centered Systems that Ensure Organizational Success

Talent is always conscious of its own abundance, and does not object to sharing.
-- Aleksandr Solzhenitsyn

To successfully initiate a change process that facilitates the development of a learning organization, leadership as a practice must be capable of emerging from within all levels of the organization. Personnel from all levels of the organization should be encouraged to change and develop their skills and talents. Leaders should demonstrate the relevance and importance of change while encouraging a commitment among followers to continuous improvement and learning. All personnel should be encouraged and taught to synergize their values with those of the organization.

In his classic work, Peter Senge (1990) demonstrated that the learning organization is a place where employees are given the freedom to succeed, to realize their personal values, and are encouraged to express those values. Learning organizations are places where all employees are given decision making power over the determination of goals and the means of achieving them; where new paradigms and knowledge are appreciated and developed, and where people use learning as a means of improving their organization, their workplace, and their lives. The goal of becoming a learning organization can be one of the most rewarding strategies of organizational renewal undertaken.

The Process of Becoming a Learning Organization

The process of becoming a learning organization is both one of the most rewarding and challenging initiatives engaged by contemporary organizations. However, since 1990 few organizations have been successful at reaching their goals of becoming learning organizations. David Garvin demonstrated that the topic remained murky, confused, and difficult to penetrate in 1993. In the fifteen years since Garvin suggested that the concept was difficult to implement, many more organizations have attempted to transform their organizational culture to that of a learning centered operation. Senge's original work, *The Fifth Discipline*, suggested that the best means of implementing a learning organization was through a systems approach to management.

As was suggested in Chapter 3, the holistic and transcendent based systems approach does not fully capture the emergent complexity of the modern organization. Applying the holistic systems based approach to implementing the learning organization restricts the ability of contemporary leaders to realize the benefits of a learning centered workplace. Attempting to implement a learning organization model within a transcendent systems based approach creates a circumstance where many current day organizations become limited by their traditional hierarchical structures. Figure 8.1 illustrates how the implementation of the triadic heterarchical strategic planning process can simultaneously initiate a cultural change toward the learning organization.

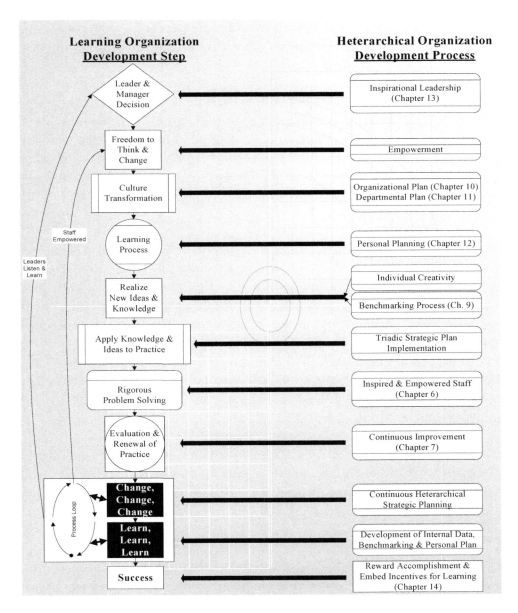

Figure 8.1. Learning Organization Development Process.

As the leaders and managers of the organization decide to transform their corporate culture into one of a learning organization, they realize the need for the unification of management and leadership principles and practices. They consciously make the decision to develop the organization into a learning centered enterprise. Once the decision of renewal is finalized, the leader/managers empower the workforce to think freely and change the daily practice of their respective roles and processes.

Through implementation of the organizational and departmental planning processes, the organization develops learning centered principles and goals that transform the existing culture of the firm. The culture of the organization and its departments change from reactive assumptions to proactive goal setting and learning centeredness. Through the implementation of the personal planning process, employees are asked to set personal and professional development goals that establish learning processes and schemas throughout the organization.

The implementation of the triadic heterarchical strategic planning process includes a process of best practice benchmarking and individual empowered freedom and creativity that will allow a significant number of stakeholders to realize new ideas and to actively acquire new knowledge. As the learning organization begins to take form, the three level strategic planning process facilitates the implementation and usage of new knowledge and new creative practices that emerge from external and internal sources.

Full-scale strategic plan implementation (i.e., the post development process) permits the organization, departments, and individuals to apply newly acquired knowledge and ideas to the practices of the organization. The firm uses benchmarking and new ideas to transform its goals from reactions and simple assumptions about circumstances to proactive continuous accomplishment. The departments refine existing business and functional practices, and the individual staff member transforms into a learner dedicated to continuous improvement. Once this transformation has taken place, the learning organization focuses its culture on rigorous problem identification and solving, both of which are accomplished by an inspired, engaged, and empowered staff.

Leader/managers implement processes of continuous improvement (described in Chapter 7 of this work) to evaluate the effectiveness of existing processes, new ideas, and the strategic planning efforts. Processes (both business and functional) are revised, reified, or discarded based on the evaluative outcomes of the continuous improvement mechanisms.

As the learning organization embarks on a direction of quality enhancement and continuous improvement, the flow of the triadic strategic planning process is reversed (now moving from the bottom-up); and a continuous strategic planning practice within a learning culture is initiated. The permanent organizational and departmental planning processes are supplemented with ongoing data development and personal planning that leads to the realization of an organizational culture of continuous learning and quality development. Quality efforts are embraced in a process loop of learn-change-learn-change-learn, which provides evaluative feedback to leaders that head toward greater levels of freedom and empowerment for the staff and all organizational stakeholders.

As the learning organization culture matures by means of continuous improvement through strategic planning, the organization will experience increasing levels of success. Goal achievement, departmental improvement, and personal growth become normal practice of the company. Leaders begin to reward accomplishment at the levels of the organization, department, and the individual. Finally, the organization should embed reward incentives within the learning organization steps, which are linked, to strategic planning goal achievement to ensure a continuous improvement culture that celebrates the values of learning, talent alignment, and knowledge attainment.

Using the Triadic Heterarchical Strategic Planning Process to Create Learning Centered Organizations

The triadic heterarchical strategic planning process fully develops and executes the organizational plan, as well as creating an environment and managerial atmosphere where the culture of a learning organization can emerge and transcend as the dominant ideology of the firm. The implementation of the personal planning process is the realization of the importance of the learner-centered organization.

The choice of becoming a learning organization is the realization and celebration of the importance of each staff member's talents and knowledge in the accomplishment of collective organizational goals. Strategic planning and the development of the learning organization are interrelated processes that when combined into a single ongoing renewal process, can move the organization to a level of unprecedented growth and expectation. The organization experiences a greater degree of accomplishment because the stakeholders of the company experience higher levels of personal and collective expectation. Members of a learning organization expect more of their leaders, who in turn expect more of their followers. The hierarchy is diminished as personal accountability is publicly acknowledged and expectations become embedded in the emergently complex heterarchy (Figure 8.2) as opposed to the traditional command-and-control reporting structures of the hierarchy in place in most contemporary organizations.

The triadic planning process can advance the organization from a reactive enterprise to a goal-centered learning organization, embedded with proactive departments implementing the organizational mission. As the personal planning process is initiated, each staff member develops a personal plan. This plan should encompass the realization of both personal life goals (e.g., family, career, finance, status, work-life balance, etc.) and professional goals (e.g., work centered skill development, knowledge acquisition, talent enhancement, etc.). The creation and realization of personal goals creates an environment where knowledge acquisition is the norm, and where learning is central to the development of both the organization and the individual.

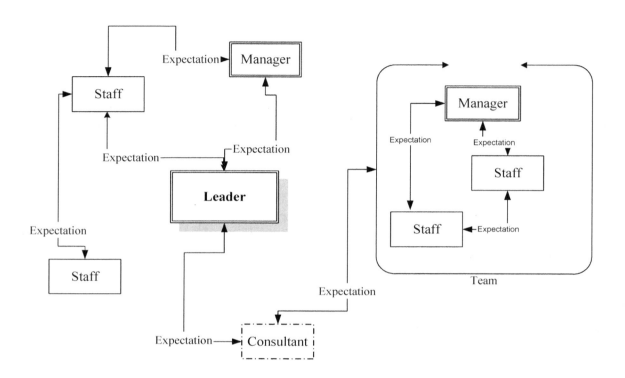

Figure 8.2. Heterarchical Learning Organization Expectation Flowchart.

As the triadic heterarchical strategic planning process completes its initial implementation sequence (organization to department to personal) and reverses sequence (personal to departmental to organizational), knowledge and talent become the driving force of organizational development. This bottom-up process relies on the realization of the learning organization prior to plan development reaching strategic levels.

The triadic heterarchical strategic planning process is specifically designed to permit organizational leaders to simultaneously develop strategic plans and create a culture of learning. As the organization progresses through the three planning processes, organizational leaders should be creating an environment where the learning organization emerges as the dominant culture.

Principles of the Heterarchical Learning Organization

O'Banion (1997) argued that for organizations to succeed in the development of a learning organization culture, the concept of learning should be linked to the planning process to ensure that the institution strategically sets goals and develops learning systems for long-term organizational success. The heterarchical learning organization thrives by implementing an ideological superstructure of ten principles that frame the management perspective of learning centeredness.

1. The learning organization implements a process of individual learner development to create a culture of continuous substantive change.
2. The organization creates a "sense of ownership" among all employees, and engages them as full partners in the planning process.
3. Employees take full responsibility for their choices, the success of their respective departments, and the fulfillment of the organizational mission.
4. The learning organization offers unlimited access to learning and personal development.
5. The learning organization focuses the attention of its workforce on talent development and alignment.
6. The learning organization engages all of its learners in collaborative learning enterprises embedded in its heterarchical team-based structures.
7. The learning organization exists neither in hierarchical or transcendent forms, rather it exists as a complex emergent heterarchy.
8. Clear expectations are established for all learning groups (at individual, team, departmental, or organizational levels).
9. The learning strategies of the organization are determined by the needs of the learners (identified in the triadic planning system), not by the management fads of the day.
10. Learning and change processes are at the center of all work and plans.

Adherence to these ten principles, coupled with the implementation of the triadic heterarchical planning process can ensure unprecedented institutional success and the attainment of the learning organization.

Creating the Culture of the Learning Organization Through a Learner Centered Approach

The achievement of the learning organization relies on the development of an organizational atmosphere of open communication and trust. It requires an inspirational leadership perspective of creativity about possibilities over a management of norms. The culture requires an emphasis on quality and continuous improvement over status quo and "the way we've always done it." Leaders and staff in the learning organization expect continuously to expand potential and to achieve new levels of excellence. Learning organizations thrive on calculated risks, because leaders and staff learn from both successes and failures. Finally, through shared responsibility, accountability, and teaming; the learning organization empowers people throughout the organization to envision a better future and gives them the power to achieve it.

The learning organization emerges when the leaders of an institution are committed to assisting all staff members in the development of their talents. Talents can be developed through a diverse agenda of learning experiences and through an emphasis on knowledge acquisition and skill development. Leaders in the learning organization set the standards for learning through their own continuous professional development. True leaders will not only believe in the learning organization concept, they will live it in everything they say and do.

The culture of the organization will filter down from the senior leaders of the firm. If the leaders are learners and acquirers of knowledge, then the followers will value learning, talent alignment, knowledge acquisition, and continuous personal and professional development. Leaders in the learning organization take a vested role in the learning activities of the company, ensuring that institutional resources are adequately dedicated to learning (training) procedures.

The acquisition of knowledge becomes paramount over the monotonous review of internal statistics and external forces that usually dominate the strategic planning landscape, and also simultaneously diminish employee morale. The new emphasis becomes the learning enterprise, and the creation of the learning environment. The learning environment centers on the development of learning activities and agendas, individual learner development, and the alignment and synergy of employee talents. Triadic strategic planning can serve as a method to reach the organization's collective learning potential, if leaders choose it as a value.

We're drowning in information and starving for knowledge. – Rutherford D. Rogers

Developing Data to Assess Effectiveness, Performance Improvement, & Organizational Success

Change must be measured from a known baseline. – Evan Shute

The development of essential information to conduct a strategic planning process is paramount in the realization and implementation of the plan. Organizations should develop baseline data (i.e., a snapshot of the present situation), and proceed to develop the strategic plan to improve their institutional standing. Often, the public relations data of an organization do not adequately capture the current situation or the need for change. Strategic planning requires a disciplined and rigorous examination of all relevant statistics of the organization, its departments, and the employees that compose the company.

Data, What is it Good For?: Basic Research & Planning

Statistics alone tell us very little, the key ingredient of any statistical analysis is the interpretation of the figures within an historical and social context. Too many bad ideas have emerged from an examination of statistics, where time and place were not properly factored into the equation. Researchers relying solely on analytic results often fail to explicate the true significance of the data's meaning in relation to decision-making.

I have witnessed many organizations develop fact books, financial spreadsheets, or satisfaction inventories without a proper comparison to baseline data, to the current marketplace, to competitor's data, or to the historical and social reality of the present time. Perhaps, the greatest example of this was that infamous Coca Cola decision to forego the classic recipe in favor of a new flavor. The decision was largely based on a study of people's preference of Pepsi's taste. They failed to really consider the social reality, branding, loyalty, or customer reaction. One simple question might have prevented this marketing situation: if people like Pepsi so much more, why do they drink more of our product? In the end, the basic premise of research and planning is to review all statistics within a common sense framework to enhance decision-making.

The goal of any research study should be to determine the relevance and reliability of anecdotal data prior to decision-making. People often ask, "What do the numbers say?" The fact is the numbers don't say anything; the people presenting the figures do all the talking. Statistics give us an indication of probability, and they are our best defense against bad decisions, but they will never completely determine the answer.

Data can suggest a best practice, but all analyses will occur within our existing paradigms of understanding (Kuhn, 1970).

It is the duty of leaders to challenge existing paradigms, and to suggest a pathway (plan) to change (success). It is the function of research to assist leaders and to suggest possible paths for planning. As a professional researcher, I will suggest a series of statistical needs that your organizational leaders may choose to fulfill prior to the initiation of your strategic planning process.

Internal Assessment: Identifying Issues to Increase Quality

In any strategic planning exercise, the organization should first determine the present state of the business. It must determine the starting point from which the plan is proposed. Companies should focus on the data that best suggests the current state of resources and the organization's future potential. The focus of internal assessment should be to determine the strengths and weaknesses of the firm. Smart planners will focus mainly on strengths that they can exploit. Often, organizations focus their attention and resources primarily on trying to overcome their weaknesses, trying to develop mechanisms to solve problems.

The focus on overcoming weaknesses leads to a reactionary culture of perceived failure and ineffectiveness. The smarter strategy is a focus on the strengths, aligning resources to ensure that the exploitation of current strengths can address some of the internal organizational shortcomings. When an organization finds an area of excellence, this area/department/practice should be nourished with increasing resources. By focusing on an area of strength and excellence, the organization is assured future and continuous quality improvement.

There are many facets of an organization, department, or professional career that can be examined. The key data reviewed in any strategic planning process should consist of analyses on: markets, customers, human resources and organizational structure, production or services, technology, finances, facilities, research and strategic outcomes, and other industry specific indicators. The table below illustrates the type of data planning teams may choose to review and consider.

The method of measurement that each organization can utilize may differ in breadth and depth. Regardless of the organization, the most effective analyses will identify key data for decision-making, will utilize the most strategic indicators necessary to create a success culture, and will identify internal data for comparison with competitive enterprises.

The successful planning enterprise will have created a series of executive summaries (as exemplified in Figure 9.1) to create a proper framework for the planning process. The breadth and depth of these summaries will depend on the ability of the organization to measure effectiveness, and the need for data to create effective plans. As a general rule the greater the number of strategic indicators that the organization can measure, the greater the relevance of statistics developed by the planning exercise.

Key Internal Indicators for Strategic Plan Development

Markets & Customers
- Branding and/or Imaging Results
- Market Strategy Effectiveness
- Marketing/Sales Performance
- Customer Loyalty (Retention)
- Diversification of Market Share
- Customer Satisfaction

Human Resources & Organizational Structure
- Staffing Levels
- Staffing Talents (*educational attainment, awards, knowledge capital*)
- Staff Tenure & Diversity
- Knowledge Capital
- Organizational Reporting Design & Management Systems

Production and/or Services
- New Product Development
- New Service Development
- Product/Service Support

Technology
- Cost & Assessment of Effectiveness
- Replacement Statistics
- Usage & Upgrade Needs

Finances
- Pricing/Costs
- Revenue, Expenditure & Balance
- Cost of Production/Delivery
- Profit Margins/Profit Analyses
- Finance Options

Facilities
- Condition of Existing Facilities
- Adequacy of Capacity
- Usage
- Capital Improvement Needs & Expenditures

The organization that plans successfully will also realize that there is no ideal (correct or incorrect) value for any given indicator. Each indicator will have a different meaning and interpretation, based in a situational reality in which the firm currently exists. The most essential factor of the interpretation of data is the understanding and realization of your current circumstances relative to the organization's historical standing, local competition, and in relation to the goals leaders have for the organization.

To demonstrate data in a usable form, the ad hoc research team or research office may elect to create a fact book of internal data for use by strategic planners. This fact book should present statistics in a simple format.

ITEM	10 YEARS AGO	5 YEARS AGO	3 YEARS PRIOR	PREVIOUS YEAR	CURRENT YEAR	3-Year Change		BENCHMARK
						#	%	
Name	#	#	#	#	#	#	#%	National or Competition Best Practice

Interpretation: The ad hoc research team or chief research officer should provide a narrative executive summary of the statistics presented in the table, statistics can be analyzed either grouped by area or measure-by-measure.

Recommendation: The ad hoc research team or chief researcher should offer an explanation of the contextual meaning of the data, and make a recommendation for the need for corrective action if necessary.

Figure 9.1. A Simple Method to Present Data.

Some organizations may want to take their data development to a higher level and conduct quality assessments and statistical analyses designed to ensure fulfillment of the organizational mission. These organizations will measure results as well as current statistical facts. In this case, the internal analysis should also be composed of goal development and performance expectations based on benchmarking best practices (an example is provided in Chapter 11 of this work). Core values will serve as a central framing reference for data development and analyses of quality.

In a quality motivated organization, data on leadership performance, public responsibility and corporate citizenship, strategy development, satisfaction, organizational performance, work systems analyses, support processes, and result orientations will also be quantified and disseminated as part of the strategic planning development and implementation processes. Quality driven organizations are interested in performance outcomes as well as basic statistical summaries. They develop mechanisms of continuous data development for decision-making throughout the strategic plan execution process.

Finally, when analyzing the organization's statistical internal data, planners should be ever cognizant of external factors such as the economy, social trends, historical trends, the local community, and political forces. External forces can have a major impact on the interpretation of data, and even on the realization of your strategic goals. External forces will in some fashion likely influence all of the key indicators and the strategic position of the firm (Taylor et al, 1990). Effective planners should incorporate external facts into the planning process.

External Assessment: Looking Outward

The strategic planning process requires that you examine those elements outside the organization that represent opportunities that can be exploited, or threats that can challenge the success of the company. Examining the essential data of external forces will allow planners to forecast a likely scenario of the future, to develop mechanisms for change, and to ensure that the firm moves from reactive chaos to a proactive culture. The two most important external data elements facing an organization are its markets (market share), and its competition.

Market Segmentation

As the organization has limited resources, it is essential that the company divide its business functions and its markets into differing segments. To do this effectively, the organizational leadership team should determine a definition of all of the markets that the business will compete to capture.

To determine the appropriate markets and business functions, the organization should determine the customer wants and needs it will fulfill. Wants describe those business products or services that customers prefer, and needs define those things customers cannot do without obtaining. Next, the organizational research team should determine the total available market size, the number of competitors, and the share of the market currently held by the organization. By doing this, research will demonstrate the number of potential customers, lost customers, and a prediction of future customers (i.e., the strategic goals). Using geo-demographic data your organization can make predictions on market growth and set goals for potential market growth as well.

Data within the following five statistical categories should be developed to assess the market and its potential:

1. Market Needs
2. Customer Wants
3. Products or Services Developed or Needed
4. Market Classification (Personal or Business)
5. Geo-demographics

As leaders of an organization that serves the public and considers itself as selling a service to the public, the leadership of the organization must consider both the demographics and the social-psychological interests of the marketplace.

To develop an effective marketing strategy it is essential to determine and understand the five distinct areas of marketing. The development and mastering of the following five areas will allow the organization to use market segmentation as a business strategy.

1) Product/Service Development & Distribution
2) Customer Satisfaction
3) Market Service Analysis
4) Expansion Into New Markets
5) Development of Effective Advertising Campaigns

Each of these five elements of the marketing process should be handled as unique and distinct parts that create a holistic process known as the market segmentation strategy. Mistakes are often made by organizations trying to resolve issues in their marketing campaign, when they attack one area or another without realizing the emergent complexity of the entire mosaic that these areas create. Simply stated, the organization attacks one area without realizing its relation to the whole or its uniqueness in the process.

As the organization progresses through this process it is important that decision makers realize the relationship between all of these factors in organizational planning. At times when the market decreases or marketing strategies become ineffective, organizations often begin to look for the "weak link" or begin to "place blame." Energy is often wasted on over examining competitors' practices or in self-doubt. A more effective approach is to re-examine and revise the strategy in a positive framework where each component is examined on its own merits and in light of the entire process and success rates of organizational competitors.

In developing an effective market segmentation strategy, questions should arise, some examples being:

a) Why are the numbers of customers decreasing, increasing remaining stagnant, or not increasing?
b) Do we have the right products or services?
c) Are products and services properly packaged?
d) Are our current locations positioned in the right places?
e) What are competitors doing better than us?
f) Should we initiate our competitors' strategy?
g) Are they successful because they do _____, and we do not?

A review of questions like these can represent a positive motivating force if raised within a context of information management and a well-developed planning process. If however, they become questions in an unorganized process or questions of defeat and self-doubt, the firm may not be able to develop new strategies for success. Often, an organization will fail to see marketing as a living process and rather view it as a one time universal strategy. In this environment, a failed marketing strategy will often be scrapped and replaced by a new "cure all" strategy instead of being revised. Members of the organization will most likely fear change and resort to the infamous, "This is the way it has always been done," mindset.

The situation noted above is a formula for failure over the long term because the organization becomes monotonous rather than innovative, duplicative rather than creative, and can become complacent rather than engaged. Energy that is spent talking and worrying about the innovations of competitors or in keeping the status quo is lost or wasted. Developing an effective market segmentation strategy requires a comprehensive properly framed understanding of the best practices of the organization's competitors and the desire to understand and transform current internal practices.

Benchmarking Best Practices of Competitors

The search for best practices among competitors should be part of the agenda of any learning organization, but it should not become the single driving force of change. Given the strong current of change manifesting itself throughout corporate America, the healthcare industry, not-for-profits, and even in educational institutions; learning organizations will need to benchmark the best practices of other companies to stay ahead of change, to propel themselves into situations of competitive advantage, and to continuously satisfy their customer base.

The intelligent organization will look not only within its own industry, but outside the industry as well. Great organizations will realize that they can develop leading and "cutting-edge" practices through an examination of best practices within their organization, within their economic sector, and throughout all business types in the global marketplace. The leaders of the next set of successful organizations will take the best practices of their competitors, or anywhere else they find them, and they will emulate them, innovate them, improve them, use them, and then renew them into the next set of best practices. The goal of any learning organization should be to become the organization within their sector that is benchmarked by others, including both their competitors and organizations outside their respective industry.

In the benchmarking process, your organization, department, or even you, will first plan to examine the practices of others. You will determine the process or practice to benchmark, and then you will need to review external data to determine the organization that is outperforming others in this area. The final step in the benchmark planning process is the development of data on the best practices of the organization being benchmarked, and for your organization's similarly related practices.

Once data have been developed, the next step is to determine the performance differential between your firm and that of the organization you are benchmarking. Next, determine if the benchmarked organization's performance is real, or an anomaly where emulation will not prove beneficial. Your organization does not want to model an anomaly, since your people will not be capable of duplicating the outstanding results.

As the data are fully developed, the manager of the benchmarking process should begin to communicate the findings and develop feedback loops to ensure that the findings are reliable and relative to the work that your organization is attempting to model. Proper communication will help to develop a "buy-in" for the proposed change that is likely to be recommended. The manager should also develop an initial set of recommendations about how best to incorporate the best practices of the other firm into the current practices, tradition, and culture of your organization.

Once the organization has substantial "buy-in" (and this will normally be developed within the framework of the three strategic planning processes), a set of action plans are developed to fully initiate the modeling phase. The action plans should be implemented and the best practices of other organizations should be modeled to produce desired results. As the implementation and modeling process is initiated, a process of progress evaluation should be implemented to potentially refine the benchmarks and best practices.

The results of benchmarking are best accomplished within the context of the triadic heterarchical strategic planning process. Too many organizations are in a constant state of benchmarking, where they rarely if ever fully implement the best practices of another organization. They, instead, engage in a series of "management fads," that tear at the culture and morale of their organization. To fully model the best practices of another organization, your organization will need to conduct the process as part of your strategic planning process, developing data prior to the initiation of strategic planning, and modeling best practices throughout the implementation timeline of your strategic plan. Benchmarking is a powerful tool if initiated in the appropriate context, and conducted with an emphasis on continuous improvement, rather than as a mechanism for exposing the "worst" practices of your own firm.

Benchmarking the best practices of your competitors or other organizations will give the firm a competitive advantage. It can transform your internal culture from one of reaction, to a progressive culture of proactivity. Employees can begin to more readily challenge the "status quo," and will begin to develop a mission of continuous improvement and enhancement.

Identifying the Best Indicators of Effectiveness & Success

When examining all of the available statistics, information, quantitative, qualitative, and anecdotal data, some indicators of success are more rewarding and informative for strategic planning effectiveness than others. In my experience, I have found the following ten indicators to be the most useful to review prior to the initiation of the triadic heterarchical strategic planning process.

1. Current Market Share of Available Markets
2. Competitive Analysis
3. Three-Year Revenue Formation (with benchmarks)
4. Three-Year Expenditure Formation (with benchmarks)
5. Three-Year Financial Balance Analysis (with benchmarks)
6. Historical & Current Customer Satisfaction (with benchmarks)
7. Educational Attainment of Organizational Human Resources
8. Retention Rates of Employees & Return Rates of Customers
9. Maintenance Backlog versus Total Value of Facilities
10. Assessment Results of Quality Assurance

An understanding of these ten indicators will serve any organization prior to entering the strategic planning process. Either an ad hoc committee or the organizational research office should produce a series of executive summaries for each of these indicators as part of the information gathering stage of organizational planning. All ten of these indicators will allow for a SWOT analysis that is rich in value for its ability to help formulate strategic proposals. Figure 9.2 demonstrates that the development of data is not part of the strategic planning process; rather, it is a preliminary development product for strategic planning.

The strategic planning process offers an organization the ability to develop baseline data, compare its current results against itself, its competitors, and its desired results. The real goals of data development should be dissemination and the productive use of the data in the decision-making process.

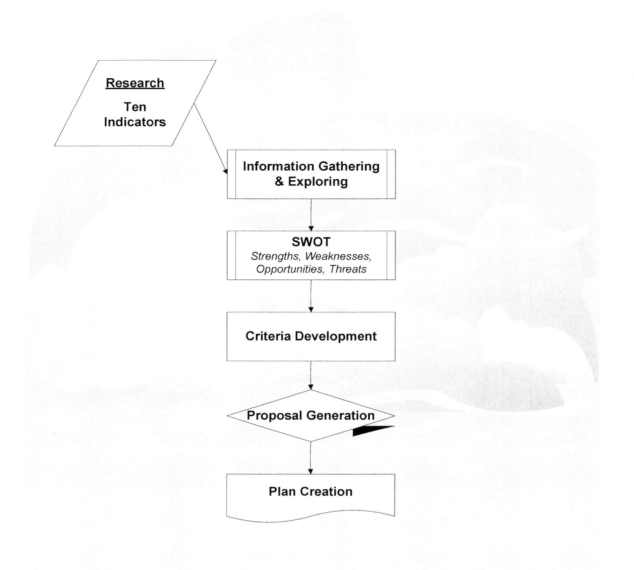

Figure 9.2. Data Development & the Strategic Planning Process.

Strategic planning offers an opportunity, not only to develop information, but also to communicate to all stakeholders and constituents of the organization. By using the data within the context of strategic planning, its usage will be more proactive and productive. The development of data may represent the first positive step toward organizational transformation that the firm has taken in many years. Leaders should never underestimate the power of information, while also never underestimating the ease of interpreting data incorrectly.

The development of data is only a small part of the strategic planning process. However, look at most strategic plans and you will notice that the majority of the document is based on the presentation of facts, with little done in the relation of these facts to the actual goals, or little on the benefit of communicating these facts across the organization. Data, although essential for proper strategic planning, is a functional requirement of the planning process; it is not the plan itself. Do not fall victim to the popular trap of assuming the presentation of statistics is synonymous with the development of an effective plan.

> *While I am busy with little things, I am not required to do greater things.*
> – St. Francis de Sales

Step-by-Simple Step Planning Section

The Triadic Heterarchical Planning Process

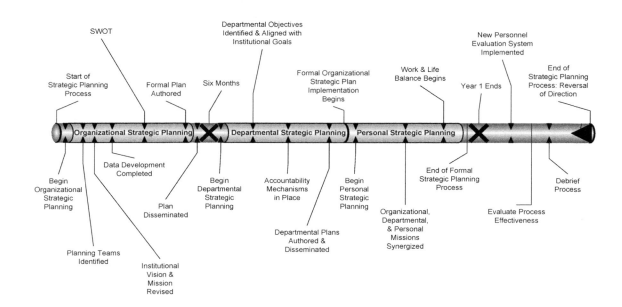

SWOT

Departmental Objectives
Identified & Aligned with
Institutional Goals

New Personnel
Evaluation System
Implemented

Start of
Strategic Planning
Process

Formal Plan
Authored

Six Months

Formal Organizational
Strategic Plan
Implementation
Begins

Work & Life
Balance Begins

Year 1 Ends

End of
Strategic Planning
Process: Reversal
of Direction

Organizational Strategic Planning

Departmental Strategic Planning

Personal Strategic Planning

Begin
Organizational
Strategic
Planning

Data Development
Completed

Begin
Departmental
Strategic
Planning

Accountability
Mechanisms
in Place

Begin
Personal
Strategic
Planning

End of Formal
Strategic Planning
Process

Debrief
Process

Plan
Disseminated

Evaluate Process
Effectiveness

Planning Teams
Identified

Departmental Plans
Authored &
Disseminated

Organizational,
Departmental,
& Personal
Missions
Synergized

Institutional
Vision &
Mission
Revised

Triadic Heterarchical Strategic Planning Timeline

Chapter 10

Strategic
Organizational Planning
Workbook

Table of Contents

Purpose of Strategic Organizational Planning

The purpose of this strategic planning initiative is to develop a process that will allow your organization to enter the 21st Century as an active agent in the realization of the competitive advantage and culture of success you currently seek. Organizational planning will allow your leaders, staff members, clients, customers, and the local community to diligently reflect on the vitality of the organization in relation to current and future relationships with stakeholders.

The strategic planning process empowers everyone in the organization to reflect on the past, present, and future, renewing the strategic vision, mission, values, and goals. The organization will work through a collaborative process to evaluate current vision, mission, values, goals, strategies, results, marketing, technology, facilities, and fiscal considerations. Planners work to evaluate the structures currently in place, while recommending necessary changes, improvements, developments, and enhancements in light of the overall triadic strategic planning process.

Organizational planning is a process of creating both short- and long-term goals. Although there have been many definitions developed to describe strategic planning, and rarely are any two processes the same (largely due to the differing stakeholders involved), for the sake of a common understanding, your organization might adopt a combined definition from Peter Drucker and the author of this book:

> *Strategic planning is the continual process of making entrepreneurial (risk-taking) decisions systematically and with the greatest knowledge of their futurity; organizing systematically the efforts needed to carry out these decisions; and measuring the results of these decisions against the expectations through systematic feedback (Drucker, 1973). Strategic planning is best accomplished when plans are tied to the mission of the organization, involve a large number of the stakeholders, are data driven, and emerge from an arena of consensus that is cross-institutional and heterarchical in authority. (Austin, 1999)*

Strategic planning, at the global level, typically results in a formal, written, structured strategic plan which projects the organization's future course for success. (Jurinski, 1993) Departmental planning results in strategic actions at a local level that map the future of the department and integrate the plans of the local and global into one interrelated set of outcomes. Simultaneously, strategic planning at the personal level will develop the staff talents and goals necessary to fully implement all plans throughout the organization, thus ensuring a greater likelihood for success. This is the first step in the larger process of value integration known as Strategic Planning. Jurinski has demonstrated that a distinction should be made between the organization's strategic planning process and subsequent strategic plans.

The two terms are not synonymous and it is important to realize that this activity requires both a formal process (detailed within this workbook) and a formal written plan (the formal outcome of the strategic planning process). (Jurinski, 1993, p. 1).

Part #1: Overview of Organizational Strategic Planning Process

<u>Overview</u>

Your organizational planning process should establish a set of planning teams that represent the core functions of the business. They should be prioritized from the most mission centered through those representing only the functional support activities of your business:

1. _____

2. _____

3. _____

4. _____

5. _____

6. _____

7. _____

8. (ADD MORE AS DEEMED NECESSARY)

Planning Tip: Planning teams can represent many facets of the operation, it is important to choose the teams that are most important to the organization's success.

Teams in *business* might include: Production, Development, Distribution, Management, Technology, Facilities, Financial, Human Resources, Marketing, Capital Development, Customer Support, etc.

Teams in *educational institutions* might include: Academic Programs, Enrollment Management, Advancement, Government Relations, Student Services, Public Relations, Business & Community Partnerships, Governance, Research, Development, Instructional Technology, Information Technology, Facilities, Financial, etc.

Teams for *not-for-profits* are likely to contain many of the above and others that are more mission driven, such as, Client Development, Customer Service, Revenue Generation, Board Development, Volunteer Development, etc.

Each of these planning teams should, at a minimum, consist of a Chairperson (leader) from the organization's senior management staff as well as a member of the Board (if at all possible), a line worker, a professional/administrative (middle management) staff member, a support staff member, a customer, and a member of the larger local community. These teams will meet over three months to complete the strategic organizational planning process defined within this workbook.

Each planning team works toward establishing an area of concentration for the organization-wide strategic plan. Teams develop and analyze the internal and external environment, develop an understanding of the current situation and strategic goals, create a supportive climate at the organization with a multi-level collaboration of ideas, and develop interactive planning networks with cross institutional responsibility and cross departmental resource sharing. The outcome of the planning process will include a formal document, the Organizational Strategic Plan, that should be implemented within a three (no more than five) year period.

Organizational planning will benefit your organization by minimizing the element of surprise, while maximizing the ability of leaders and decision makers to manage change effectively and efficiently. Organizational planning allows for the change in institutional management from a reactive enterprise to one of action, and from command-and-control styles to one of emergent heterarchy. It creates a better understanding of the competition and the external economic environment to ensure that the organization achieves its goals. Organizational planning can help identify potential internal problems on paper, before action must be taken. Finally, this level of planning is a mechanism for continually measuring performance against established standards. It should serve as a valuable communication tool that provides each stakeholder and/or staff member with a common base of information and expectations.

Planning Tip: When developing any team it is important to realize that teams should not consist solely of members from the department that most closely relates to the function of the strategic planning area. I suggest that the teams have only a few members from departments directly related to the planning team area. I further suggest that the team leader should be the department head most closely associated with the planning team charge, and that the total number of members of the planning team that are from a related departmental area not exceed 25% of the total team membership. This will ensure that a cross-institutional cross-functional perspective is guiding the planning process, thus leading to more cross-organizationally based plans and expectations.

Each team should select members to fill the following essential roles. These roles assist in the management of the process and the fulfillment of the planning objectives within an aggressive timeframe.

1. **Team Leader** -- This individual, selected from the senior management team, is responsible for setting agendas, guiding the team through the process, and making decisions when consensus cannot be reached or when there is not sufficient information to warrant a decision about a particular goal. The leader makes all final decisions regarding the outcome of the planning process, and is the driver of the team's charge.

2. **Team Facilitator** -- This individual, selected for his/her ability to keep the group on task in a diplomatic way, is responsible for leading discussions and moving the team through the process in a timely fashion. The facilitator also acts as a mediator in the consensus process.

3. **Team Timekeeper** -- This individual, selected for an ability to complete projects and tasks in a timely and efficient manner, is responsible for keeping the team focused on the task of completing the process by the quickest most efficient means. The timekeeper continuously reminds the facilitator of the time remaining and the amount of material still to be covered.

4. **Team Recorder** -- This individual, selected for his/her ability to write quickly and neatly as well as the ability to retain and summarize what is heard, is responsible for highlighting the discussion points on flip charts for future review.

5. **Team Transcriber** -- This individual, selected for an ability to keep detailed records, will keep minutes, complete the official set of worksheets, and prepare the first draft of the team's planning document.

6. **Team Educator** -- This individual, selected for the ability to understand and interpret data, as well as to conduct rudimentary level research, is charged with ensuring that the team uses information and data to guide discussions. In instances where anecdotal storytelling is relied upon over quantifiable information (i.e., data or statistics that contradict the qualitative information), the educator should alert the team to this fact.

7. **Team Motivator** -- This individual, selected for his/her ability to inspire others and create a sense of camaraderie, is selected to provide refreshments, rewards, and other motivational reinforcements for team members.

8. **Team Editor** -- This individual, selected for their ability to edit and summarize large amounts of information as well as a tendency to be a perfectionist, is charged with preparing the final team report.

Planning Tip: People are often chosen for these roles by the positions they hold in the organization; more effective outcomes are often reached by choosing members with appropriate skill sets rather than by position.

Timeline of Stages

Organizational Planning Kickoff

State of the Organization Dinner   – Friday (5:30-8:00 PM)

- Publicly Display Key Statistics of Organization.
- Have CEO deliver State of the Organization Address.
- Envision a Common Positive Future and Publicly Express It.

Vision & Mission Evaluation   – Saturday (8:30 AM – 11:00 AM)

- Invite public commentary on the current vision & mission.

Workbook Training   – Saturday (12:00 PM – 3:00 PM)

- SWOT
- Consensus
- Planning Proposal Development
- Plan Implementation Matrix
- STOP Matrix
- Final Plan Format

Vision, Mission Evaluation & Development   (SET DATE_____)
Planning Team Meeting (2 Hours)   – Determined by Teams
Team leaders, Senior Staff (or Board) Meeting   – Special Public Meeting

Stage #1: Information Gathering & Exploring   (SET DATE_____)
Planning Team Meetings   – Determined by Teams

> Two meetings 2-3 hours in length; or whatever is deemed necessary to complete task.

Stage #2: Identify Alternative Goals for Action   (SET DATE_____)
Planning Team Meetings   – Determined by Planning Teams

> One or two meetings 2-3 hours in length; or whatever is necessary to complete task.

Public Report of Progress by Team Leaders to CEO (SET DATE_____)

Stages #1 and #2 should be completed.

Stage #3: Create Criteria for Choosing Goals for Action (SET DATE_____)

      Planning Team Meetings   – Determined by Planning Teams

Two meetings 2-3 hours in length; or whatever is necessary to complete task.

Stage #4: Proposal & Plan Implementation Developed   (SET DATE_____)

      Planning Team Meetings   – Determined by Planning Teams

Two to four meetings 2-3 hours in length; or whatever is necessary to complete task; completed by no later than third month of process.

Public Report of Progress by Leaders and First Draft delivered to President/CEO
      Stages #1-#4 Completed; initial draft of Planning Team Proposals presented.

First Draft of Organization's Plan Summarized from Team Drafts and Returned to Planning Teams as One Document (*END OF THIRD MONTH*)

Planning Teams Review Draft and Present Comments via Leader to President/CEO

Organizational Plan Finalized and Formally Presented to Organization Next Time (SET DATE_____)

Plan Implementation Begins Through Formalized Departmental Planning & Personal Planning (*FOURTH MONTH OF PROCESS*)

Preparation Guidelines

All staff members at an organization should be asked to volunteer as a Planning Team member to enhance both the departmental and institutional levels of the organization. Planning effectiveness relies on certain essential preparations. These are:

A.   **Personal level preparations**
- Open minded and voluntary readiness to participate in process.
- Considerations of personal reasons for joining a planning team.
- Identification of personal goals for strategic organizational planning.
- Willingness to work beyond both the departmental and personal levels.
- An understanding that strategic planning is not just an addition to current job, but an essential element of current work and future success.

B.   **Departmental and Organization level preparations**
- Alerting of supervisors to staff participation & time considerations.
- Consider readiness of individual staff members to participate.
- Determination of time schedule to complete process with limited effect on workplace production.
- Identify major opportunities and threats that could be encountered as part of the process.
- Senior management accepts responsibility to lead and empower staff.

To assist in the preparation of the Planning Teams, the organization should host a kickoff weekend planning orientation. The first night will consist of a catered dinner, and a statistical summary of the organization. This "State of the Organization" presentation will review relevant statistics, identify the broad long-term objectives of the organization planning process, and orient planning team members to the task at hand. The Saturday orientation should begin with light refreshments, proceed with an evaluation of the current vision and mission of the company. Following lunch, the afternoon session should review this workbook, and answer questions before the teams proceed.

Planning Tip: The weekend kickoff is used to ensure that all participants have self-selected to be part of the process. This quickly identifies organizational planning as a volunteer process that will require work beyond normal routines and hours. People will volunteer if they understand that planning will influence their work life later in the form of departmental and personal planning. If done well, this event will result in the timely completion, essential buy-in, and a sense of ownership by staff members. Take the preparation time to make this a rewarding and professional event.

Part #2: Vision & Mission Evaluation & Development

Scott Adams, in his book <u>The Dilbert Principle</u>, defines a mission statement as "a long awkward sentence that demonstrates management's inability to think clearly." (Adams, 1996, p. 36). Jurinski defines a mission statement as a brief, general description of the direction a company is taking. In strategic planning: the vision, mission, and mission statements are often confounded and confusing. A mission will be defined as a description of the task we face, the service we offer, and those who we serve. The mission statement should consist of no more than a few sentences that enthusiastically articulates your mission to stakeholders.

In addition, a vision should be defined as the direction or path that sets the pace for excellence in our organization (i.e., what you hope to achieve). Values should represent the abstract principles that guide your organization through an increasingly complex economy, while goals are the specific targets you hope to achieve, and strategies or objectives will be the mechanism devised to meet goals. Note well, that each of these are separate components; good mission and vision statements do not contain specific details about the objectives that will be reached, who does the work, or how much it will cost. These are the details that are defined in the strategic organizational plan.

Planning Tip: Use the definitions above. Do not get caught up in semantically oriented arguments over the difference between a mission and a vision, or an objective or a goal. In the end, ask yourself, are the definitions really as important as the success of our firm?

VISION

A DIRECTION OR PATH THAT SETS THE PACE FOR EXCELLENCE IN AN ORGANIZATION. WHAT YOU HOPE TO ACHIEVE

MISSION

A DESCRIPTION OF THE TASK WE FACE, THE SERVICE WE OFFER, AND WHO WE SERVICE

VALUES

THE MOST SACRED IDEALS

GOALS

THE ESTABLISHMENT OF SPECIFIC TARGETS

STRATEGIES / OBJECTIVES

DEVISING WAYS TO MEET YOUR GOALS

Identify the Organization's current vision, mission, and value statements:

Vision Statement

_____

_____

Mission Statement

_____

_____

_____

_____

_____

_____

_____

_____

Value Statements

1. _____
2. _____
3. _____
4. _____
5. _____
6. _____
7. _____
8. _____

(ADD MORE AS NECESSARY)

Planning Tip: If your organization does not posses strategic values, you can use other abstract principles that guide the organization (e.g., Institutional Priorities, Abstract Goals, etc.)

Upon a reflection of these statements and principles, the Planning Teams will complete a series of worksheets (Worksheets #1 & #2). These worksheets will measure and evaluate the expectations of the current vision and mission of the organization, while the goals will be evaluated as part of the larger planning process. These sheets are designed to give the planning teams the framework and ability to suggest changes to current statements. As part of the morning exercise of the Saturday retreat, Planning Teams will complete and discuss Worksheets #1 and #2; the final results of this section will be completed at a later meeting, and subsequently discussed at the senior management-planning meeting.

The vision of the organization should be a direction or path that sets the pace for excellence in the organization. It should be that which the organization hopes to achieve. Henry M. Boettinger, retired Director of Corporate Planning at AT&T stated that: "To manage is to lead, and to lead others requires that one enlist the emotions of others to share a **vision** as their own." To this end, please review your Vision Statement and answer the following questions:

- Do all stakeholders share our vision?
- Would you say that we share a common unspoken vision?
- Do individuals have differing visions?
- Do departments have differing visions?
- Do we share a common language?
- What are the barriers to a common language and a common vision?

In addition to examining the vision, mission evaluation is crucial to the final strategic planning process, in that, it will set a major mark for the Planning Teams to base criteria for goal selection upon. The mission of an organization is critical to the measurement of its success. To be truly effective, a mission and mission statement must tell us who we are, and we as stakeholders must believe it. Unfortunately, the vast majority of mission statements currently in use are leading their organizations in the same fashion that a hood ornament leads a car.

How would you rate your organization's mission statement in terms of this metaphor?

Proceed to Worksheet #1

After you have completed Worksheet #1, review your response, repeat the steps substituting the word vision for mission, and please answer the following questions:

1) Are our Vision and Mission Statements assets to our organization?

_____

_____

_____

2) Should we keep or change the current Vision?

_____

_____

_____

3) Should we keep or change the current Mission?

_____

_____

_____

4) Is there room for improvement in our current mission or should we begin again?

_____

_____

_____

_____

If you believe the organization would improve by a re-development of the Vision and Mission, please proceed to Worksheet #2.

After you have completed Worksheet #2, complete the following section:

Using the ideas and concepts you developed in Worksheet #2, please write a vision and mission statement for the company in the space below. If you accept the current vision or mission statements, see if you can improve upon them.

_____

_____

_____

_____

_____

Complete proceeding task both as an individual and within the context of your Planning Team, repeat the exercise for the Vision statement below as well. Deliver to the leader via the senior staff planning meeting.

_____

_____

_____

_____

_____

_____

_____

Planning Tip: The involvement of as many staff members as possible in this process is essential to build the case of ownership that can make both your vision and mission relevant to the organization.

MISSION STATEMENT
Worksheet #1: Recognize the Perceptions[1]

Rate your organization from 0 (lowest) to 5 (highest) on the following:

_____ Our mission includes elements that will endure beyond the tenure of anyone currently working here.

_____ We are very careful not to confuse our mission with our mission statement.

_____ We developed our mission completely before trying to write a mission statement.

_____ We don't try to substitute strategies, plans, and goals for mission.

_____ All employees gave input to the development of the mission (1 if 20%, 2 if 40%, etc.)

_____ Our Mission could easily be understood by a twelve year old.

_____ After thirty days of working here, each employee can passionately articulate our mission in their own words.

_____ Our employees think our mission is worthy.

_____ Our mission is achievable in total as well as in parts.

_____ Our customers and suppliers know, understand, and agree with our mission (again, ask them).

_____ The public we serve, know and understand our mission.

_____ Our mission clearly differentiates us from our competitors.

_____ We refuse to borrow our mission from anyone or buy it from a consultant.

_____ Our mission is a declaration of what we want to be, not a statement of what we think others expect us to be.

_____ Our mission has the passion to make people excel, work harder, and develop professionally.

_____ We really believe that we could not operate successfully without our mission or mission statement.

_____ We proudly and publicly display our mission.

_____ Our CEO believes and embodies our mission.

_____ We use our mission to guide all major discussions at the firm.

---

[1] *Revised from Lucas, J. (1997). Fatal Illusions. New York: American Management Association.*

MISSION STATEMENT
Worksheet #2: Identifying Organization Characteristics[2]

1. What overall business are we in and what business are we likely to be in five years from now?

_____

_____

2. What are our most important services?

_____

_____

3. What will our most important services be in the next five years?

_____

_____

4. Who are our most important customers?

_____

_____

5. Why or how are we different from our main competitors?

_____

_____

6. How do we think our business will change over the next five years?

_____

_____

7. How do we judge the organization's ultimate success? Why are we in existence?

_____

_____

---

[2] _Revised from Jurinski, J. (1993). Strategic Planning. New York: American Management Association._

Part #3 Meeting Guides for Organizational Planning

Stage #1: Information Gathering & Exploring

Purpose

- To gather information about the company and your respective area of general concern.
- To appreciate what has previously been accomplished in this area, to build on the past, and to improve and excel.
- To review information/data about the organization in general and about your Planning Team's charge in particular.
- To identify the external opportunities and threats that exist in general and in your Planning Team's charge in particular.
- To identify assumptions about the future of the organization in general and in your Planning Team's charge in particular.

The Planning Team

- Gathers information about the charge.
- Examines information provided by the designated research office or committee.
- Requests additional information from the designated research office or committee when appropriate (Worksheet #3).
- Identifies external opportunities and threats.
- Makes assumptions about the future in general and their Planning Team's charge in particular.

> **Expected Outcome:** *"Based on the Planning Team's assumptions, the specific issues that this **organizational** plan must address to be successful are ..."*

Meeting #1

Preparation

- All Planning Team members bring their Organization Planning Workbook and their institutional information to all of the meetings.
- Each member should come prepared to discuss the information/data provided by the Research Office or ad hoc committee.
- Members should complete the appropriate worksheets prior to the first meeting (#3, #4, & #5).

Discussion

The Team Lists on Easel Paper

- What external opportunities exist beyond the internal organization community that could help us carry out the mission?
- What external threats exist beyond the internal organization community that should be addressed to help us carry out the mission?
- What are our assumptions about our future in relation to our charge? (Brainstorm)
- Can we verify these assumptions, opportunities, and threats based on the information provided to us by the Research Office or ad hoc research committee?
- Are their additional sources of information that we need to consult?
- What data do we need to begin to collect for guidance in future planning initiatives?

Decision Making

- What opportunities does the team believe exists here?
- What threats does the team believe exists here?
- What are the valid and verified assumptions that the team believes will influence the progress over the next 3-5 years?
- What are the common assumptions that we share?

Responsibility

- The leader identifies additional information that is needed for the next meeting.
- The leader designates one person to bring the additional information needed from the Research Office or ad hoc committee to the next meeting.
- Facilitator debriefs process.
- Transcriber emails each department within 2 days and gets organization's IT office to post on web.
- Motivator ensures that all team members are prepared to be fully engaged at the next meeting.

Meeting #2

<u>Preparation</u>
- Each team member will complete appropriate Worksheets (#6, #7, #8).
- Each team member will review his/her notes from previous meeting.
- Each team member will be prepared to identify the internal strengths and weaknesses of the organization.
- The designated team member will bring either the information or a report on its availability from the designated research office or committee.

<u>Discussion</u>

The Team Lists on Easel Paper
- What internal strengths exist, that help us carry out the mission of the organization?
- What internal weaknesses exist that should be addressed to help us carry out the mission of the organization?
- What are our assumptions about the future of firm in relation to our charge, the external threats and opportunities, and the internal strengths and weaknesses? (Brainstorming Process)
- Can we verify these assumptions; strengths and weaknesses based on the information provided to us by the designated research office or committee?

<u>Decision Making</u>
- What strengths does the team believe exists here?
- What weaknesses does the team believe exists here?
- Given all of the information/data and discussions, are there any other valid and verified assumptions that the team believes will influence progress over the next 3-5 years?

<u>Responsibility</u>
- The leader identifies and lists all of the External Threats, External Opportunities, Internal Strengths, and Internal Weaknesses (SWOT).
- The leader designates one person to type these lists in MS Word and deliver a copy of this file to the Chief Planning Officer; and to bring a copy of the lists to the next meeting.
- The Leader distributes handouts on SWOT (Situational) Analysis.
- Facilitator debriefs process.
- Transcriber emails each department within 2 days and gets organization's IT office to post on web.
- Motivator ensures that all team members are prepared to be fully engaged at the next meeting.

INFORMATION GATHERING
Worksheet #3:
Additional Information/Date/Statistics Needed from the Research Office or ad hoc Team

-
-
-
-
-
-
-
-
-
-
-
-
-
-
-

INFORMATION GATHERING
Worksheet #4:
External Opportunities to the Organization Relating to Our Charge

1.

2.

3.

4.

5.

6.

7.

8.

9.

10.

11.

12.

13.

14.

15.

INFORMATION GATHERING
Worksheet #5:
External Threats to the Organization Relating to Our Charge

1.

2.

3.

4.

5.

6.

7.

8.

9.

10.

11.

12.

13.

14.

15.

INFORMATION GATHERING
Worksheet #6:
Internal Strengths of the Organization Relating to Our Charge

1.

2.

3.

4.

5.

6.

7.

8.

9.

10.

11.

12.

13.

14.

15.

INFORMATION GATHERING
Worksheet #7:
Internal Weaknesses of the Organization Relating to The Charge

1.

2.

3.

4.

5.

6.

7.

8.

9.

10.

11.

12.

13.

14.

15.

INFORMATION GATHERING
Worksheet #8:
The Critical Assumptions that this Plan must address are:

-
-
-
-
-
-
-
-
-
-
-
-
-
-

Stage #2: Identifying and Assessing Alternative Goals

Purpose

- To affirm and understand the revised vision and mission of the organization (if necessary).
- To specify the general expectations that each planning team should address, and the characteristics of a vital and vibrant mission driven organization.
- To identify and prioritize common goals for the Planning Team's charge.
- To begin to develop a list of alternative actions (GOALS: strategies: objectives) to achieve these common goals.
- To brainstorm as many possible goals and directives as possible for the organization.

The Planning Team

- Understands, accepts, and embraces the Vision and Mission Statements.
- Identifies and prioritizes common goals for the Planning Team's charge.
- Develops a list of alternatives to accomplish these goals.
- Prioritizes goals and begins to develop subsequent objectives, strategies, and action steps.
- Realizes that these actions should be based on real quantifiable data.
- Realizes that the ideas of the team will influence the direction of our company for the next three years.

Expected Outcome: "The Planning Team has identified these common goals and proposes a range of alternative goals (strategies/objectives) including..."

Planning Tip: Teams normally enter this part of the process concerned with generating the best ideas and goals. The purpose of this stage is to generate as many alternatives as possible. The next stage will prioritize and validate the ideas, while the final stage represents "wordsmithing". Feel free to exercise creativity in this stage.

Meeting #3

<u>Preparation</u>

- Examine and become familiar with the situational analysis process using external opportunities and threats, internal strengths and weaknesses with respect to the Planning Team's charge.
- Review notes from training session on conducting a SWOT (Situational) Analysis.
- Review Worksheets #9, #10, #11, #12, complete as an individual and come prepared to complete as a team.

<u>Discussion</u>

- The Planning Team leader will review the (SWOT) situational analysis methodology and review handouts supplied in this workbook.
- The Planning Team leader will review Worksheets #9-#12.
- The Planning Team will discuss each of the Worksheets in detail; identifying alternative actions that may be necessary based on the situational analysis.
- The Team develops a set of goals that cover the four areas:

  1. Expand and Invest
  2. Originate and Improve
  3. Join and Amplify
  4. Change and Integrate

(Note that, no goals for a given area is a legitimate response).

<u>Decision Making</u>

- Using the multi-vote process (covered in the glossary) the group will come to consensus on a list of at least twenty prioritized alternative goals (goals/strategies/objectives) for each planning team area.

<u>Responsibility</u>

- The Planning Team leader will prepare the list of the prioritized alternative actions (goals/strategies/objectives) and a report on the Team's progress to date for distribution and discussion at the next senior management meeting.
- The Planning Team leader will summarize response of Senior Staff, CEO, and other Planning Team leaders, and return a response summary to team members prior to next meeting.

Goal Development

	Internal	
	Strengths	**Weaknesses**
Opportunities	**SWOT (+,+)** Expand & Invest	**SWOT (-, +)** Join & Amplify
Threats	**SWOT (+, -)** Originate & Improve	**SWOT (-, -)** Change & Integrate

External

Worksheet #9
Choosing Alternative Goals

List strengths and opportunities, then comparing the two, develop a list of alternative goals. For example, how will you leverage the internal strengths of your organization to exploit the external opportunities available to your organization?

"Nurture and Guard for Rewards."

Internal Strengths (+,)

1. _____

2. _____

3. _____

4. _____

5. _____

External Opportunities (,+)

1. _____

2. _____

3. _____

4. _____

5. _____

SWOT (+,+)
Expand & Invest for Success

1. _____

2. _____

3. _____

4. _____

5. _____

Use Additional Space as Necessary

Worksheet #10
Choosing Alternative Goals

List strengths and threats, then comparing the two, develop a list of alternative goals. For example, how will you leverage the internal strengths of your organization to overcome the external threats currently confronting your organization?

"New Ideas will Bring New Rewards."

Internal Strengths (+,)

1. _____

2. _____

3. _____

4. _____

5. _____

External Threats (, -)

1. _____

2. _____

3. _____

4. _____

5. _____

SWOT (+, -)
Originate & Improve for Success

1. _____

2. _____

3. _____

4. _____

5. _____

Use Additional Space as Necessary

Worksheet #11
Choosing Alternative Goals

List weaknesses and opportunities, then comparing the two, develop a list of alternative goals. For example, how will you overcome your internal weaknesses in the organization to leverage the external opportunities currently available to your organization?

"Together We Can Earn Rewards."

Internal Weaknesses (-,)

1. _____

2. _____

3. _____

4. _____

5. _____

External Opportunities (, +)

1. _____

2. _____

3. _____

4. _____

5. _____

SWOT (-, +)
Join & Amplify for Success

1. _____

2. _____

3. _____

4. _____

5. _____

Use Additional Space as Necessary

Worksheet #12
Choosing Alternative Goals

List weaknesses and threats, then comparing the two, develop a list of alternative goals. For example, how will you overcome the internal strengths of your organization to manage the external threats currently confronting your organization?

"Embrace Challenges to Gain Rewards."

Internal Weaknesses (- ,)

1. _____
2. _____
3. _____
4. _____
5. _____

External Threats (, -)

1. _____
2. _____
3. _____
4. _____
5. _____

SWOT (- , -)
Change & Integrate for Success

1. _____
2. _____
3. _____
4. _____
5. _____

Use Additional Space as Necessary

Stage #3: Creation of Criteria for Choosing Goals

Purpose
- To consider and revise the goals in light of Senior Staff Meeting discussions.
- To develop criteria that must be met by any proposed goals.
- To test the proposed alternative goals against the criteria and the organization's mission.
- To develop additional alternative goals that meet the criteria and eliminate all that do not meet the criteria.
- To evaluate all goals, choosing those most appropriate for the organization at this time.

The Planning Team
- Considers the response of other Planning Team leaders, The President/CEO, The Board of Trustees, and the Chief Planning Officer regarding the alternative actions, and revises these goals as needed.
- Develops criteria for testing the feasibility of proposed alternative goals (goals/strategies/objectives).
- Tests the proposed goals against the criteria.
- Revises goals, adds and eliminates goals as needed.
- Identifies alternatives for future structures, activities, services, and programs in relation to the defined charge in particular and the organization in general that are, ideally, both desirable and feasible.
- Creates a final list of proposed alternative actions (goals/strategies/objectives) that have been tested against the criteria and reviewed at the Senior Staff meeting for the development of all strategic planning initiatives.
- Uses Worksheet #13 as needed.

Expected Outcome: "We, the Planning Team, submit these proposed goals to fulfill the organization's mission in the form of these specific goals, objectives, strategies, and actions..."

Planning Tip: In this stage, the team identifies the best goals to achieve over the next three years. It is important to realize that many "great" ideas will need to be discarded because the time and circumstances of reality and context diminish the ability of the organization to achieve them at the present moment.

Meeting #4

<u>Preparation</u>
- Review the outcomes, worksheets, and notes from Stages #1 & #2.
- Review the comments and suggestions from the senior leaders.
- Consider the true meaning of the mission of the organization.

<u>Discussion</u>
- The Planning Team reviews outcomes of Stages #1 & #2, within the context of the leadership responses, and considers if any changes should be made to the identified alternative goals in light of these discussions.
- The Team comes to final consensus about the possible goals (strategies/objectives/actions).
- A finished list of final alternatives is posted on easel paper.
- The Team identifies essential criteria (Worksheet #13) for testing the proposed goals.

<u>Decision Making</u>
- Planning Team members use easel paper and post the alternative goals, objectives, and criteria, walk past them and mark those they support. The Team comes to a final consensus on the goals and criteria that they have chosen to support.

<u>Responsibilities</u>
- Review the final list of alternative actions (**GOALS: objectives: strategies**)
- Review the list of essential criteria that were identified as part of this meeting.
- Facilitator debriefs process.
- Transcriber emails each department within 2 days and gets organization's IT office to post on web.
- Motivator ensures that all team members are prepared to be fully engaged at the next meeting.

Planning Tip: When developing the essential criteria, consider the following contextual points:
1. Mission
2. Costs
3. Desire to Implement
4. Resources Available
5. ROI

Meeting #5

<u>Preparation</u>
- Review the final list of Goals of the Team.
- Review the list of criteria identified at the previous meeting.
- Come prepared to discuss your rationale for removing goals.

<u>Discussion</u>
- The Planning Team finalizes the essential criteria through multi-voting and consensus building.
- The Planning Team tests the goals against the criteria, and prioritizes a set of no more than five to seven goals to be implemented over the next 3 years.

<u>Decision Making</u>
- From the final list of alternative actions (GOALS: objectives: strategies), the Planning Team will come to consensual agreement on at least three and no more than seven proposed goals that meet the criteria established, further the mission of the organization, move the institution toward its vision, and will receive support of the entire organization.
- All other goals will be descended.
- If some goals are borderline, keep a record of them but remove them from final plan

<u>Responsibilities</u>
- The Planning Team leader works to move the group through the process to a level of consensual agreement.
- The Planning Team leader and transcriber create a final formal list of GOALS to be met, objectives to be accomplished to fulfill goals, and a set of strategies to meet the objectives; which are delivered to team prior to next meeting.
- Facilitator debriefs process.
- Transcriber emails each department within 2 days and gets organization's IT office to post on web.
- Motivator ensures that all team members are prepared to be fully engaged at the next meeting.

Planning Tip: It is important to remember that not all goals are strategic in nature. Many are tasks that should be addressed by departmental planning and some are "pet" projects. The idea here is to rationally choose the goals that are truly strategic (i.e., will have the greatest positive impact on the organization) without alienating fellow team members.

Creating Criteria & Choosing Goals
Worksheet #13
GOALS that meet the Criteria Test are in this Order of Priority

Alternative Goal	Criteria Met	Chosen as Strategic Goal (Yes/No)

Stage #4: Planning Proposal Development

Purpose

- To draft a portion of the Organizational Plan based on the elements of the particular charge of this Team. Identify Goals, Narrative Explanations, Potential Outcomes, Measurement Vehicles, Timelines, Possible Strategies, Reason for Selecting Strategies, Responsible Parties, and a Summary of Actions to be Taken & Resource Requirements.
- To share the draft portion of the plan with the Board of Trustees, President/CEO, other Planning Team leaders, and the organizational review committee (made up of non-active planners from organization personnel).
- To revise the plan as needed and submit the Team's portion of the plan to the Chief Planning Officer, who will compile the final document and present it to the President/CEO for implementation.

The Planning Team

- Comes to meeting with Worksheets 14, 15, and 16 completed.
- Considers all of their work to date and develops a planning component that includes:
  1. Goals
  2. Explanatory Narrative of the goal's importance
  3. Anticipated Outcomes
  4. Procedure for measuring the success of the plan.
  5. Explanation on how goal will improve the organization's effectiveness or efficiency.
  6. Timeline
  7. Chosen objectives and action items for reaching the goal
  8. Responsible Persons
  9. Summary of Action Plans and Resource Requirements.
     (See Part #4 for detailed descriptions)

Expected Outcome: "We propose the following plan of goals and objectives. We propose that the following actions be taken by the organization that will help us reach our vision and fulfill our mission: "

Planning Tip: In this stage, all editing and "word-smithing" will occur. This is a critical stage. Remember this is how you will publicly demonstrate the competence and hard work of your team. Do a good job here to impress others.

Meeting #6 & #7

<u>Preparation</u>
- Review the final list of GOALS to be met, objectives to be accomplished to fulfill goals, and a set of strategies to meet the objectives.

- Use Worksheets #14, #15, #16 as necessary to place goals into context.

- Be prepared to identify and review:
    1. Goals
    2. An Explanatory Narrative of the goal's importance
    3. Anticipated Outcomes
    4. Procedure for measuring the success of the plan.
    5. Explanation on how goal will improve the organization's effectiveness or efficiency.
    6. Timeline
    7. Chosen Strategies for reaching the goal
    8. Responsible Persons
    9. Summary of Action Plans and Resource Requirements.

<u>Discussion</u>

Meeting #6
- The Planning Team leader works to develop a consensus on each of the nine plan components identified above.
- Two Team members volunteer to take notes and compose a first draft of the plan, following the template presented in **PART #4: Strategic Plan Format** (Team Template)

Meeting #7
- The Planning Team reviews the draft and makes necessary revisions for presentation to the Chief Planning Officer.

<u>Decision Making</u>
- A general consensus on the Goals, Narrative Explanations, Potential Outcomes, Measurement Vehicles, Timelines, Possible Strategies, Reason for Selecting Strategies, Responsible Parties, and a Summary of Actions to be Taken & Resource Requirements is reached by the Planning Team.
- Consensus on plan drafters is reached.
- A draft formal written document is created.

<u>Responsibilities</u>

- The Planning Team Leader is responsible for bringing the group to consensus on Goals, Narrative Explanations, Potential Outcomes, Measurement Vehicles, Timelines, Possible Strategies, Reason for Selecting Strategies, Responsible Parties, and a Summary of Actions to be Taken & Resource Requirements.
- Volunteer plan drafters are identified, and they develop both the first and second drafts. (at least one member from each team)
- The Leader makes revisions as deemed necessary.
- The Leader delivers both a paper copy of the document and an electronic copy to the Chief Planning Officer.
- The Chief Planning Officer compiles the first draft of the Organizational Plan, incorporating the work of the Planning Teams. The Chief Planning Officer returns the first draft of the plan to the Planning Team.

Meeting #8

<u>Preparation</u>

- Review entire Organization Plan, noting in particular the Team's charge and its relation to other goals of the organization and the Firm's Mission.

<u>Discussion</u>

- Make recommendations on further revisions to the Strategic Organizational Plan

<u>Decision Making</u>

- Come to consensual agreement on the Strategic Organizational Plan.

<u>Responsibility</u>

- The Leader helps the team reach consensus.
- The Leader delivers the recommended revisions.
- The Chief Planning Officer in consultation with the President/CEO, drafts the Final Strategic Organizational Plan.

Worksheet #14
Strategic Planning Proposal Worksheets
I) Organizational Value #_____:

1) Strategic Goal:_____

   a) Objective:_____

      1) Action Item:_____

      2) Action Item:_____

      3) Action Item:_____

   b) Objective:_____

      1) Action Item:_____

      2) Action Item:_____

      3) Action Item:_____

   c) Objective:_____

      1) Action Item:_____

      2) Action Item:_____

      3) Action Item:_____

The data/information that support the implementation of this goal are:

The critical assumptions that support this goal are:	
1)	2)
3)	4)
5)	6)

2) Strategic Goal:_____

    a) Objective:_____

        1) Action Item:_____

        2) Action Item:_____

        3) Action Item:_____

    b) Objective:_____

        1) Action Item:_____

        2) Action Item:_____

        3) Action Item:_____

    c) Objective:_____

        1) Action Item:_____

        2) Action Item:_____

        3) Action Item:_____

The data/information that support the implementation of this goal are:

The critical assumptions that support this goal are:

1)   **2)**

3)   **4)**

5)   **6)**

3) Strategic Goal:_____

    a) Objective:_____

        1) Action Item:_____

        2) Action Item:_____

        3) Action Item:_____

    b) Objective:_____

        1) Action Item:_____

        2) Action Item:_____

        3) Action Item:_____

    c) Objective:_____

        1) Action Item:_____

        2) Action Item:_____

        3) Action Item:_____

The data/information that support the implementation of this goal are:

The critical assumptions that support this goal are:

1)   **2)**

3)   **4)**

5)   **6)**

4) Strategic Goal:_____

    a) Objective:_____

        1) Action Item:_____

        2) Action Item:_____

        3) Action Item:_____

    b) Objective:_____

        1) Action Item:_____

        2) Action Item:_____

        3) Action Item:_____

    c) Objective:_____

        1) Action Item:_____

        2) Action Item:_____

        3) Action Item:_____

The data/information that support the implementation of this goal are:

The critical assumptions that support this goal are:	
1)	2)
3)	4)
5)	6)

Planning Tip: Complete a proposal development worksheet for each of the values and teams that are part of the process.

Worksheet #15
Strategic Plan Implementation Matrix

Descriptor	Accountable Position	KRA* Pledge	Complete Timeline	Percent Complete	STOP
Strategic Value					
Strategic Goal #1:					
Strategic Goal #2:					.
Strategic Goal #3:					
Strategic Goal #4:					
Strategic Value					
Strategic Goal #1:					
Strategic Goal #2:					
Strategic Goal #3:					
Strategic Goal #4:					

* KRA – Key responsibility area (departments or positions).

Descriptor	Accountable Position	KRA* Pledge	Complete Timeline	Percent Complete	STOP
Strategic Value					
Strategic Goal #1:					
Strategic Goal #2:					
Strategic Goal #3:					
Strategic Goal #4:					
Strategic Value					
Strategic Goal #1:					
Strategic Goal #2:					
Strategic Goal #3:					
Strategic Goal #4:					
Strategic Value					
Strategic Goal #1:					
Strategic Goal #2:					
Strategic Goal #3:					
Strategic Goal #4:					

* KRA – Key responsibility area (departments or positions).

Descriptor	Accountable Position	KRA* Pledge	Complete Timeline	Percent Complete	STOP
Strategic Value					
Strategic Goal #1:					
Strategic Goal #2:					
Strategic Goal #3:					
Strategic Goal #4:					
Strategic Value					
Strategic Goal #1:					
Strategic Goal #2:					
Strategic Goal #3:					
Strategic Goal #4:					
Strategic Value					
Strategic Goal #1:					
Strategic Goal #2:					
Strategic Goal #3:					
Strategic Goal #4:					

* KRA – Key responsibility area (departments or positions).

Worksheet #16
Strategic Outcome Performance Worksheet

STOP Item	Quantifiable Measurement	Time 1 Goal	Result	Time 2 Goal	Result	Time 3 Goal	Result

Part #4: ORGANIZATIONAL PLAN FORMAT (TEAM TEMPLATE)

The following template is designed to provide you with a standard framework for developing your Planning Team's area of concentration. The following template should be followed as to ensure consistency throughout the Planning Teams:

You will complete an entire template for each of the goals you have selected to be part of the strategic plan (at least 3, but no more than 5).

GOAL #1: *(TEAM CHARGE)*

State your first goal here (each goal should be listed and developed in this template separately).

EXPLANATORY NARRATIVE

In a single, detailed, concise paragraph explain why this goal is important. Explain the external opportunities and threats, internal strengths and limitations that were considered. Finally explain the criteria you tested this goal against.

ANTICIPATED OUTCOMES

List the potential outcomes that will be generated by the successful completion of this goal.

MEASUREMENT VEHICLE

List the measurement tools, instruments, or methods that will be used to assess the successful completion of this goal.

EFFECTIVENESS & EFFICIENCY

Explain how the successful completion of this goal will improve the organization's effectiveness and efficiency.

TIMELINE & MILESTONES

Report a timeline and identify outcome milestones for the accomplishment of this goal. Be as specific as possible.

OBJECTIVE AND ACTION ITEMS

Report the strategies that will be necessary to implement to accomplish this goal. Use the following format, provided on Strategic Planning Proposal Worksheet #14 in prior section:

MISSION FULFILLMENT: Describe how this goal fulfills the mission in a sentence.

I) Organizational Value #_____:

    1) Strategic
Goal:_____

        a) Objective:_____

            1) Action
        Item:_____

            2) Action
        Item:_____

            3) Action
    Item:_____

RESPONSIBLE DEPARTMENT or PERSON

List those departments and/or position titles that will be responsible for the successful implementation of the goal.

SUMMARY OF ACTION AND RESOURCE REQUIREMENT

In a narrative form describe this goal and the actions necessary to successfully accomplish this goal. In addition, indicate any additional operational costs to the institution to implement this goal (i.e., new hire, money for program, new department, etc.).

"Give me a level long enough . . . and single-handed I can move the world," a simplistic expression of common sense details how we can change our world and our organization. To this end, you will want to make a plan detailed enough to make your organization more successful. Still, be aware of another not so famous metaphor: "Give me a plan simple enough . . . and it might actually happen." Please limit your entire written plan to two pages per goal; be detailed, simple, and concise. More detail will be provided at the departmental level, this planning document should be written to be easily understood by a high school graduate (as they represent most of our customers/clients/students).

Part #5: ORGANIZATIONAL PLAN FORMAT (FINAL TEMPLATE)

The following template is designed to provide you with a standard framework for developing your Strategic Organizational Plan.

Introduction

Briefly trace the history of the organization to the current status and situation of the firm.

Vision & Mission of the Organization

Review the process used to revise or reaffirm the vision and mission of the organization.

Situational Analysis

Detail findings of the macro-level analysis of the organization and its key statistical descriptors.

Organizational Values

Review process used to develop strategic values, and list them.

Organizational Strategic Plan

Using each value as a framing subsection, divide identified team goals by value and publicly expresses strategic goals in the following format:

Value Statement

State strategic value. Develop a value statement that embodies each strategic value and display it here.

Strategic Issues

Develop a list of bulleted questions that emphasize the reasons for choosing your strategic goals.

Historical Context

This section should identify the factors that led to the selection of the strategic goals within the historical context of the organization.

Strategic Goals

Complete the following table for each goal.

State Goal: _____			
State Objective: _____			
Strategic Action	**KRAs**	**Timeline**	**Total Cost**
1.			
2.			
3.			
4.			
5.			

Message from CEO

Create section that displays a message from the organizational CEO supporting the planning process, the plan, and that envisions a shared and prosperous future.

Strategic Plan Goal Accountability Checklist

Develop a table that summarizes the goals for each strategic value and creates an accountability system for presentation to CEO or corporate board.

STATE STRATEGIC VALUE			
STRATEGIC GOAL	**LIST KRAs**	**TIMELINE**	**DATE COMPLETED**

Overview of Planning Process & Acknowledgements

Develop a section that details the planning process your organization used, while acknowledging all those that made the process a success.

Statistical Appendix

Create appendices as deemed necessary by your organization. At least include an appendix that offers key statistical data detailing the state of your organization.

APPENDIX A
General Expectations and Principles that Guide the Planning Process

The general expectation of every Planning Team is that it promotes the best interest of the organization above any individual or departmental agenda. Through this process all of the members of the Planning Team are expected to become more aware of the elements that influence the life of the firm, and why some decisions are chosen over others. The Strategic Organizational Plan is intended to describe how the organization will excel and succeed in its endeavors and become increasingly vital to the community over the next three to five years.

It is expected that for the company to be successful it must accept the recommendations of its Planning Teams, and integrate its resources and leadership to become a more synergistic enterprise. To this end, it is important that each Planning Team member be an advocate of proper planning and proper procedural implementation. Use the following checklist to check the process for accuracy and validity:

_____ Have we asked the fundamental questions?
_____ Have we completed a complete situational analysis?
_____ Have we chosen the right subjects to investigate in the situation analysis?
_____ Have we correctly interpreted data from the situation analysis?
_____ Did we correctly estimate the time it takes to plan and the cost of the plan?
_____ Did we have and follow the planning manual (Workbook)?
_____ Did we adequately communicate the strategic planning process to all participants?
_____ Did we include all stakeholders in the planning process or at least periodically communicate its progress to them?
_____ Did we not copy the plan or planning process of another organization.
_____ Did we not create too much paperwork?
_____ Did we pay careful attention to the time factor in strategic planning.
_____ Did we select the right objectives?
_____ Did we allocate the necessary amount of resources?

If at any time, you as a participant feel these objectives are not or were not met, please alert your fellow Team members.

APPENDIX B
Glossary of Strategic Organizational Planning Terms in this Workbook

Action – process of doing or performing in a specific way to produce a desired effect or to achieve an objective. Synonymous with strategies in this planning process

Alternative – an idea expressed in the form of objective(s) and actions intended to move
the organization closer to the goal(s) identified by the Planning Team and the organizational mission. Synonymous with goal in this planning process.

Brainstorming – a method for generating ideas that allows everyone on a team to speak and encourages everyone to listen. All ideas are to be evaluated at a later time.

Consensus – a process of arriving at a decision after a time of thoughtfulness and study; characterized by a general agreement as opposed to a majority vote; results in the recommendation that all, or nearly all, of the members of the Planning Team agree to accept and support the decision.

Decision Making – the act of choosing one alternative from among more than one. The decision making process includes recognizing and defining the nature of the decision situation, identifying alternatives, choosing the "best" alternative, and putting the decision into practice. A decision making group may be most effective when members openly discuss and agree on the best alternative.

Facilitator – a person identified to have the responsibility of keeping the Planning Team clearly focused on the discussion at hand and in an ordered, purposeful way so that the Team members' time together is more productive.

Goal – the establishment of specific targets, a purpose toward which an endeavor is directed, a desired end or achievement. In this planning process goals are specific achievable outcomes of the planning process.

Group – two or more individuals in face-to-face interaction, each aware of his or her membership in the group, each aware of others who belong to the group, and each aware of their positive interdependence as they strive to reach mutual goals.

Mission – a description of the task we face, the service we offer, and who we service.

Mission Statement – a concise expression of the organization's fundamental purpose.

Multi-voting – a method of reducing a list to the most important issues by allowing each member a number of choices (usually about 1/3 of the total on the list) and reorganizing those items that all or most of the group identify as important.

Objective – devising ways to meet your goals, the purpose or aim of a specific action, something to be worked toward as a step in accomplishing a goal.

Planning – a process of selecting a rational course of collective action to achieve a future state of affairs. It includes setting goals, gathering and analyzing information, evaluation information, making decisions, and acting.

Planning Team Leader – senior staff member identified by the President to serve as the leader of a specific Planning Team.

Priority – an established sequence by order of importance or urgency.

Resources – something that can be looked to for support or aid of organization vitality; available assets, operational budgets, customers/students/clients, personnel, community members, faculty, consultants, community size, the number and usefulness of buildings, technology, knowledge, the current and future fiscal situation, other institutions in the community associated with the mission of the organization, etc.

Situational Analysis (SWOT) – a precise and careful look at the community and its environment to determine the primary external opportunities and threats, and the primary and related internal strengths and weaknesses.

Strategies/Activity – ways or methods of meeting objectives.

Vision – a direction or path that sets the pace for excellence in an organization. What you hope to achieve.

Chapter 11

Strategic
Departmental Planning
Workbook

Table of Contents

Purpose of Strategic Departmental Planning

The departmental level strategic planning process will permit your organization to implement a procedure to allow your business to enter the 21st Century as an active agent in the advancement of your goals. The departmental component of strategic planning will allow your staff to diligently reflect on the outcomes of the strategic plan development phase of organizational planning.

The departmental planning process empowers employees to reflect on the past, present, and future practice, and to systematically discuss newly defined vision, mission, values, and goals of the organization. Each department in your organization should work through a collaborative process to evaluate the impact and influence of the organizational vision, mission, values, and goals on the functions and objectives of department. Planners work to evaluate the structures, procedures, practices, and processes currently in place, while proactively recommending necessary changes, improvements, developments, and enhancements in light of the Strategic Organizational Plan.

This workbook is designed to serve as an implementation guide for managing the strategic planning initiatives articulated in the Strategic Organizational Plan (developed as part of the exercises in Chapter 10). This workbook is written as a combined departmental planning process and a strategic planning management model. It illustrates an eight point system of implementing the organizational strategic plan through the development of both a framework for and process of departmental planning. The seven key points for implementing the Strategic Organizational Plan are:

1. Developing a Departmental Vision, Mission, Values, & Business Definition
2. Creating a System of Change through Leadership
3. Relating Departmental Structures: Managing Key Business Functions
4. Managing the Process Functions
5. Defining & Matching Employee Talents
6. Setting the Departmental Objectives
7. and, Pledging to Do the Best

Relating Your Departmental Plan to the Institutional Plan: An Implementation Guide

Throughout the organizational planning process, your institution worked diligently to establish a new vision for the future, a mission to guide all present and future initiatives, and a to develop a set of key values to guide decision making and planning. The vision, mission, and values of the organization should serve as a baseline and guide for developing departmental plans. All planning should be viewed as a participatory process where both departmental and organizational stakeholders are given an equal stake in the success of the institution and its respective departments.

The key to successful plan implementation is the realization that each member of the department is vested and interested in the success of the organization. This departmental planning process is designed to meet the goal of creating a sense of ownership in the institution, the planning process, and the successful outcomes of individual and collective performance. This process was designed with the realization that strategic plans can be implemented if organizational leaders effectively orchestrate and direct a diverse range of people, resources, programs, and actions over the next three years across a number of organizational boundaries (Fogg, 1999).

It is critical for the departmental planning process to incorporate the seven essential ingredients into implementing the Strategic Organizational Plan. These seven ingredients are illustrated below. Overall, departmental plans should assist in the development of a systematic definition of the business functions, the core processes, leadership practices, accountability and reward systems; the positive reallocation of all resources and personnel coupled with the redefinition of duties and structures; the re-articulation of culture; the empowerment of all existing staff; and the desire and ability to publicly declare a quest for excellence that comes with a sense of ownership.

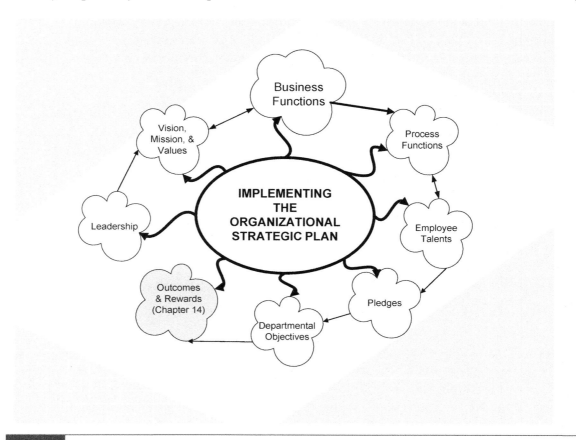

Section #1: Vision, Mission, Values, & Business Definition Development

Identify the organization's current vision, mission, and value statements in the space below:

Vision Statement

_____

_____

Mission Statement

_____

_____

_____

_____

_____

_____

_____

_____

Value Statements

1. _____
2. _____
3. _____
4. _____
5. _____
6. _____

(ADD MORE AS NECESSARY)

Upon a reflection of these statements and principles, department members should consider and evaluate the expectations of the current vision and mission of the organization. They should review the following series of questions and place their thoughts into perspective.

- Do department members support the vision, mission, and values of the organization?
- Would you say that department members share a common unspoken vision for the department?
- Is this departmental vision reflective of the organization's vision, mission, values, and goals?
- Do individual department members have differing visions?
- Do department members have counter productive objectives and goals?
- Do department members share a common language and philosophy?
- What are the barriers to a common language and the common vision for this department?
- What do we value as a group?

In addition to examining the vision and mission of the organization, evaluation is crucial to the departmental planning process, so that members develop a common vision and mission to determine the most appropriate departmental objectives. These objectives should complement the organizational vision, mission, and goals. The mission of the department is critical to the measurement of its success. To be truly effective, a mission and mission statement should tell us who we are, and we as team members need to believe it. Unfortunately, the vast majority of mission statements are an abysmal failure.

After you have considered the section above, review your response, repeat the steps substituting the word vision for mission, and please answer the following questions:

1) Are our departmental vision and mission statements assets to our department (or do we even have a mission)?

_____

_____

_____

2) Should we keep or change the current departmental vision?

_____

_____

_____

_____

_____

3) Should we keep or change the current departmental mission?

_____

_____

_____

_____

_____

4) Is there room for improvement in our current mission or should we begin again?

_____

_____

_____

_____

_____

If you believe the department would improve by a re-development of the vision and mission, please proceed below. If you are happy with the current vision & mission, please proceed to the next section of the workbook.

Please write a vision and mission statement for your department in the space below.

(If you accept the current vision or mission statements, see if you can improve upon them.)

_____

_____

_____

_____

Complete the proceeding task both as an individual and in a conversation with fellow department members. Repeat the exercise for the vision statement below as well.

_____

_____

_____

_____

_____

_____

_____

Planning Tip: The involvement of as many staff members as possible in this process is essential to build ownership that can make both your vision and mission relevant to the department.

Identifying the Departmental Business Definition

1. What overall business is our department in and what business is it likely to be in three years from now?

   _____

   _____

2. What are the most important services this department provides to the organization?

   _____

   _____

3. Who are our most important customers (are they other departments or the community)?

   _____

   _____

4. Why or how is our department different from similar departments at our main competitors; and are we better than them in any area of our business?

   _____

   _____

5. How do we think our core functional processes will change over the next five years?

   _____

   _____

6. How do we judge the organization's ultimate success? Why are we in existence?

   _____

   _____

7. Do our people have any special talents that can help us grow our business and our department's importance within the organization?

   _____

   _____

Section #2: Creating System Change Through Leadership

Your organization can succeed in its efforts if proper leadership and staff development are incorporated into the departmental planning process. If your department measures outcome success against past practice and national standards, it can challenge the existing status quo more effectively. Your department should desire a move from top-down hierarchical mandates to emergent empowerment that is driven by consensus and shared authority.

Hierarchical structures limit the role of leadership among those who do not possess power based on authority. "This is the true reason that top-down, hierarchical style of leadership is widely perceived as doomed to failure, even by those who aren't sure precisely why this should be so." (Hesselbein, et al., 1996, p. 22). Many articles on leadership practice implicitly suggest the need to incorporate heterarchical structural approaches into all administrative initiatives designed to transform modern organizations. The emphasis on change currently in practice is often misguided, since the belief is that change is necessitated of employees. The case is that change is really necessitated in business functions, management style, and the lack of leadership in many departments and organizations. As planning commences in your department, leaders will need to put forth a challenge to the management status quo, and the current practice of accomplishing work. Management, although necessary, is not the best means to motivate people, inspiration is.

To challenge the decision-making process currently in effect, there will be a need for increased leadership by the organization's Board, CEO, senior leaders, and department leaders; this leadership will need to transform many practices from the form of top-down mandates into practices of inspirational change and empowerment.

To challenge the process leaders are compelled to ask:

> Why do we cling to the view that only the top can initiate significant change? Is it our unwillingness to give up a familiar mental model? Is it the fear of stepping out of line without the imprimatur of the hierarchy? (Hesselbein et al., 1996, p. 42).

Your department can act as an agent of change for your organization, only if your leaders can introduce a structure of emergent heterarchy, individual accountability, and shared responsibility. Contemporary theories on leadership and organizational transformation demonstrate that any successful planning initiative should occur within a heterarchical structure with lateral processes and shared leadership. To inspire a shared vision of change, departments need to present the objective findings of newly developed data within an historical context that does not violate the past tradition of the organization.

To lead this change movement and to become the model of leadership in planning, each department should develop a vision of success that is incorporated in a shared decision-making Leadership should emerge among many stakeholders. To measure the effectiveness of current leadership practice, the section below "Leadership & Change: Choosing to Lead, to Change, & to Inspire" should be completed and discussed among all planners and staff members in the department.

Leadership & Change: Choosing to Lead, to Change, & to Inspire

Rate our department with (A) Agree, (N) Neutral, (D) Disagree, NC Don't Know (No Communication) for each of the following:

_____ Leaders in our organization inspire us to see change as a positive motivating force.

_____ Leaders in our organization choose to *listen* to our suggestions and input prior to making a decision.

_____ When our leaders *hear* our fears, they quickly and directly address them to ensure a work environment of open communication.

_____ Our leaders expect us to balance home and work lives.

_____ Leaders in our department move prudently and swiftly to make decisions before problems arise.

_____ Our leadership team promotes a positive motivating presence in our workplace.

_____ Leaders in our department inspire us, creating a passion in each of us to do our best work.

_____ Our leaders stress a workplace management method of personal accountability and collective responsibility.

_____ Our leaders represent the best of what our department and/or organization has to offer.

_____ Leaders in this department fully understand the after effect of each decision they make, and they work to ensure that employees are ready to embrace change.

_____ Our leaders set priorities for themselves, the organization, and our department.

_____ Our leaders expect each of us (in the context of mutual responsibility) to set priorities for ourselves and to help set them for our department, and the organization.

The Role of the Inspirational Leader

A leader, if he or she wishes to become an inspiration to the staff, has eight essential challenges to face.

1. Create a Quest for the "Holy Grail"
2. Create a Sense of Urgency
3. Trust Instinct over Figures
4. Hold the Line on Integrity
5. Break the Management Rules
6. Believe in Your People
7. Demonstrate through Results
8. Share the Wealth

To lead an effective planning process the leader should be willing to publicly challenge the status quo, to challenge ineffective bureaucratic procedures, and to examine past practice and process, and to create new dynamic models of transformation. The inspirational leader will see the future (preferably a healthier and happier workplace coupled with increased profit margins), communicate it often and loudly, and convince others to see it and want it. Thus, the leader will set a quest for the "Holy Grail," or that culture which no previous leader could achieve.

Next, the leader will work to create a sense of urgency. Urgency is not panic, not doom and gloom, not a disaster. A sense of urgency is creating a strong desire within employees to want something better, to want change, to want improvement in their lives and in their work. The leader can create this sense of urgency through a careful examination of the numbers.

However, looking at the numbers does not mean leading by the numbers. The inspirational leader will privately examine the numbers and figures. She will digest them, she will sleep on them, and she will have a profound understanding of the organizational and departmental statistics. Once she has this, she will lead by instinct, she will know what to do to fix the numbers, but she will not concentrate on them, rather she will only talk the talk of vision and quest.

Inspirational leaders will not only talk about trust, honesty, and trustworthiness; they must live it. Inspirational leaders will have a strong sense of character, and a "right things first" agenda. They will place the benefit of their institution and its people above their own needs, wants, and agenda. However, inspirational leaders will not follow the typical management rules. They will be honest and fair, but they will choose favorites (i.e., the best employees, the ones they want all others to emulate). Inspirational leaders will match good employees' work with their talents. Inspirational leaders will have the courage to remove untrustworthy elements and poor employees from their institution.

Inspirational leaders believe in the ability of their people, they empower all their people (largely because they have removed those that cannot be trusted with authority and decision making). They show results. Inspirational leaders pick both small and large goals. They strategically align the goals to ensure that people are constantly in a state of success and achievement that ensures that they can do more. Finally, an inspirational leader never looks for credit, rather he shares it with his staff. Inspirational leaders understand that they get the credit for the work of their staff and/or team. They have the self-confidence to inspire others to action and success, they don't need glory, and they realize that they are already successful. *More detail on these eight challenges is provided in Chapter 13 of this book*

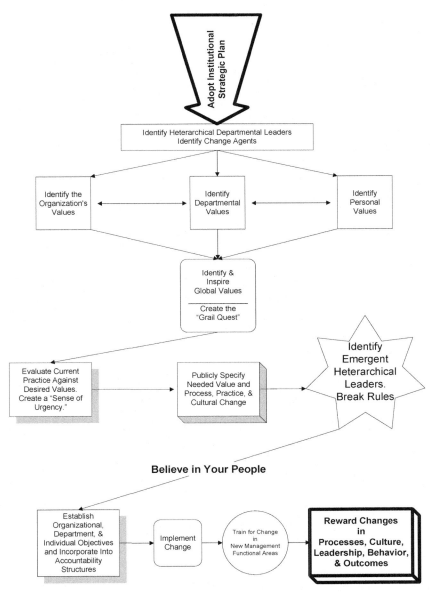

Creating the Culture of Change & Quality Improvement

Change by Means of Empowerment

Prior to creating a situation of empowerment, departmental leaders and staff should ensure that all members of the department share a common set of values. A shared set of values should be created collectively, communicated publicly, and embraced wholeheartedly.

Common Values: Identifying Our Shared Values: I Know What I Feel

Rate our department with (A) Agree, (N) Neutral, (D) Disagree, NC Don't Know (No Communication) for each of the following:

____ This organization and my department have a value set that I believe in.

____ When asked to set a future direction for the organization, leaders work with employees to determine what is most important.

____ I feel a sense of belonging in this organization.

____ The work we do in this department and at this company, fulfills part of my life, soul, and being.

____ I value the work we do together.

____ Our customers/clients/students know we value them.

____ People value one another and the opinion of others in this department.

____ We work to balance life and work in our department, it is something each of us holds precious.

____ We work together to achieve shared goals and dreams.

____ When I arrive at work, I am excited, anxious, and determined that it will be a great day.

____ The work I am asked to do is important, is rewarded, and is appreciated by my supervisors, my co-coworkers, and this organization.

____ My values and the values of this department are related.

____ The values of our department and the organization are complementary.

--CUT HERE---

Planning Tip: This worksheet is designed to create awareness in the need for shared values. It will serve as a means to begin a discussion about departmental values, and the need for a shared meaningful list of departmental values.

Organizational transformation can emerge only through the empowerment of all staff. As stated previously; leadership, planning, and change should be developed on the central principle of empowerment. However caveats on implementing empowerment initiatives, as well as all of the examples of failed attempts at empowerment should be viewed critically. "Empowerment is a popular word for a very old and important concept – defining and delegating responsibility, then holding people accountable for carrying out their responsibilities successfully." (Fogg, 1999, p. 279).

The staff at any organization and at any level should be empowered to accomplish the goals of both the departmental and organizational strategic plans; they should be included in the development of the planning outcomes. Fogg demonstrates that within the business world, one frightening misconception about empowerment is that it gives people the freedom to do anything they want, any way they want, in order to get their jobs done. This is not the case; empowerment is a type of freedom, a freedom to improve the organization, not one to run wild. A proper vision will ensure common objectives and outcomes, and proper planning will serve as a mechanism for incorporating accountability and responsibility. Empowerment will allow the staff to change practice, to improve, to reach new goals but not to turn the organization inside out.

Implementing a first time empowerment initiative is like handing the keys of the car to an adolescent. It is freedom, but it is freedom within a system of guidelines, with rules, with oversight, and with insurance. Trust, and a desire to see people become independent are as paramount to the initiation of an empowerment culture, as they are to watching a son or daughter pull out of the driveway for the first time.

The following worksheet is designed to measure the culture of empowerment in your department. It can serve to identify empowerment goals, to identify empowerment practice, and to begin an empowerment dialogue. The level of empowerment obtained by a given department will depend on the self-confidence of the leader, the trustworthiness of the people, and the culture of the organization.

Setting Goals: The Dichotomy of Accountability & Responsibility

When leading a culture change movement, leaders should identify two main principles: individual accountability and shared responsibility. Individual accountability will involve the establishment of goals for each employee (as demonstrated in the Personal Planning Workbook (Chapter 12). Each person will be asked to identify personal goals of achievement that will directly influence the success of both the departmental and organizational strategic plans.

Shared responsibility is the principle of establishing a departmental level culture, where each staff member feels a sense of belonging and personal importance. Each staff member should become aware of how their actions and inactions influence the success of their colleagues and other departments. Rewards should be established to ensure that shared responsibility becomes an important cultural trait. In essence, the goal for the leader is to convince the staff that they are their "brother's keeper." This will create an effect of peer accountability, group success, and teamwork. This concept was fully developed and explained in Chapter 6.

Empowerment: Power to the People

Rate our department with (A) Agree, (N) Neutral, (D) Disagree, NC Don't Know (No Communication) for each of the following:

_____ Our leaders use words like empowerment, then give us the responsibility to make our own decisions.

_____ I feel a bond with my coworkers, like we are working toward the same goals.

_____ I feel like I own a unique part of this company.

_____ I feel strongly that if I fail, I have not only let myself down, but my fellow workers as well.

_____ My co-workers and I embrace change, in fact we demand it to make our workplace better and our organization more competitive.

_____ Organizational charts are not important in our department, rather a shared sense of teamwork and accomplishment are the motivating forces.

_____ My supervisor does not tell me what to do, rather I tell him/her what needs to change to make this department better (and then it is changed).

_____ Our leaders are more like cheerleaders of our success, and less like the constant bearers of bad news, or barriers to change.

_____ Our department and company has abandoned the standard vertical, departmental, and hierarchical forms of organization, and is embracing more heterarchical, virtual, project and matrix based forms of organizational management.

_____ Leaders discusses consequences (intended and unintended) thoroughly with the workforce before making any decision or change.

_____ Each of my fellow employees understands the implications of failing performance.

_____ Everyone is free to question every decision, publicly.

_____ Our department assumes that its problems were not the result of anyone else's mistakes or practice, rather our own.

Expected Outcomes: The department will examine is current culture of empowerment and begin a discussion to determine the exact level of empowerment that is appropriate for the desired level of success.

Section #3: Relating Structures: Developing the Business Functions

The essential means of establishing an effective plan is to determine the core businesses that you will pursue. Keeping and managing functions that do not improve the viability of your department cannot help your department or staff. The first thing your department should do is decide the strategic business areas that you perform. I have found that no more than eight strategic business functions can be effectively preformed by any one department.

The legendary GE CEO, Jack Welch, transformed his company by choosing to keep only the businesses in his conglomerate that could be either number one or two in the marketplace.

> These are the businesses that we really want to nourish, he said. These are the businesses that will take us into the twenty-first century. They are inside the circles. Outside the circles you have the businesses that we would prefer not to pursue any further. (Slater, 1999, p. 62).

Using the figure below, what key business functions will your department choose to pursue.

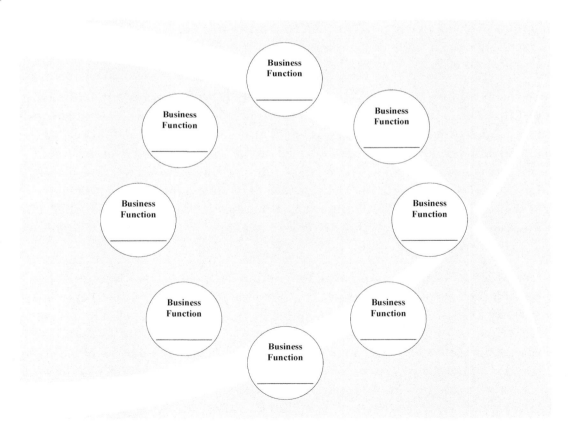

Choosing the best business functions, enlisting all your resources into them, and growing the people staffing these functions will make your department a success. Wasting time and resources on business functions that have no future will ensure that all members of your department can expect hard times for years to come. In the competitive global markets of today's world, those that transform and challenge the business systems will succeed, those that embrace the past are doomed to failure.

What will the destiny of your department be? You are setting the plan, you control your future.

Section #4: Managing Process Functions

Process functions illustrate the means that work is done to move customers/clients/ students from entering the business enterprise through their exit from being served by the company. At each level there exists a set of processes that are encountered and navigated by the customer. These processes are the backbone of the business; regular analysis and understanding of the processes of the department are essential to improving and transforming the business. The most efficient means for moving from understanding the processes in the abstract to the concrete is the drawing of a map of each process (usually in the form of a flowchart).

The first step in the process mapping procedure is the illustration of a macro-conceptual framework for understanding the paradigm of processing and its implications of the department. The goal is to move from the level of the institutional strategic plan to the level of evaluating the department through its individual departmental processes.

Prior to the development of the departmental plan, each department should identify its current processes, map the related functions, benchmark the processes against its competitors and global best practices, map all alternative actions, define needed talent, plan and develop new processes based on knowledge gained from process mapping procedure, and review and evaluate changes in performance. The most common type of process mapping that you are likely to complete is the workflow process review, however there are numerous processes in your department that may need a systemic review, the planning exercise should demonstrate where employees believe a closer look is warranted.

Department leaders will need to realize that employee tasks are not the equivalent of business functions or process functions. As a general rule, it takes at least five tasks completed by at least three separate people to have reached the level of a process function. Often in a review of processes, managers actually review tasks and the employee performance of tasks. A review of processes is an examination of the logical and strategic alignment of tasks. To conduct a process mapping exercise to merely review staff task assignments does not add value to the strategic planning process. Managers should try to remove tasks that add no value to the process or end goal. In addition to asking if tasks are necessary, managers and leaders should ask whether the processes themselves add value to the department.

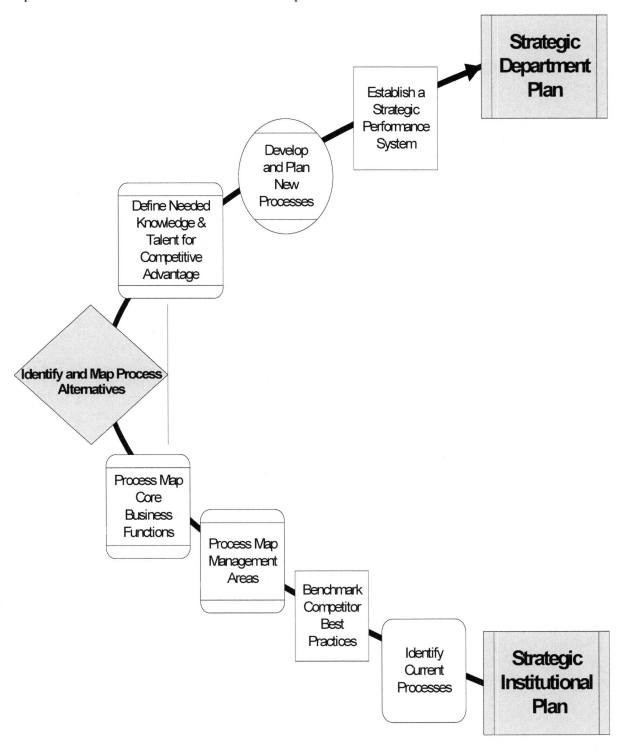

The Pathway of Functional Process Mapping

Planning Tip: Departmental planners will need to review all functional processes completed by the department, choosing which functions represent the talent areas of the operation, and making improvements to those functions. Examples of process functions might include:

1. Cross-Functional Processes
2. Customer Intake Processes
3. Relationship Processes
4. Information System Processes
5. Billing Processes
6. Hierarchical Reporting Processes
7. Facility Maintenance Processes
8. Sales Lead Follow-up Processes
9. Departmental Procedure Processes
10. Past Practice Processes

Additionally planners should predetermine the anticipated result of the process under review, process mapping outcomes might include:

1. Cost Reduction
2. Production or Service Time Reduction
3. Quality Enhancement (TQM)
4. Information Collection, Design, Evaluation, & Dissemination
5. Customer Satisfaction
6. Management Effectiveness
7. Measurement System Evaluation
8. Process Reengineering & Staffing
9. Benchmarking Best Practices
10. Departmental Reorganization

Process mapping is not likely to be accomplished prior to the completion of a one-year departmental plan, but each of the processes should be considered and made part of the long-term goals of any formal Strategic Departmental Plan. Process mapping will allow each department to streamline its current activities, discard useless or outdated practices, and become more deliberate in meeting both its strategic and operational goals. Still, prior to the completion of the planning method, you should develop a set of workflow process maps and determine if each step is valued-added or if the step adds little to no value to the department. Nonvalue-added processes should be eliminated from the departmental procedures, as discarding useless steps will increase productivity, efficiency, and cost effectiveness.

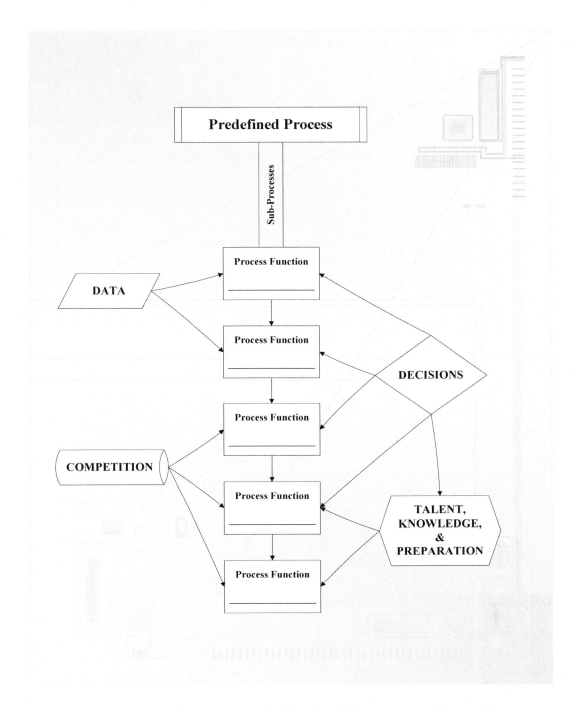

Realizing the Complexity of Process Mapping

Planning Tip: A process map can be illustrated in many formulations and diagrams. The importance is not on the attractiveness of the diagram, or its adherence to traditional flowchart rules; rather, the goal of the mapping exercise is to represent a flow of processes that can be understood throughout the organization and within the department.

Section #5: Defining the Core Talents Needed to Secure the Competitive Advantage

As the organization and department moves toward implementing its plan; redefining its vision, mission, and values; and in creating a culture of change; leaders will need to match employee talents with the work needed to be done. As departmental leaders find themselves in an ever-increasing situation of resource scarcity, exploiting the known talent of your employees will provide you with a competitive advantage.

Marcus Buckingham has demonstrated that the most effective managers are the ones that match the skills and talents of their staff to the needs and wants of their departments and customers (Buckingham and Coffman, 1999; & Buckingham and Clifton, 2001). Their Gallup studies demonstrate that current command-and-control mechanisms focus on fixing problems and fixing broken employees. They suggest that we should not waste time fixing inadequacies, rather we should identify the strengths of each staff member and match them with the work that needs to be done to reach our organizational goals and the respective departmental objectives.

Try to remember the many managers and supervisors in your career, whom during a conversation (usually in the form of a performance review) had briefly mentioned your talents (usually as a courtesy) and then spent the remainder of the hour (usually 55 minutes) reviewing in great detail all of your weaknesses and short-comings. Wouldn't it be a better working environment if we matched the talents of our people and colleagues to the work we have to do? Wouldn't they be happier? Wouldn't we all do a better job? Wouldn't our customers benefit? Why is so much emphasis spent on changing people instead of changing situations?

To match employee talents to the work at hand we must first identify the objectives and core needs of each of the business (management) functions we identified in Section #3 of this workbook. Then we need to ask each employee to review their own unique set of talents and to suggest ways in which they might provide increasing levels of quality service to the department.

Supervisors, managers, and leaders alike should begin to ask whether or not their best employees are being used effectively. They should also question whether the department's least performing employees have talent in the areas they are asking them to excel. If they do not, the managers should move them into situations where they can excel and achieve excellent performance. If more of our employees are performing at higher levels, then we can expect to achieve a competitive advantage, as long as we have appropriately defined both our key management business functions and our core process functions.

The worksheets on the following two pages are designed to frame discussions toward this end. The third worksheet "The Talent Needs Analysis" is designed to allow the department to make a public inventory of the talent pool. This will allow for each member of the department to suggest talents that are needed for long-term success.

This talent should be acquired either through staff hiring's or in staff replacement as positions open. Managers should develop a second talent inventory to ensure that they know what talent is lost as employees resign and retire. The development of a talent inventory will allow the department to achieve its objects through the proper use of personnel.

I Know I Can: Identifying Needed Departmental Talents & Knowledge

1. What do we believe are the most important services our department provides to the institution and/or to our customers?

   _____

   _____

   _____

2. Who are our most important customers, and can we serve them better?

   _____

   _____

   _____

3. Why or how are our talents different from those of our main competitors?

   _____

   _____

   _____

4. What skills and/or talent do we share with the rest of the company, and what are the skills/talent unique to our department?

   _____

   _____

5. Which three phrases best describe the knowledge needed to be successful in our marketplace?

   _____

   _____

   _____

Keeping Up with the Jones's: Do We Have A Competitive Edge?

Rate our department with (A) Agree, (N) Neutral, (D) Disagree, NC Don't Know (No Communication) for each of the following:

_____ Department leaders are committed to the employees they lead.

_____ Our leaders and staff often ask, "How can we use our vision to promote positive change?"

_____ Our leaders and staff often ask, "What makes us the best in our business?"

_____ Our leaders and staff often ask, "How can we learn from what our competitors do, and serve the customer better?"

_____ Our leaders and managers, work hard to align employee talents with workplace objectives and expectations.

_____ We strive to create a department that is better than any other.

_____ We often choose to break the "traditional bureaucratic rules" that hold our organization back.

_____ We don't let the difficulty of assessing our performance limit our growth.

_____ We encourage our people's differences, and match their talents to the work we ask of them.

_____ We are encouraged to measure our performance against ourselves, rather than other people, or other organizations.

_____ We have set a vision to be the department that sets the symbol for others to benchmark.

_____ We benchmark the best practices of others to improve our processes, not to engage in self-loathing or self-pity.

_____ Leaders evaluate us on the basis of our own previously established goals, rather than on comparisons with peers or universal standards.

_____ We are benchmarked by our competitors.

Copy this page for each planner or staff member

Talent Needs Analysis Worksheet

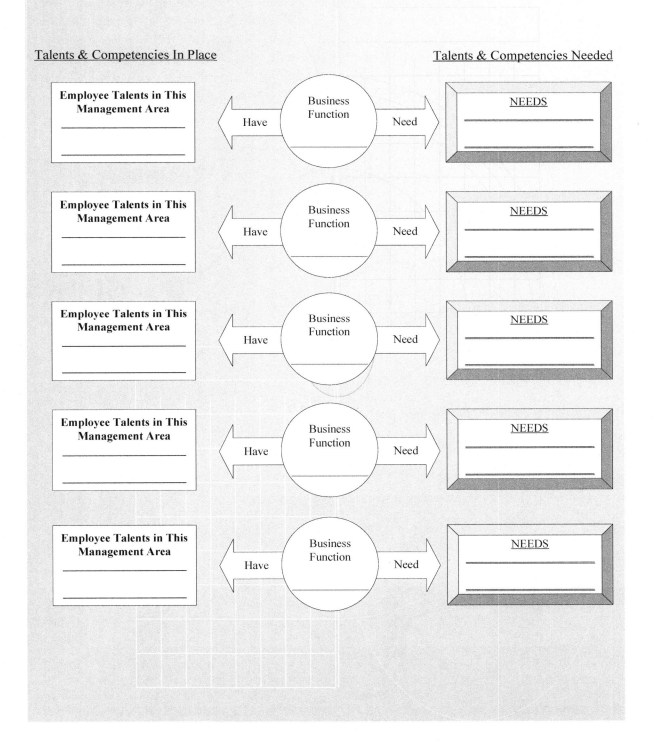

Talents & Competencies In Place

Talents & Competencies Needed

Employee Talents in This Management Area

Business Function

Have

Need

NEEDS

Section #6: Setting Key Departmental Operating Objectives

Using the same SWOT analysis method that was used in the organizational planning workbook (Chapter 10), list the internal strengths and weaknesses of the department; and also list the external opportunities and threats to departmental success. External opportunities and threats may be inside or outside the organization, as long as they are external to the department. Match these strengths, weaknesses, threats, and opportunities to develop a set of alternative strategic objectives for the department.

		Internal	
		Strengths	**Weaknesses**
External	**Opportunities**	 **SWOT (+,+)** Expand & Invest	 **SWOT (-, +)** **Join & Amplify**
	Threats	 **SWOT (+, -)** **Originate & Improve**	 **SWOT (- , -)** **Change & Integrate**

Worksheet #1
Choosing Alternative Objectives

List strengths and opportunities, then comparing the two, develop a list of alternative objectives. For example, how will you leverage the internal strengths of your department to exploit the external opportunities available to your department?

"Nurture and Guard for Rewards."

Internal Strengths (+,)

1. _____

2. _____

3. _____

4. _____

5. _____

External Opportunities (,+)

1. _____

2. _____

3. _____

4. _____

5. _____

SWOT (+,+)
Expand & Invest for Success

1. _____

2. _____

3. _____

4. _____

5. _____

Use Additional Space as Necessary

Planning Tip: Using the organizational goals developed in the organizational planning component of this book as ground zero will serve to develop integrated departmental objectives.

Worksheet #2
Choosing Alternative Objectives

List strengths and threats, then comparing the two, develop a list of alternative objectives. For example, how will you leverage the internal strengths of your department to overcome the external threats currently confronting your department?

Internal Strengths (+,)

1. _____

2. _____

3. _____

4. _____

"New Ideas will Bring New Rewards."

5. _____

External Threats (, -)

1. _____

2. _____

3. _____

4. _____

5. _____

SWOT (+, -)
Originate & Improve for Success

1. _____

2. _____

3. _____

4. _____

5. _____

Use Additional Space as Necessary

Worksheet #3
Choosing Alternative Objectives

List weaknesses and opportunities, then comparing the two, develop a list of alternative objectives. For example, how will you overcome your internal weaknesses in the department to leverage the external opportunities currently available to your department?

"Together We Can Earn Rewards."

Internal Weaknesses (-,)

1. _____
2. _____
3. _____
4. _____
5. _____

External Opportunities (, +)

1. _____
2. _____
3. _____
4. _____
5. _____

SWOT (-, +)
Join & Amplify for Success

1. _____
2. _____
3. _____
4. _____
5. _____

Use Additional Space as Necessary

Worksheet #4
Choosing Alternative Objectives

List weaknesses and threats, then comparing the two, develop a list of alternative goals. For example, how will you overcome the internal strengths of your department to manage the external threats currently confronting your department?

"Embrace Challenges to Gain Rewards."

Internal Weaknesses (- ,)

1. _____

2. _____

3. _____

4. _____

5. _____

External Threats (, -)

1. _____

2. _____

3. _____

4. _____

5. _____

SWOT (- , -)
Change & Integrate for Success

1. _____

2. _____

3. _____

4. _____

5. _____

Use Additional Space as Necessary

Section #7: The "Pledge" Matrix

Strategic Outcome Performance Item Department Level	Action Needed Intradepartmental Staff*	Action Needed Interdepartmental Cross-Institutional	Action Needed Form External Entity
1.			
2.			
3.			
4.			
5.			
6.			
7.			
8.			
9.			
10.			
11.			
12.			
13.			
14.			
15.			

* Be certain to name responsible parties as well as actions.

Planning Tip: Use this matrix to develop an understanding of the complex interrelationships that dominate the modern corporate landscape. It can be used to demonstrate to employees the value of their work and its impact on the success of the entire organization.

The Departmental Planning Template

DEPARMENTAL DIRECTION

Departmental Vision Statement: Develop a one sentence positive statement that describes where this department will be at the end of the planning cycle.

We will_____

_____

_____

_____.

Departmental Mission Statement: In no more than one paragraph, define the central mission of the department during the planning cycle timeframe. Review the institutional mission and be certain that the two missions are at least complimentary in nature.

The _____ department provides _____

_____

_____

_____

_____

_____

_____

_____

Reframing Questions:
> What is the purpose for this department?
> What is our reason for existing, what do we do, what is our central task?
> Where do you want the department to be in the future?
> What role do we have in the advancement of the organization?
> What type of institutional enterprise would we like our department to become?

Departmental Values: List a set of no more than seven to nine words that capture the essence of what is important to the members of this department.

1. _____
2. _____
3. _____
4. _____
5. _____
6. _____
7. _____
8. _____
9. _____

Reframing Questions:

What are the values of our department, what is important to our staff?

What are the driving beliefs that define the culture of our department?

What type of culture do we believe will produce the performance we desire and need to succeed?

What set of no more than nine single words encompasses the culture we want and those beliefs we hold most precious?

Competitive Tactics: List the six key customer wants that your department plans to meet better than the competition during this plan; or those tactics and processes that your department will review and revise to ensure a competitive advantage.

● _____by_____

● _____by_____

● _____by_____

● _____by_____

● _____by_____

● _____by_____

Business Definition: Develop those business and process functions that you will leverage to gain a competitive advantage to fulfill your department's purpose and achieve the institutional and departmental visions.

In a narrative form describe the key management or business areas that this department will concentrate its resources on growing, flourishing, or achieving during this plan. Resources should be applied to the key business strategies that will be used to gain the competitive advantage.

_____

_____

_____

_____

_____

_____

_____

_____

_____

List the business functions, that that will leverage the department to gain a competitive advantage to fulfill the department's mission and achieve the institution's vision:

1. _____

2. _____

3. _____

4. _____

5. _____

6. _____

7. _____

8. _____

List the five key process functions that the department will map, review, and revise over the next year.

1. _____

2. _____

3. _____

4. _____

5. _____

Using the paradigm model below, create a relevant cross-functional flowchart for your department illustrating the core management/business functions and core process functions that your department will rely on to gain a competitive market advantage. (Return to the circle worksheet and apply management processes and relationships developed to this flowchart. The flowchart as it appears below is only a model; your unique enterprise may need to be expressed differently).

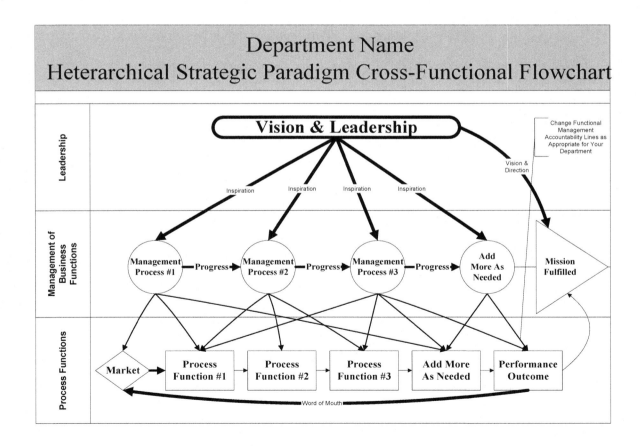

Shared Strategic Goals

List out those goals from the institutional strategic plan that your department will need to either directly or indirectly work to accomplish over the life of this strategic planning cycle (i.e., during the duration of this plan).

1. _____

2. _____

3. _____

4. _____

5. _____

6. _____

7. _____

8. _____

9. _____

10. _____

OTHERS:

Planning Tip: Return to your organizational plan, and review the goals. Which of the strategic goals of the institution will need either direct or indirect support from this department. The emphasis of your departmental objectives (next page) should be to realize the goals of the institution. Listing the goals in your plan will help focus the staff, institutional leaders, and anyone else reading your plan.

Departmental Strategic Goals and/or Key Departmental Operating Objectives

List out the strategic department objectives as developed in the SWOT analyses.

1. _____by_____

2. _____by_____

3. _____by_____

4. _____by_____

5. _____by_____

6. _____by_____

7. _____by_____

8. _____by_____

9. _____by_____

10. _____by_____

11. _____by_____

12. _____by_____

13. _____by_____

14. _____by_____

15. _____by_____

Planning Tip: In this section you will list the alternative objectives you developed in your examination of the internal strengths and weaknesses of the department and the external threats and opportunities of the organization and the marketplace. The objectives of this section are designed to meet the goals of the institutional strategic plan, and to expand the scope of responsibility and accomplishment of the department.

Your departmental objectives should be strategic in nature. Far too often, departmental plans are filled with daily actions or annual operating objectives. This plan should be strategic, if you need to list operating actions, create another sheet to detail what your department does (or create and appendix).

Pledge Card

Pledged to Others

- List the eight essential items, products, or services that your department will need to provide to other departments to fulfill the planning objectives of the organization.

1. _____

2. _____

3. _____

4. _____

5. _____

6. _____

7. _____

8. _____

Pledged to Our Department

- List the six essential items, products, or services that your department will need have pledged by others to fulfill the planning objectives of the organization. *Always try to give more than you get.*

1. _____

2. _____

3. _____

4. _____

5. _____

6. _____

OTHER:

List of Quantifiable Outcomes & Departmental Goals

STRATEGIC ITEM	Measurement Mechanism	Timeline	Goal	Comments

Add Items & Pages as Necessary

Key Figures & Statistics

ITEM	Actual			Goals		Anticipated Change	
	Year Before Last	Last Year	This Year	Next Year	Year After That	#	%
Customer Counts							
Choose Appropriate							
Statistical References							
That Should be Reviewed							
To Understand Both The							
Planning Priorities And							
The Quantifiable							
Outcomes							
Revenue & Costs							
Total Revenue							
Costs							
Budget Data							
Selected Statistics							
Information Capital							
Facilities							
Knowledge Capital							
Process Data							
Management Data							
Other Client Data							
Cost per/Item							
Revenue per/Item							
Evaluation Data							
Etc.							
Staffing							
Human Resource							
Statistics							

Planning Tip: Remember to use relevant statistical data (attempt to keep this section to less than one page). Plan implementation will be accomplished with vision and leadership, not with a constant review of the numbers. However, if you work in an organization that is numbers driven, you may want to make this section an appendix and provide detail on a wide variety of statistics. Chosen statistics might include: budget figures; income or revenue; profit analyses; five year operating expenses and revenues; needs assessment data; customer satisfaction summaries; customer or market projections; cost projections; quality assessment figures; current & future market shares; local, regional, and national demographic data; competition analyses; technology assessments; benchmarking data; human resource data; information/knowledge data; process mapping data (costs per input, output, and steps; time data; complexity analyses; variability analyses; systems analyses; market research; comparative analyses); etc. Positives (strengths) as well as weaknesses should be highlighted (*see Chapter 9 for more explanation*).

Objectives (by month in order of priority):

YEAR: _____ (JANUARY)

Objective	Timeline	Responsibility / Participants	Status*	Cost	Comments**
STRATEGIC INSTIUTIONAL OBJECTIVES					
STRATEGIC DEPARTMENTAL OBJECTIVES					

*Status Options: C (Completed), D (Disregarded), SWT (Still Working Toward)
**For Status "D" or "SWT", explanation is provided in the comments column.

Objectives (by month in order of priority):

YEAR: _____ (FEBRUARY)

Objective	Timeline	Responsibility / Participants	Status*	Cost	Comments**
STRATEGIC INSTIUTIONAL OBJECTIVES					
STRATEGIC DEPARTMENTAL OBJECTIVES					

*Status Options: C (Completed), D (Disregarded), SWT (Still Working Toward)
**For Status "D" or "SWT", explanation is provided in the comments column.

Objectives (by month in order of priority):

YEAR: _____ (MARCH)

Objective	Timeline	Responsibility / Participants	Status*	Cost	Comments**
STRATEGIC INSTIUTIONAL OBJECTIVES					
STRATEGIC DEPARTMENTAL OBJECTIVES					

*Status Options: C (Completed), D (Disregarded), SWT (Still Working Toward)
**For Status "D" or "SWT", explanation is provided in the comments column.

Objectives (by month in order of priority):

YEAR: _____ (APRIL)

Objective	Timeline	Responsibility / Participants	Status*	Cost	Comments**
STRATEGIC INSTIUTIONAL OBJECTIVES					
STRATEGIC DEPARTMENTAL OBJECTIVES					

*Status Options: C (Completed), D (Disregarded), SWT (Still Working Toward)
**For Status "D" or "SWT", explanation is provided in the comments column.

Objectives (by month in order of priority):

YEAR: _____ (MAY)

Objective	Timeline	Responsibility / Participants	Status*	Cost	Comments**
STRATEGIC INSTIUTIONAL OBJECTIVES					
STRATEGIC DEPARTMENTAL OBJECTIVES					

*Status Options: C (Completed), D (Disregarded), SWT (Still Working Toward)
**For Status "D" or "SWT", explanation is provided in the comments column.

Objectives (by month in order of priority):

YEAR: _____ (JUNE)

Objective	Timeline	Responsibility / Participants	Status*	Cost	Comments**
STRATEGIC INSTIUTIONAL OBJECTIVES					
STRATEGIC DEPARTMENTAL OBJECTIVES					

*Status Options: C (Completed), D (Disregarded), SWT (Still Working Toward)
**For Status "D" or "SWT", explanation is provided in the comments column.

Objectives (by month in order of priority):

YEAR: _____ (JULY)

Objective	Timeline	Responsibility / Participants	Status*	Cost	Comments**
STRATEGIC INSTIUTIONAL OBJECTIVES					
STRATEGIC DEPARTMENTAL OBJECTIVES					

*Status Options: C (Completed), D (Disregarded), SWT (Still Working Toward)
**For Status "D" or "SWT", explanation is provided in the comments column.

Objectives (by month in order of priority):

YEAR: _____ (AUGUST)

Objective	Timeline	Responsibility / Participants	Status*	Cost	Comments**
STRATEGIC INSTIUTIONAL OBJECTIVES					
STRATEGIC DEPARTMENTAL OBJECTIVES					

*Status Options: C (Completed), D (Disregarded), SWT (Still Working Toward)
**For Status "D" or "SWT", explanation is provided in the comments column.

Objectives (by month in order of priority):

YEAR: _____ (SEPTEMBER)

Objective	Timeline	Responsibility / Participants	Status*	Cost	Comments**
STRATEGIC INSTIUTIONAL OBJECTIVES					
STRATEGIC DEPARTMENTAL OBJECTIVES					

*Status Options: C (Completed), D (Disregarded), SWT (Still Working Toward)
**For Status "D" or "SWT", explanation is provided in the comments column.

Objectives (by month in order of priority):

YEAR: _____ (OCTOBER)

Objective	Timeline	Responsibility / Participants	Status*	Cost	Comments**
STRATEGIC INSTIUTIONAL OBJECTIVES					
STRATEGIC DEPARTMENTAL OBJECTIVES					

*Status Options: C (Completed), D (Disregarded), SWT (Still Working Toward)
**For Status "D" or "SWT", explanation is provided in the comments column.

Objectives (by month in order of priority):

YEAR: _____ (NOVEMBER)

Objective	Timeline	Responsibility / Participants	Status*	Cost	Comments**
STRATEGIC INSTIUTIONAL OBJECTIVES					
STRATEGIC DEPARTMENTAL OBJECTIVES					

*Status Options: C (Completed), D (Disregarded), SWT (Still Working Toward)
**For Status "D" or "SWT", explanation is provided in the comments column.

Objectives (by month in order of priority):

YEAR: _____ (DECEMBER)

Objective	Timeline	Responsibility / Participants	Status*	Cost	Comments**
STRATEGIC INSTIUTIONAL OBJECTIVES					
STRATEGIC DEPARTMENTAL OBJECTIVES					

*Status Options: C (Completed), D (Disregarded), SWT (Still Working Toward)
**For Status "D" or "SWT", explanation is provided in the comments column.

APPENDIX A: Suggested Reading List

To develop the most effective departmental strategic plan, you many want to review the following titles prior to completing this workbook. These resources may help you to become a more effective planner, leader, and/or manager prior to beginning this process.

- Bardwick, J. (1998). <u>In praise of good business: How optimizing risk rewards both your bottom line and your people.</u> New York, New York: John Wiley & Sons, Inc.

- Belasco, J. A., & Stayer, R. C. (1993). <u>Flight of the buffalo: Soaring to excellence, learning to let employees lead.</u> New York, NY: Warner Books.

- Blanchard, K, & Bowles, S. (1997). <u>Gung-ho: Turn on the people in any organization.</u> New York, NY: William Morrow & Company.

- Bradford, D., & Cohen, A. (1998). <u>Power up: Transforming organizations through shared leadership.</u> New York, New York: John Wiley & Sons, Inc.

- Buckingham M., & Coffman, C. (1999). <u>First break all the rules: What the world's greatest managers do differently.</u> New York, NY: Simon & Schuster, Inc.

- Covey, S. (1992). <u>Principle-centered leadership</u> [CD]. New York, NY: Simon & Schuster, Inc.

- Damelio, R. (1996). <u>The basics of process mapping.</u> Portland, OR: Productivity, Inc.

- Fogg, C. D. (1999). <u>Implementing your strategic plan: How to turn intent into effective action for sustainable change.</u> New York, New York: American Management Association.

- Goold, M., & Campbell, A. (1998, September-October). Desperately seeking synergy. <u>Harvard Business Review,</u> 130-143.

- Hammer, M. (1996). <u>Beyond reengineering: How the process-centered organization is changing our work and our lives</u> [Cassette Recording] New York, NY: Harper Audio.

- Johnson, S. (1998). Who moved my cheese?: An amazing way to deal with change in your life and work. New York, NY: Putnam Publishing Group.

- Pinchot, G. & Pinchot, E. (1994). <u>The end of bureaucracy & the rise of the intelligent organization.</u> San Francisco, CA: Berrett-Koehler Publishers, Inc.

- Scholtes, P. R. (1995). <u>The team handbook: How to use teams to improve quality.</u> Madison, WI: Joiner.

- Wheatley, M. J. (1996). <u>Leadership and the new science: Learning about organization from an orderly universe</u> [Cassette Recording]. San Bruno, CA: Audio Literature.

Chapter 12

Personal Planning
Workbook

"If you want to make minor improvements in life, work on behavior and attitude. If you want to make quantum leaps, work on paradigms."

-- Stephen Covey

Preface

Organizations glibly use terms like *empowerment, teamwork,* and *sharing power*: but they vastly underestimate the gap between providing a description of the desired behavior and people really behaving in that way. Management, for example, was taught for decades to evaluate, judge, punish, and reward subordinates. Those behaviors are intrinsically different from coaching, motivating, and delegating responsibilities to subordinates. The newly desired behaviors are too foreign to many people's experience for normal training to be anything but words, words, words. – Judith Bardwick

Dr. Bardwick's words resound with an uncanny ring of truth. Over the past decade, many organizations have moved toward success, achieved, transformed, and grown. Leaders use words like empowerment, cross-functional teaming, heterarchy, learning organization, and trust; yet does your organization share a common language, a set of common definitions, or a common understanding of the social construction and structure of your vision, mission, and values? Do your supervisors and leaders share a common understanding with each other, in your departments, or with you?

This personal planning process is designed to create a common language, to engage the entire organization in a dialog on empowerment, and to assist in opening the lines of communication, trustworthiness, and trust. For you to maintain the current level of excellence and to continue to improve your overall individual performance, you will need to begin a common journey that moves interdependent relationships from evaluation and judgment to teamwork, motivation, and shared decision-making. Please remember that to the community you serve, you are all equal, you must come to see yourselves as one common entity.

TABLE OF CONTENTS

INTRODUCTION

At this point, you have developed and implemented a systemized organizational strategic planning process as well as a systematized departmental planning process. These processes have allowed your organization to embark on a new journey with a renewed sense of purpose at both the institutional and departmental levels.

On the lines below, record just a few examples of success that your organization has achieved since implementing your organizational planning efforts:

_____

_____

_____

_____

_____

_____

_____

Goal of Personal Planning

You have completed the process of articulating a common vision, mission, and value statements, now there needs to be a process in which each of us is able to internalize and communicate the vision, mission, and values. The nature of the problem that keeps most plans from ever being realized is the gap between individual accountability, and departmental/institutional responsibility.

The goal of the personal planning initiative is to create a process of individual (personal/professional) planning and evaluation that will complement the existing strategic planning efforts of your organization and department. The personal planning and evaluation process will close the final chapter in strategic planning.

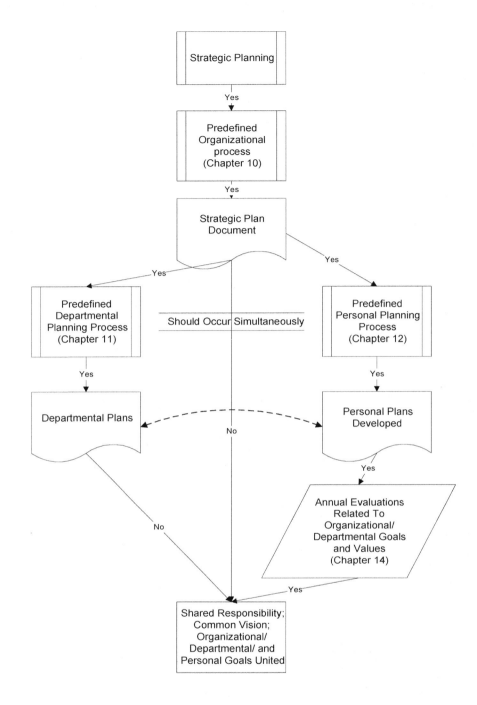

GOAL: BECOME A LEARNING ORGANIZATION

<u>Figure 1</u>. Institutional Planning Process Gap.

All leaders, managers, professional and support staff members of the organization will be asked to realize through an analysis of past ineffectiveness that hierarchical structures limit the role of leadership among those who do not possess power based on authority. Leaders are being asked to implement a system of personal goal development and evaluation that will unite the organizational and departmental values with those of the people who will implement them. This will create a system that is more heterarchical and more likely to have a shared vision and a system of shared responsibility.

> "We need to become learning organizations. Learning organizations use 'learning disciplines' that are concerned with a shift of the mind from seeing parts to seeing wholes, from seeing people as helpless reactors to seeing them as active participants in shaping their reality, from reacting to the present to creating the future." (Senge, 1990).

We need to move our firm from an organization that asks us for service, to one where we decide the best service to give to assist our stakeholders and community. We need to realize that we, the employees, are the embodiment of this institution. Becoming a learning organization can help us do that.

The core of the learning organization is based upon Senge's five learning principles:

1. *Personal Mastery* – this is the ability to expand our personal skill base and our personal capacities. It is the ability to use our skills to create the results and outcomes we want, and to create an organizational culture that encourages all of our stakeholders to personally and professionally develop themselves toward the goals and purposes we have chosen.

2. *Mental Models* – the paradigms and images of reality and the world that exist within our minds. Understanding our mental models is the ability to see how our conception of the world shapes our actions and decisions.

3. *Shared Vision* – this is the creation of a sense of commitment in a group through the development of shared mental models and a shared sense of personal mastery. It is the development of a shared sense of the future.

4. *Team Learning* – is the transformation of communication and collective thinking skills so that a group of people can develop an intelligence and understanding that is greater than the sum of the individual's talents.

5. *Systems Thinking* -- a means of conceiving, understanding, and describing the forces of the interrelationships that shape the behaviors of our

organization. This discipline can help us to see how to improve our organization and our internal systems more effectively.

Our organizational planning process assisted us in addressing the discipline of creating a shared vision. Departmental planning assisted us in team learning, and personal planning will help us in addressing personal mastery and mental models. United, these three planning processes can give us the common understanding and common language to address our future from a heterarchical systems thinking approach, so that we may become a learning organization, and better serve our community.

TRIADIC HETERARCHICAL STRATEGIC PLANNING

In 1982, Baldridge and Okimi suggested that higher education personnel were influenced by a gap between planning and budgeting and planning and the daily operational activities of specific departments (p. 15). Little has changed in almost thirty years. The diminishing of these gaps was of central importance to the planning design of the organization (Figure 2). This design is focused on creating a system of planning tied to the three elements that comprise our organization: the whole (institution), the local (units or departments), and the one (each of us individually). However, there still is a difference between organizational planning and the individual understanding of the goals of the organization.

As Stephen Covey (1992) argued in his work, *Principle Centered Leadership*, the world class competitive organization of the future should concern itself with four levels of natural laws: personal (principle centered), interpersonal (relationships), managerial (leadership, supervision), and organizational (structure). Covey suggests that these four departments are governed by four principles: personal governed by trustworthiness, interpersonal governed by trust, managerial governed by empowerment, and the organization governed by alignment.

To Covey, these levels and related principles must be aligned and synergized for the organization to succeed. His principles demonstrate the underlying point of the planning effort: any planning strategy must be incorporated into every level of the organization; otherwise empowerment is merely a shiny method of command-and-control, and systems thinking is merely a practiced method of restructuring the hierarchy. The implementation of personal planning will fulfill the missing component of our organization's comprehensive planning process, thus uniting the three levels of the organization and the four principles described by Covey.

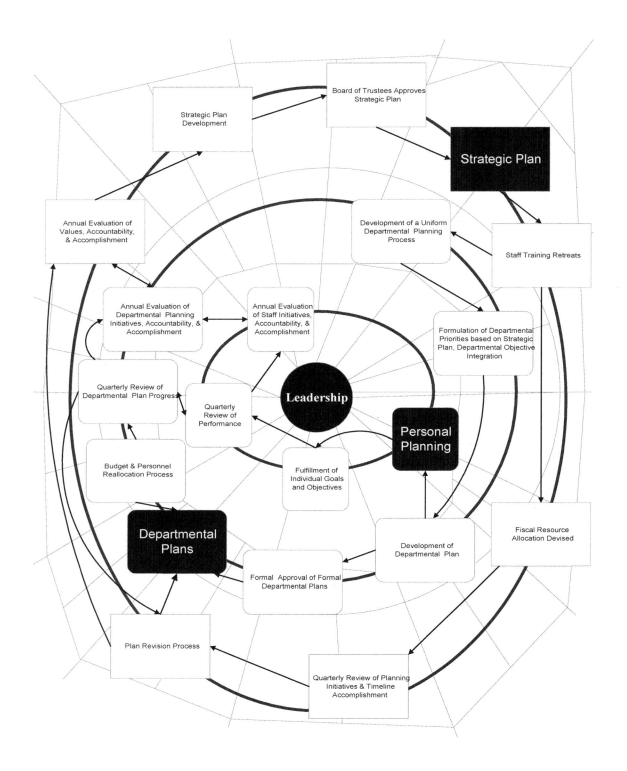

Figure 2. The Triadic Strategic Planning Design.

The completion of this workbook will allow you to develop a systems approach to your work, your career, and your commitment to serving our customers/clients/students. As each of us creates our personal plan, we are in essence creating a plan for our department, and drafting a future for the organization. As our departments are updated, so too is our institutional plan, thus creating an ongoing system of strategic planning throughout the organization.

By aligning our personal plans to the institution, we are demonstrating that the institution is a collection of our commitment and our efforts toward service. This process will help us to create an organization that possesses synergy throughout its being (i.e. emergent from the level of each employee, through its departments, and toward shaping the vision and mission of the entire organization).

THE CASE FOR ORGANIZATIONAL SYNERGY

The best example of the importance of this process and the need for organizational synergy can be paraphrased from a story told by Brian Dumaine:

> In the days of misty towers, distressed maidens, and stalwart knights, a young man, walking down a road, came upon a laborer fiercely pounding away at a stone with hammer and chisel. The lad asked the worker, who looked frustrated and angry, "What are you doing?" The laborer answered in a pained voice: "I'm trying to shape this stone, and its backbreaking work." The youth continued his journey and soon came upon another man chipping away at a similar stone, who looked neither angry nor happy. "What are you doing?" the young man asked. "I'm shaping a stone for a building." The young man went on and before long came to a third worker chipping away at a stone, but this worker was singing happily as he worked. "What are you doing?" the young man asked. The worker smiled and replied, "I'm building a cathedral." (Dumaine, 1994, p. 196).

It is time for a system and process that helps the workers see that they are building the future, and doing it through the betterment of themselves. The completion of the organization's triadic planning process will lead to the development of personal plans and objectives for you that will create an organizational collective with a set purpose of serving customers.

This purpose is best illustrated in the organigraph pictured in Figure 3, it suggests the need to view our organization and its planning processes as a system of hubs and webs based around actual person-to-person work strategies that not only chart an organization but provide a conceptual map as well. This picture illustrates the relationship between internal and external stakeholders, the organizational mission and vision, departments (units), and each of us, demonstrating the system as a whole and our role in making the organization function productively and synergistically. Only together can we fulfill our mission and achieve our vision.

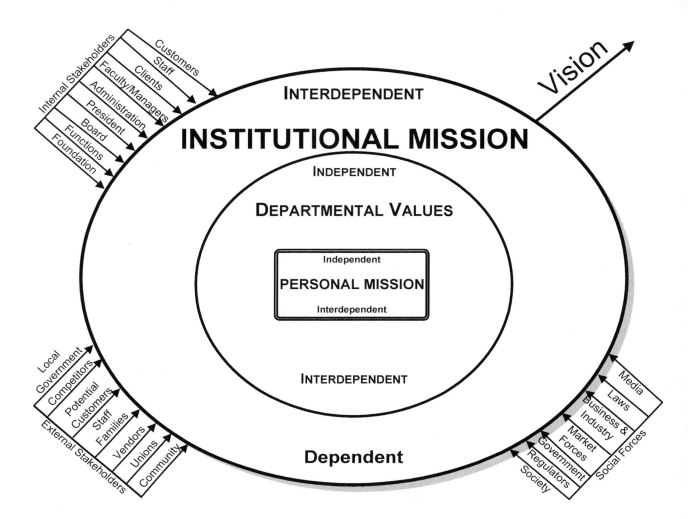

Figure 3. Triadic Heterarchical Strategic Planning Organigraph.

"The definition of insanity is doing the same thing over and over expecting different results."

-- Albert Einstein

PUTTING PROFESSIONAL LIFE INTO PERSPECTIVE

Your goal in developing a mental framework and perspective for your personal plan is the realization of physical, mental, and emotional health. This should be a primary focus in reaching your potential and in improving your performance and the performance of the organization. We should begin to view life holistically and systemically, asking the right questions, and developing the life skills that allow us to reach our goals. The objective is to work for long-term goals over short-term temporary solutions. To guide you in a journey to better health, a sense of work/life balance, and the development of essential principles for success, your organization should adopt "Principles for the Successful High Performance Employee," such as the ones presented below.

10 Principles of the Successful High Performance Employee

1. **Take Risks & Become Entrepreneurial**

   - Be informed, vigilant, and continuously flexible.
   - Be passionate and engaged.
   - Think unconventionally.
   - Look for the opportunity.
   - Be constructively discontent.

2. **Learn to Love the Work You Do**

   - Make your workplace the place you want to work.
   - Develop the skills to be highly successful at your chosen profession.
   - Develop a personal portfolio of skills.
   - Identify your strengths and work toward them.
   - Discover and adapt to changes in the workplace.
   - Take a leadership role whenever possible.

3. **Communicate Constantly**

   - Share information continuously.
   - Tell the story whenever possible (aim for daily).
   - Zero in on the key concepts.
   - Actively clear up any and all misconceptions constantly.
   - Dialog, Dialog and Dialog: Do not give commands or orders.
   -

4. Keep on Learning

- Develop new skills.
- Acquire a love of learning.
- Take classes whenever possible.
- Develop new personal and professional capacities.

5. Create Internal Competence

- Learn new and innovative skill sets.
- Embrace new technology and practices.
- Develop skills of self-reflection and goal setting.
- Practice, Practice, and Practice.

6. Achieve Financial Goals & Independence

- Develop sound long-term financial goals.
- Set goals for salary, personal savings, and retirement.
- Develop the skills and acquire the knowledge to earn these goals.

7. Live Healthy

- Control stress and strain in work and family life.
- Develop a sound perspective.
- Exercise your mind, body, and soul.
- Work safely.
- Develop an overall healthy lifestyle.
- Develop a sound social support system.
- Decide to have a positive mental attitude.

8. Manage Time Effectively

- Determine which projects/duties/activities are important and not important.
- Determine which projects/duties/activities are urgent and not urgent.
- Learn to say no at the right times.
- Organize your work and your workspace.
- Avoid unnecessary interruptions.
- Use technology to save time.
- Schedule your time effectively.

9. Develop People Aptitude for Better Interpersonal Relationships

- Be flexible and understanding.
- Work on communication skills.
- Value others thoughts and opinions.
- Use this workbook to develop a sense of personal balance.
- Realize the limitations of others and yourself.
- Concentrate on the "win-win."
- Be mindful of the feelings of others.
- Be self-reflective about your communication & behaviors.

10. Always Look Toward the Future While Attending to the Present

- What do I want to be?
- Where am I going?
- What personal and professional options do I have or can I develop?
- How can I change to achieve my personal and professional goals?
- How can I increase my service?

"One can choose to go back toward safety or forward toward growth. Growth must be chosen again and again; fear must be overcome again and again."

--Abraham Maslow

WORKPLACE TREND MATRIX

The workplace of the future will be redefined, job titles and descriptions will diminish in importance. Each employee will need to begin to develop a value-added set of transferable skills and comprehensive talents. Single dimensional positions will no longer exist, rather each of us will move from project to project, activity to activity, objective to objective, and goal to goal. Your job and responsibilities will remain in a constant state of transformation and change. Your personal success will depend on your ability to redefine yourself, change your practice, and professionally and personally develop. In contemporary times, you are responsible for the management of your destiny and your place within our organization. You are becoming an empowered employee who is expected to take leadership responsibility for the realization of your goals. The following matrix is designed to illustrate the desired transformation at your organization.

WORKPLACE TREND MATRIX

PAST	PRESENT/FUTURE
One-Time Degree Attainment	Lifelong Learning
Dependence & Subordinate	Interdependent—Thinker—Project Leader
Blind Institutional Loyalty	Work/Life Value Balance & Integration
Skill Sets	Talent Portfolio/Inventory
Job	Career Goals
Hierarchy	Heterarchy
Transformational Leaders	Inspirational Leaders

* Adapted from Portillo, J. (1997). <u>Strategic Personal Planning.</u>

"When one door closes, another opens; but we often look so long and so regretfully upon the closed door that we do not see the one which has opened for us."

-- Alexander Graham Bell

PERSONAL KNOWLEDGE/SKILL DEVELOPMENT FRAMEWORK[1]

In order to come to an understanding and to develop a perspective on creating a balance between the obligations of life and work it is important to consider a set of framing questions that can assist you in the development of your personal goals and objectives.

1. Examine your attitude toward yourself, toward your personal success, toward your role in the organization, toward your interpersonal relationships, toward your interactions with others, toward your health (mental, physical, and emotional), and toward your life in general. What thoughts come to mind? Write down some notes for your own consideration and to help you with the development of your plan at the end of this workbook.

    _____

    _____

    _____

    _____.

2. Consider ways in which you would like to improve your attitude, start with your workplace, then examine your other roles and personal relationships. What thoughts about attitude improvement come to mind? Write down some notes for your own consideration and to help you with the development of your plan at the end of this workbook.

Area of Improvement	Strategy
Workplace	

OTHER:_____

_____.

---

[1] Many of the questions in this section of the workbook were developed as modified framing questions from the classic work: Nightingale, E. (1990). *Lead the Field.*

3. Over the course of the next year, how would you like to increase your personal and professional knowledge and skills in the place you currently find yourself? What self-improvement ideas come to mind? Write down some notes for your own consideration and to help you with the development of your plan at the end of this workbook.

    _____

    _____

    _____

    _____.

4. How can you immediately improve your attitude and workplace performance? What thoughts come to mind? How can you develop skills into a lifelong talent? Write down some notes for your own consideration and to help you with the development of your plan at the end of this workbook.

    _____

    _____

    _____

    _____.

5. How would you like to expand your current scope of responsibility in the organization? What thoughts and ideas come to mind? Write down some notes for your own consideration and to help you with the development of your plan at the end of this workbook.

    _____

    _____

    _____

    _____.

6. Evaluate yourself on how effectively you think you are providing service to the customers/clients/students, stakeholders, and other employees of the organization. Write down some notes for your own consideration and to help you with the development of your plan at the end of this workbook.

_____

_____

_____

_____ .

7. Write down the duties of your current job that you think are difficult, unpleasant, or an utter waste of time.

_____

_____

_____

_____ .

(When completed, resolve to do them to the best of your ability, just for the sake of self-accomplishment. Also resolve to discuss them with your supervisor during your next annual evaluation.)

8. Consider the key people in your life, those that have a direct or indirect impact on you, your work, your family, and your community. Which of these people would you choose to emulate? What qualities do they have that you want to possess? Write down some notes for your own consideration and to help you with the development of your plan at the end of this workbook.

_____

_____

_____ .

9. How productive do you currently feel in your work? What can you do to increase your productivity? Are your talents matched with the work you are asked to perform? How can you better express your productivity and what you need to be productive to others? Write down some notes for your own consideration and to help you with the development of your plan at the end of this workbook.

_____

_____

_____

_____

_____.

10. When these words are mentioned (physical fitness, attitude, mental focus, health, emotional well being, time, trust, communication, pressure, and stress) what thoughts come to mind? Consider each word separately and write down some notes for your own consideration and to help you with the development of your plan at the end of this workbook.

_____

_____

_____

_____.

11. If someone were to say to you: "you should find ways to make yourself more valuable at your workplace." What thoughts come to mind? Write down some notes for your own consideration and to help you with the development of your plan at the end of this workbook.

_____

_____

_____.

12. Do you feel you currently have the skills, education, productivity, talent, and/or knowledge to earn the financial rewards you desire? What will you do over the next year to develop these skills and to ensure you are valued professionally and personally so that you can reach your financial goals? Write down some notes for your own consideration and to help you with the development of your plan at the end of this workbook.

_____

_____

_____

_____

_____.

13. If someone were to suggest that you need goals for the following: personal fulfillment, relationships with family, relationships with co-workers, relationships with friends, and your health and well-being. What thoughts come to mind, what goals would you set? Write down some notes for your own consideration and to help you with the development of your plan at the end of this workbook.

Item	Goals
Personal Fulfillment	
Relationships with Family	
Relationships with Co-workers	
Relationships with Friends	
Health and Well Being	

14. What goals will you set to improve your level of service to the organization? How can you become a leader/teacher/mentor/friend/asset to others at the firm next year? Write down some notes for your own consideration and to help you with the development of your plan at the end of this workbook.

_____

_____

_____

_____

_____

_____

_____

_____

_____

_____

_____ .

"New knowledge is of little value if it doesn't change us, make us better individuals, and help us to be more productive, happy, and useful."

■ Hyrum W. Smith

Personal Knowledge/Skill Development Worksheet

Talents/Knowledge I Now Possess	Skills/Knowledge I Need to Develop/Acquire to Improve My Talents

Sometimes I lie awake at night, and I ask, "Where have I gone wrong?" Then a voice says to me, "This is going to take more than one night."

-- Charlie Brown

PERSONAL IDEALS WORKSHEET

Looking back on your notes in this workbook, complete the following worksheet.

1. The three new skills I will learn this year are:

    A. _____ .

    B. _____ .

    C. _____ .

2. The perspective I will change about my work attitude over the next year is:

    _____

    _____

    _____

    _____

    _____ .

3. When I leave my current job, I will be remembered for (or the legacy I will leave is)?

    _____

    _____

    _____

    _____

    _____ .

4. My greatest accomplishment in my work thus far has been:

_____

_____

_____

_____

_____.

5. At my workplace, no one can do _____

_____

_____

_____

_____

_____better than I can.

6. The aspect of working that I like best is:

_____

_____

_____

_____

_____

_____.

7. The aspect of working at my current organization that I like least is:

_____

_____

_____

_____

_____.

8. This year I will do the following to change the thing I like least about working

here:

_____

_____

_____

_____

_____.

9. If I accomplish nothing else this year, I will at least:

_____

_____

_____

_____

_____.

10. The five significant things I want to accomplish before I retire are:

- _____.

- _____.

- _____.

- _____.

- _____.

You are beginning to take your world into your hands.

"The illiterate of the year 2000 will not be the individual who cannot read and write, but the one who cannot learn, unlearn, and relearn."

-- Alvin Toffler

"To each of us, at certain points of our lives, there come opportunities to rearrange our formulas and assumptions -- not necessarily to be rid of the old, but more to profit from adding something new."

—Leo Buscaglia

PERSONAL MISSION STATEMENT DEVELOPMENT FRAMEWORK

"The most effective way I know to begin with the end in mind is to develop a *personal mission statement* or philosophy or creed. It focuses on what you want to be (character) and to do (contributions and achievements) and on the values or principles upon which being and doing are based." – Stephen Covey (1989)

The development of a personal mission statement is essential in the establishment of personal values and goals. Your individual mission is a profession of your beliefs and values, of your relationship to others, and to the roles in which you chose to live your life. It publicly expresses the meaning of your life, and how you plan to fulfill all of the respective roles of your life, how you will prioritize and manage your most valuable resource (time), and how you will create a balance between the work you have chosen (your service) and your life. As Covey illustrates, your mission is what you really want to be, not necessarily what you are. Remember, your mission is a goal, not easily achieved or realized; but nonetheless what you strive to become.

Personal Mission Statement Development Worksheet

First think of the members of your family, your personal friends, and all of your social relationships. Now ask yourself a question: "What do I want them to remember about me when I am gone?" Write down some notes for later reference:

_____

_____

_____

_____

_____

_____

Next think of your workplace and your role in it and ask yourself: "how do I want my co-workers to feel about me?" Again write down some notes for later reference.

_____

_____

_____

_____

_____

Finally, consider other people you relate to in each of your roles (community leader, organization member, neighbor, etc) and again ask: "what is the impression I choose to leave?" Again write down some notes for later reference.

_____

_____

_____

_____

_____

_____

After you have answered these questions, reviewed the components of this workbook, considered all of your personal and professional roles, your values, and your beliefs you are ready to draft a personal mission statement. The format of the statement is not important, the length is not important, the literary value and style is not important. The values, goals, personal meaning, and your personal commitment to them are important and the key to understanding how you will balance your life and work. How you will lead yourself through your busy life, how you will achieve the life goals you desire, and the legacy you will leave are equally important.

Sample Personal Mission Statements

"I shall not fear anyone on earth. I shall fear only God. I shall not bear ill toward anyone. I shall not submit to injustice from anyone. I shall conquer untruth by truth. And in resisting untruth, I shall put up with all suffering." – Mahatma Gandhi

"I came, I saw, I conquered." – Julius Caesar

"I will provide exceptional service everyday. I will value each person I come into contact with, treating each of them as the most important person in the world (because they are). I will value what I have over what I want. I will approach each situation under the motto of "Do no harm." I will succeed under the direction of these values alone." – William Austin

"My personal career mission is to master the leading GUI software development tools and gain a greater understanding of business application development." -- Unknown

" To live content will small means, to seek elegance rather than luxury, and refinement rather than fashion; to be worthy, not respectable, and wealthy, not rich; to study hard, think quietly, talk gently, act frankly; to listen to stars and birds, to babes and sages, with open heart; to bear all cheerfully, to do all bravely, wait occasions, hurry never. In a word to let the spiritual, unbidden, and unconscious, grow up through the uncommon. This is to be my symphony." – William Ellery Channing

---

The essential criteria/components of a personal mission statement[2]:

- Comes from inside of me.
- Appeals to my best instincts and interests.
- It says something that applies to me, it is not general, it is unique, and it is what I want to be.
- It gives a sufficiently clear direction and purpose for you, that you will be able to discuss and consider in real terms and specifics one year from today.
- It will stand the test of time. It is not an achievable objective, but a goal for life. It can remain an appropriate statement for years to come.
- It is something I wish to become and to be.

(If you are still in need for help, there are numerous web sites that will assist you in the development of a personal mission statement).

---

[2] Revised from Scholtes, P. R. (1998). The leader's handbook: Making things happen, getting things done. New York, NY: McGraw-Hill, Inc.

You are ready to write your mission statement. Review it often to revisit your goals, your mission, and your values.

MY MISSION STATEMENT

Use Extra Space and Paper if Needed

"Man transforms himself into the things he loves. When the time arrives for his sun to set, he has become that which, during the course of his life, he has consciously or unconsciously chosen to be."

-- Alexis Carrel

The Personal Planning Template

Instructions: This template is designed for you to create a formal personal plan for implementation over the next year. This plan should emerge from the completion of the personal planning workbook. This plan should not be a rearticulation of your existing job description; rather this plan will be used as part of your annual professional performance assessment. The plan is designed to provide you, your supervisor, and the organization with realistic expectations for your personal growth over the next year. The goal of personal planning is based on the leadership principle that your personal growth and development are essential to the fulfillment of the organization's mission. Whenever possible you should try to align your goals with those of the department and the organization, or to examine the goals of the department and the organization from within the framework of your professional goals and development.

<u>In paragraph form complete each of the following for your plan:</u>

Personal Mission Statement: Copy your personal mission statement from your planning workbook for the official plan.

_____

_____

_____

_____

_____

Personal Mission, Department Purpose Alignment: Explain how your personal mission will help you to fulfill the purpose of your department.

_____

_____

_____

_____

Personal Mission, Organizational Mission Alignment: Explain how your personal mission will assist you to help fulfill the mission of the organization:

_____

_____

_____

_____

Professional Development: List those areas that you believe you need to develop yourself professionally over the next year to fulfill your mission, your department's purpose, the organization's mission, and to enhance your personal core talents.

1._____

2._____

3._____

4._____

5._____

Personal Pledges & Goals

Develop the following table; wherever possible list personal goal objectives, timelines, and costs to the institution:

Pledge or Goal	Completion Timeline	Estimated Cost

Use the table below to list the cross-institutional, cross-functional teams that you plan to have a significant role in over the next year.

Team Participation & Development

1. _____

2. _____

3. _____

4. _____

5. _____

Performance Area	Rate	Examples from Previous Year's Work	Planned Goals for Improvement for the Upcoming Year	Goal Development Methods
Planning – sets objectives, establishes strategies and action oriented goals. Demonstrates adequate effort in achieving personal, unit, and institutional plans.				
Organization – adequately groups activities, achieves desired results, delegates when appropriate, uses available resources wisely.				
Identify Other Areas – The two examples above suggest areas to develop performance objectives. The supervisor and staff member should dialog to develop agreed upon goals and objectives.				

Personal Plan Summary

In paragraph form narrative, describe the significant accomplishments that you believe you will achieve over the next year.

MY COMMITTMENT

I agree to the goals identified in this plan, I realize that every goal may not be accomplished, but I also realize that eventually I will reach my personal/professional goals, because nothing can stand in the way of a well developed plan and my desire to fulfill my goals.

_____   _____

Signature   Date

APPENDIX A: DAILY PLANNING TEMPLATE

Purpose: Now that you have completed your annual personal plan, use this worksheet on a daily basis to improve your daily performance. Completion of this worksheet should take no longer than five minutes and should double your daily professional performance.

Instructions: Think of what is most important to the organization, your department, and to you. Create in your mind, an integrated, holistic sense of what tasks are most important for you to complete today. Choose the five most important achievable items and list them on the lines below. Once you have listed them order them in the order of most important (1) through least important (5).

Tasks to be Completed Today	**Order**
1. _____	_____
2. _____	_____
3. _____	_____
4. _____	_____
5. _____	_____

Now spend the rest of your day completing these tasks in the order of their importance. Remember that you may not complete all six but you will likely complete those tasks that are most important to your organization.

In completing these tasks what talents did I use and improve today?

1. _____

2. _____

3. _____

(COPY THIS PAGE AND COMPLETE IT EACH MORNING BEFORE YOU START YOUR DAY)

** Adapted from Nightingale, E. (1990). <u>Lead the field.</u> Niles, IL: Nightingale-Conant Corporation.

APPENDIX B: GLOSSARY

Decision Making. Decision-making is the act of choosing one alternative from among more than one. The decision making process includes recognizing and defining the nature of the decision situation, identifying alternatives, choosing the "best" alternative, and putting the decision into practice. A decision making group may be most effective when members openly discuss and agree on the best alternative.

Departmental Planning. Departmental planning is the systematic identification of strategic priority issues, coupled with the development of accountability systems and timelines for each organizational department.

Goal. A goal is the establishment of specific targets, a purpose toward which an endeavor is directed, a desired end or achievement.

Heterarchy. A heterarchy is a complex phenomena that not only illustrates the levels of a structure (organization) but also demonstrates the emergent complexity of social networks, and situational characteristics of contemporary organizations.

Learning Organization. A learning organization is an organization skilled at creating, acquiring, and transferring knowledge, and at modifying its behavior to reflect new knowledge and insights (Garvin, 1993, p. 80).

Organigraph. The term organigraph, which comes from the French term for organizational charts: organigramme, is a combination of a picture and a map to explain the complex networks, systems, and structures that comprise contemporary organizations.

Organizational Synergy. Organizational synergy is defined as a leadership desire for cross-functional, cross-institutional, cross-structural system designed to promote knowledge sharing, best practices, customer satisfaction, and process standardization. Synergy is further defined as the desire to align institutional, departmental, and personal values and goals.

Ownership. Ownership is defined as the ability of the staff and decision-makers at an organization to take possession of an integrated data based planning process. It suggests across the board empowerment and accountability standards that give a significant percentage of the current staff a "buy-in" and control over organization-wide and departmental initiatives.

Personal Planning. Personal planning is a system of strategic planning that occurs at the level of the individual. It is synergistic with the mission of the department and the institution.

Planning. Planning is a process of selecting a rational course of collective action to achieve a future state of affairs. It includes setting goals, gathering and analyzing information, evaluation information, making decisions, and acting.

System. A system is a set of two or more interrelated elements of any kind. It is a deliberately designed synthetic organism comprised of interrelated and interacting components, which are employed to function in an integrated fashion to attain predetermined purposes (Banathy, 1968).

Systems Thinking. Systems thinking is a discipline for seeing wholes. It is a framework for seeing interrelationships rather than things, for seeing patterns of change rather than static snapshots (Senge, 1990).

APPENDIX C: Suggested Reading List

To develop yourself personally and professionally, you many want to review the following titles prior to completing this workbook. These resources may help you to reach your long-term goals.

- Belasco, J. A. (2001). <u>The ten commandments of success.</u> Beverly Hills, CA: New Millennium Press.

- Blanchard, K., Carlos, J. P., & Randolph, A. (1996). <u>Empowerment takes more than a minute.</u> San Francisco, CA: Berrett-Koehler Publishers.

- Brassard, M., & Ritter, D. (1994). <u>The memory jogger II: A pocket guide for continuous improvement & effective planning.</u> Methuen, MA: GOAL/QPC.

- Buckingham M., & Clifton, D. (2001). <u>Now, discover your strengths.</u> New York, NY: Simon & Schuster, Inc.

- Carlson Learning Company. (1994). <u>DISC: Personal profile system: A plan to understand yourself & others.</u> Minneapolis, MN: Author.

- Covey, S. (1989). <u>The 7 habits of highly effective people: Powerful lessons in personal change.</u> New York, NY: Simon & Schuster.

- Jaworski, J. (1996). <u>Synchronicity: The inner path of leadership.</u> San Francisco, CA: Berrett-Koehler Publishers.

- Knowdell, R. L. (1998, June-July). The 10 new rules for strategizing your career. <u>The Futurist,</u> 19-24.

- Losyk, B. (1997, March-April). Generation X: What they think and what they plan to do. <u>The Futurist,</u> pp. 39-44.

- Niebrand, C., Holmes, R., & Horn, E. (1999). <u>Pocket mentor: a handbook for teachers.</u> New York: Allyn & Bacon.

- Nightingale, E. (1990). <u>Lead the field.</u> Niles, IL: Nightingale-Conant Corporation.

- Portillo, J. (1997). <u>A step by step approach to strategic personal planning.</u> Lake Quivira, Kansas: Terrace Trail Press.

- Roberts, W. (1991). <u>Leadership secrets of Attila the Hun.</u> New York, NY: Warner Books.

- Scholtes, P. R. (1998). <u>The leader's handbook: Making things happen, getting things done.</u> New York, NY: McGraw-Hill, Inc.

- Zachary, L. (2000). The mentor's guide: facilitating effective learning relationships. San Francisco, CA: Jossey-Bass.

Chapter 13

Leading the Process: Beyond the "Hero-Myth" toward the Inspirational Agenda

To get others to come into our ways of thinking, we must go over to theirs; and it is necessary to follow, in order to lead. – William Hazlitt

On December 1, 1955, a little old woman named Rosa Parks boarded a bus after a hard day's work as a seamstress in a Montgomery, Alabama department store. She refused to relinquish her seat to a "white" man, and created an historical moment that led to the emergence of one of America's most inspirational leaders. In what seemed to be one of the greatest moments of synchronicity, a great leader emerged.

Upon a closer examination, this little old woman turns out to be a forty-two year old activist, trained at the famous Highlander Folk School for passive resistance, who had served as an officer of the Montgomery NAACP and had been a secretary for the Alabama NAACP (Burns, 1990, p. 4). As inspirational as the legendary (now almost mythical) story has become, the reality of the moment is far more fascinating. Local leaders staged this event using a professional activist who could be admired by the nation as a sympathetic victim of segregation and racism. Her plight created a sense of urgency to address an inequality that had been present in the Southern states for over one hundred years.

A local minister, aware of the facts, used the situation to propel himself into the national spotlight.

> After prayers and scripture readings King walked to the pulpit, gazed out at the television cameras, put aside his scribbled notes, and gave an electrifying speech that retold the story of Parks and all others who had been abused on the buses, [he] exhorted the boycotters to use persuasion and not coercion, and ended by proclaiming: "If you will protest courageously, and yet with dignity and Christian love, when the history books are written in future generations, the historians will have to pause and say, 'There lived a great people – a black people – who injected new meaning and dignity into the veins of civilization.' This is our challenge and our overwhelming responsibility." (Burns, 1990, p. 7).

The Reverend Dr. Martin Luther King Jr. chose at that moment to move from being the manager of a simple bus boycott, reviewing the facts of the incident, to proclaiming a vision of freedom and equality for the nation that would become the trademark inspirational agenda for future generations. He set a standard for inspiration, vision, and personal responsibility that remains today. He used the "hero-myth" (i.e., strong man saves helpless woman) to his advantage, but his ability to sustain momentum, engage a nation of followers, and to create a reality of remarkable change was pure inspiration.

Although you may never possess the oratory skills, willingness to sacrifice, or charismatic character of a Dr. Martin Luther King Jr., your world will have moments in need of inspiration. Your business will need a leader to arise, to take control of a situation, and to provide a vision of what is right and what is possible. You will have your opportunity to create an inspirational agenda to change your organization and to reach your full potential. Remember, you already have one precious and luxurious element that Dr. King did not have; you have the freedom to reach your goals.

Summarizing the Theories of Leadership

When leadership was first viewed as a phenomenon worthy of study, historians examined the most well known leaders. This group consisted largely of European men, who appeared larger than life. Thus, the concept of the "Hero Myth" was formulated. In the "Hero Myth" theories, scholars looked at leadership traits, at how men emerged to levels of prominence and authority, and to what tactics they employed to be charismatically inspirational.

As time went on, and scholars began to focus less on historical figures, and more on contemporary business leaders (known as mangers), they noticed people trading service for money. This gave rise to the theory of the transactional leader, or someone who had followers and loyalty based on the rewards provided. Scholars of the transactional leader suggested that leadership was a matter of quid pro quo, that it was situationally obtained and defined, and that it was largely a matter of autocratic and bureaucratic functions.

In contemporary times, where reductions in force constitute the norm, change is everywhere, and no one expects to ever again receive that gold watch at retirement. The concept of the transformational leader has emerged. Scholars of the transformational leadership school of thought, suggests that these leaders rely on team theory, a group centered approach, collaboration, and humanism to define their management and leadership styles. This remains the dominant theory of leadership today.

In looking at all three leadership theories holistically, I am suggesting that in each case, a single type of person emerges as the dominant leader archetype of the theoretical framework. In 2002, I called this person the leader with the inspirational agenda, today I might just call him Barack Obama and you would likely have a clearer picture. I believe that leaders, who reach the highest level of performance, whether they were charismatic hero-myths, transactional practitioners, or transformational change agents, all possess a strong internal desire to inspire others to follow them. As noted prior, President Barack Obama is the contemporary master of this craft.

Figure 13.1 illustrates the three dominant leadership theories, the theory of the inspirational agenda, and the non-leadership practices of laissez-faire managers. The remainder of this chapter reveals my thoughts on the emergence of the inspirational agenda in the new century.

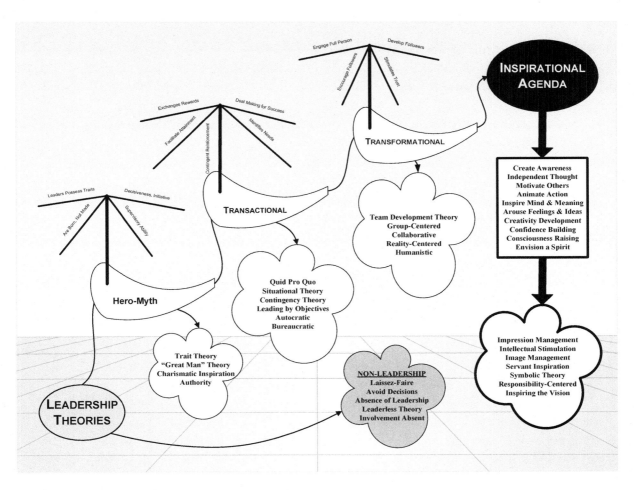

<u>Figure 13.1</u>. Illustrated History of Leadership Theories.

<u>Who are Essential, Managers or Leaders?</u>

Coupled with scholars' recognition of the evolution of leadership theory and practice, exists the management versus leadership debate. Various pundits, writers, practitioners, scholars, and consultants continuously argue about the role of the managers versus the role of leaders. The legendary CEO of General Electric, Jack Welch, has stated that managers exist to create bureaucracy and limit the effectives of the progressive organization.

> Jack Welch, the CEO of General Electric, once said that managers try to overcomplicate the simple, they equate management with sophistication, attempting to sound smarter than their employees. They fail to inspire anyone; rather, they control, stifle, hold back crucial information, breath down their necks, and waste employee time on trivia, minutia, and useless reporting (Slater, 1999, p. 28).

H. Ross Perot, has also suggested that the role of the modern manager should be the examination of processes, while the development of human relations are the responsibility of leaders.

> People cannot be managed. Inventories can be managed, but people must be led. (H. Ross Perot).

Jack Welch further suggests that the role of the leader is to interact with employees to create a shared and common vision of organizational accomplishment.

> Managers talk to one another, write memos to one another. Leaders talk to their employees, talk *with* their employees, filling them with vision, getting them to perform at levels the employees themselves didn't think possible. Then . . . they simply get out of the way. (Slater, 1999, p. 29).

Scores of books have been written to demonstrate the differences between being a leader and being a manager. Some authors (Block; Buckingham & Coffman; Carr, Hard, & Trahant; & Drucker) have favored managers and management, some have favored the role of leaders and leadership (Bass; Bolman & Deal; & Covey), some both (Blanchard), and some pundits have suggested that both managers and leaders are generally misguided (Adams, 1996). Rost has detailed the difference, suggesting that leaders primarily possess influence based relationships, possess followers, make change, and reflect mutual purposes; while managers possess authority based relationships, have subordinates, produce and sell, and coordinate activities (Rost, 1991).

I would suggest that although these works are often very useful, the separation of leadership and management is not. Although being a leader in an organization does not necessitate hierarchical authority from position, those that possess traditional predefined authority will find their leadership efforts more fruitful. The heterarchical structural model will allow for more leaders to arise in the organization. However, under this model, as they gain influence, they will still have to effect change on processes (i.e., manage a project, team, process, or initiative such as strategic planning).

The issue for most organizations is simple. The successful organization of the future will find a means to get natural leaders into key management positions, while simultaneously getting the best managers to become better leaders. Leaders and managers should evolve into the same being, the same entity. The thought that there are leaders and managers separate and not equal, but both essential, is not an appropriate or effective use of human resource capital. In the land of the blind, leaders that can manage will become the "one-eyed" masters of the successful organization.

The future sages of our organizations will possess traits and talents in the areas of process and functional management as well as human and social relations (leadership). A litany of talents will be necessitated by the transformational learning centered workplace that is evolving in contemporary America.

As leaders, managers will need to possess the skills to set a vision or future course, strategically align financial and human resources, motivate, inspire, promote ideas, develop a following, establish and define core values, encourage the culture, set a pace for performance, suggest norms for the operation, and possess a willingness to break rules when appropriate. Simultaneously, as managers, leaders will need to possess the skills to create and implement plans and budgets, organize, set appropriate staffing levels, set agendas, make rules and prevent bad ideas from being implemented, hire employees, enforce policy, control and define the normative behavior patterns, and solve problems as they emerge.

The duality and often-adversarial self-conception of leader/manager role is becoming more complex as our organizations move from production and service centered to learning centered. The complexity of the role and the duality of the ideals are illustrated in Figure 13.2. This diagram illustrates that the successful organization will possess senior leaders (managers) that are capable of balancing the best elements of each role into a forthright and determined change agent of success.

The implementation of a successful strategic planning process necessitates a team of such people, who can balance their roles of leadership and management to move their organization toward a new culture and unprecedented levels of quality, excellence, & success. These people will come to be known as inspirational leaders. They will rise when the organization needs them, and return to the group when their service is no longer warranted.

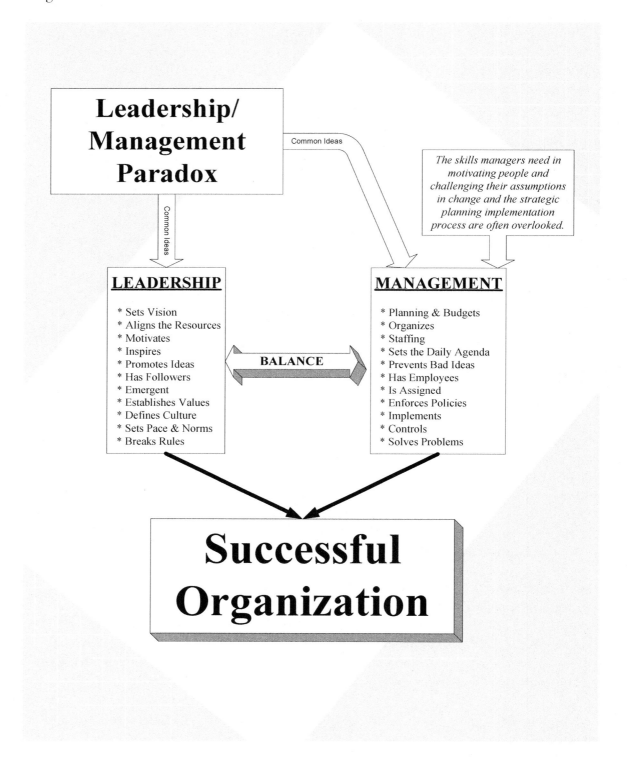

Figure 13.2. Management versus Leadership: The Most Common Misconception.

The Ideal Inspirational Model

The ideal leadership model of the future is one where a leader inspires his/her people to do their best, coaches them to prosperity and success, and listens to their problems while offering no mandated solutions. The inspirational leader realizes the necessity of letting people learn and continuously improve.

> Unlike the bureaucratic manager, the inspirational leader, as described by Welch will not be a thoughtful in the corner office guru, or a moderate policy expert, rather, he or she will be moving, dynamic, and on the lunatic fringe (Slater, 1999, p. 42).

The inspirational leader does not desire acclaim or credit, rather, he/she understands the long-term value of offering credit to others. A leader, if he or she wishes to become an inspiration to the staff, has eight essential challenges that (s)he must face.

1. <u>Create a Quest for the "Holy Grail"</u>

The inspirational leaders understand the value of a common cause, a common enemy, and/or a common goal. They envision a robust future of excellence and accomplishment. To inspire others to reach the full potential of the collective (i.e., leader and followers), the inspirational leader develops a common cause (the "Grail Quest"). A "Grail Quest" is more than just a common vision; it is a common journey of personal and professional growth.

In the learning institutions of the future, people (the followers) will come to see their work as a constant journey of personal discovery and growth (especially if your organization has instituted the personal planning process). Unlike an individual journey of self-discovery, a "Grail Quest" is a group journey toward a common end. Not, unlike the knights of Camelot, some people will take the journey alone, others will take it together in groups (known as teams), but all will see one common end, the discovery of enlightenment and glory.

The inspirational leader, shares a common vision, and develops the quest (known more appropriately as the mission). The role of the inspirational leader is to then encourage people to join the quest, to guide them along the journey, and to rescue them in times of great need. If one is familiar with the legend, then you will realize that the inspirational leader is not only the King Arthur character; the inspirational leader is also the energetic, somewhat naive, determined and righteous leader (known as the peerless knight, Sir Galahad). Like all great quests, the inspirational leader publicly acknowledges the existence of the quest, and their determination to succeed at the respective goals (be they personal, departmental, or organizational). The inspirational leader not only calls for the quest, but she/he makes the journey, and seizes the reward for the good of all. When the quests are large, the inspirational leader does not journey alone, others rise in support of the quest (mission).

Let us consider the example of King Alexander, who over twenty-three hundred years ago led his troops across a scorching desolate plain. After eleven days into the desert, he and all his followers were near death from dehydration and thirst. Alexander pressed on. At midday, two scouts brought him what little water they had been able to find. It barely filled the cup, but to all who looked on, it represented the most priceless commodity on Earth. Alexander's troops stood and watched as he poured the water into the hot sand. Alexander looked at his followers and spoke with conviction: "It is of no use for one to drink when many thirst." He knew that he had only one thing to offer his followers to help them overcome their situation and peril: inspiration to engage the mission of the day. Alexander aspired to significance and those he led followed him into history. To this day his name is hardly remembered as Alexandros III Philippou Makedonon, rather he is known throughout the world as Alexander the Great. His strength of leadership character is spoken of so often but emulated in far too few circumstances.

2. <u>Create a Sense of Urgency</u>

Once the people have "bought" into the quest, and begun the journey, it is the role of the inspirational leader to create a sense of urgency[1]. The leader examines the situation and looks for an opportunity to solve an immediate issue through the involvement of many stakeholders. The inspirational leader will first choose problems that he/she is assured success in addressing, saving the more difficult challenges for when the trust and loyalty of the people have been retained.

The 2008 election of Barack Obama again offers a clear example of how to create urgency in one's followers. In his case he used the urgency of an American need for hope and change for the better, hardly negative driving forces. People respond more to a positive mission then to the gloom and doom reactive propositions of so many contemporary leaders. Great leaders inspire a call to engage in proactive positive actions.

The inspirational leader continuously looks to improve the organization, department, or his/her fellow staff members by identifying problems to be solved. The inspirational leader is not a staunch critic; rather, the leader identifies problems and proposes solutions simultaneously. As the people grow in self-confidence, the inspirational leader will see them identify problems and create urgent situations. Eventually the leader will see fellow leaders emerge from among the followers (and all that needs to

---

[1] A sense of urgency is not a disaster or crisis, rather it is a positive focused motivating mechanism where the leader has already inspired change, and ensured a general level of "buy-in." Thus, the sense of urgency is the issue that the leader publicly identifies to motivate people into immediate action over passive reflection.

be done then, is for the leader to get out of the way and support others). The inspirational leader not only envisions the future, he/she participates in shaping that future for the organization, his/her department, for the followers, and for him/herself. This leader then allows others to lead.

3. Trust Instinct over Figures

Not, unlike the example of Dr. Martin Luther King Jr., often all the incidents, examples, statistics, and figures in our notes should be occasionally placed to the side, and we should speak from our heart to the hearts of others. The inspirational leader will learn the figures, know their true meaning, and understand their true implication, but will not dwell upon them. This leader will explain the situation to people in terms of stories that better illustrate the key points, problems, resolutions, and conclusions.

The inspirational leader has a concise and complete understanding of the situation, the assumptions, the criteria, and all possible outcomes. Once this understanding is reached, the leader is relaxed knowing the preparation work is complete. The leader should consider the reality of the world taken for granted, and allow instinct to evolve. People are moved and motivated more by a leader that understands reality, without struggling to do so. Inspirational leaders sweat, struggle, and work hard; however, they see the inspirational value in allowing it to look easy.

If the inspirational leader has done the homework, prepared the materials, and been on a lifelong learning journey of self-discovery, his/her level of instinctual ability will continuously increase. Instinct is derived from hard work, experience under good mentors, the ability and experience of following excellent leaders, and the ability to let go of the situation and not take one's self too seriously.

In the end, the figures are important, they show people many things, but the instinctual leader knows the right numbers form the many potential statistical anomalies. They can "read between the lines," and they realize that numbers are only correct if they are understood correctly. This leader often experiences moments of eureka in the decision-making process; he/she appears to always have the right answer.

4. Hold the Line on Integrity

The inspirational leader, by definition, creates an atmosphere of trust and trustworthiness. The idea of doing the "right things right," is not just a slogan, it is a way of life. The inspirational leader arouses support through the highest levels of integrity, in his/her life, business operations, relationships, communications, and in all aspects of everyday human interaction.

We have witnessed many lapses in personal integrity in recent years, especially in National and statewide politics. It is not only this integrity to which I speak, but it is also integrity to yourself, the ability to find your authentic self. Once you embrace your true self you may then find the words, work, and power to inspire others to action.

The inspirational leader believes that personal integrity and accountability are the raw materials of good character. The emphasis on integrity and honesty in everything that is done makes this leader the example to be emulated. The followers of the inspirational leader put full faith and trust into their leader, for they know that he/she will never let them down. The inspirational leader has values and beliefs that are not compromised for politics, money, or personal gain.

5. Break the Management Rules

The rules of management call for a fair and impartial leader that is compassionate and has a desire for equality among all of the people in an organization. Buckingham and Coffman (1999) have discovered that the best managers, break these rules; they play favorites, and they realize that not all employees are equal, nor should they be treated that way.

Although leaders should be fair, honest, and have the best interest of their people at the forefront of their personal values, they should publicly identify and greatly reward their top performers. The best performing staff have earned more, and rewarding them sends the right message to the rest of the stakeholders of the organization. It inspires poor performers to do better, to go the extra mile, and to excel. Rewarding all people equally, creates mediocrity in the organization, it is more likely to create a sense of diminishing satisfaction among top performers than it is to make poor performers excel.

The inspirational leader will take risks, lots of them. He or she will remember the old parable in the Bible where three men get a sack of money, one buries it, one loses it, and the third one invests and makes a profit. The story ends with the master being satisfied with the looser and the winner, while holding disdain for the coward. Inspirational leadership follows the same path; few people who try but fail are ever punished as severely as those that do nothing at all. Inspirational leaders love to compete, they love to win; therefore, they are compelled to take calculated risks that will return great rewards.

Finally, the inspirational leader will not hold information and autocratic power as a motivation tool over their people. They will shower their people with freedom and responsibility while holding them accountable for agreed upon success. The inspirational leader does not merely believe in the concept of empowerment, they continue to define and redefine the practice of empowerment at the workplace. They extend the limits of freedom. They can do this as they have removed the poor performers and surrounded themselves with fellow leaders (all of whom have excellent management skills).

Traditional management rules call for leader/managers to conduct themselves very discreetly, to not make promises, and to suggest all the reasons why they may fail prior to beginning any quest. The inspirational leader will practice the principle of refusal. The principle of refusal, stated simply, is that inspirational leaders refuse to fail, they refuse to be outdone by competitors, and they refuse to be anything less than completely successful in every endeavor. Refusing to fail, they charge forward into the abyss headstrong on their quest. They have prepared prior to the start of any journey, they are ready for action, and they have planned well. Therefore, they know they cannot fail and they share that fact publicly and openly.

6.   Believe in Your People

Inspirational leaders have the ability to create followers because they believe in the ability of their people to succeed. Leaders cannot inspire anyone unless they have faith and trust in their followers' ability to realize needs, overcome obstacles, grow into something better, and achieve in new ways. Inspirational leaders have the courage to allow others to make mistakes and learn from those errors.

Many leaders feel it is their responsibility to micromanage, preventing their followers from making the mistakes they have made in life. They feel compelled to advise people of potential missteps before they are made. These actions create cultures of follower dependency, where people are afraid to act, where they hide mistakes, and where they fail to ever learn how not to make errors. These organizational cultures are unhealthy, and often when the leader is gone, the legacy of dependency reveals a practice of inaction, incompetence, and fearfulness.

The inspirational leader observes mistakes being made, allows these mistakes to happen, and then encourages people to learn from the errors. The inspirational leader does not punish minor infractions; rather, he/she uses them as a learning exercise. The inspirational leader realizes that the best staff members are those that have learned from their mistakes, been self-motivated to improve, and have sought out mentoring, guidance, and education designed for continuous self-improvement. The inspirational leader does not fear his/her staff's mistakes, he/she realizes the value of each person, and the ability that each of his/her future successors brings to the organization[2].

---

[2] The inspirational leader also understands the negative influence of a bad, untrustworthy, and/or incompetent employee. The inspirational leader has the forthright courage to remove these destructive elements from the culture and environment.

Once the leader learns to trust his/her followers, he/she can begin to look for inspirational moments from the staff. Each day there are moments of inspiration and celebration in the complex organization. The inspirational leader realizes the necessity of recognizing those moments, learning from them, and sharing their meaning with all of the followers. It is the development of trust that allows the inspirational leader to allow his/her followers to become leaders.

7. Demonstrate through Results

The inspirational leader does not make empty promises of a brighter future that never arrives. This leader follows through on commitments. He/She understands that rewards are earned by hard work and good results. This leader will not accept credit, praise, or accolades that have not been earned.

The inspirational leader is savvy enough to understand that successful results can be found in all aspects of work. The inspirational leader quantifies his/her work, celebrates accomplishment, publicly proclaims victory, and ensures a path to success through strategic planning. The inspirational leader only seeks rewards when the quest has been completed and when the results warrant celebration and bounty.

8. Share the Wealth

The inspirational leader chooses to reward his/her people before ever rewarding the his/herself. The inspirational leader takes more pleasure from achieving rewards for followers than from personal gratification or fulfillment. The inspirational leader's fulfillment is the achievement of rewards for colleagues, followers, and the organization. The inspirational leader has a natural tendency to promote altruism. He/She realizes that the rewards given to followers should match their needs and desires, not those of the leader. The inspirational leader rewards generously, not to buy the support of followers, but to inspire them to willfully choose yet another more difficult quest for success.

Learning to Lead & Inspire Others

Leading people and developing a presence of inspiration is a lifetime goal for anyone engaged in organizational change and strategic planning. No one person is born a great leader or an inspirational presence, these are talents developed from practice, and improved by learning from mistakes. The ability that each of us has to inspire others, comes mainly from our desire to be an inspiration, to teach others, to learn from errors in practice and judgment, and to always be completely and fully prepared. Each of us on a quest for leadership ability must first choose to make it a priority. We should choose to first fail, in order to later succeed and lead. Leaders choose mentors to lead them, and they choose inner-circle followers who have already developed leadership talent.

We learn to lead by taking our organizations, departments, and selves through a change process, through deep introspection, and through our ability and willingness to communicate with others. We share our ideas openly with as many people who will listen. In every instance possible we try to see the future, to use our imaginations to picture a better place (be it a home-life, workplace, organization, or self). When it is fully envisioned, we tell others about it, and invite them on our journey (quest).

> Inspiring visions create value for others: employees, customers, and the community at large. Inspiring visions motivate people. People need to see use of the vision as a way to accomplish some greater good. (Belasco and Stayer, 1993, p. 93).

Once the inspirational leader has created value for others; he/she begins to change the organization. Change is realized through first transforming the mental models (paradigms), through creating the heterarchy, by empowerment tied to accountability, and through the development of rewards and praise.

The inspirational leader is first viewed as a heroic figure, a change agent, and a person of vision. As the leader begins the structural and cultural transformation process, they are defined as a transformational leader. Finally, when the leader has completed the change process (i.e., strategic planning process), he/she empowers the staff and holds them accountable. At this point the central role of the leader is to get out of the way, to support, and to coach. When the final stage is reached (as illustrated in Figure 13.3), the leader has become an inspiration, and has left a legacy that the organization will benefit from for years to follow.

Figure 13.3 demonstrates the transformational sequence of an organization moving from the hierarchical authority based charismatic hero leadership (in fact, most organizations never experience a charismatic leader), to the transformational change process, to the organization that plans heterarchically and is managed through empowerment across all levels of the firm. In time one, a particular leader will manage the planning process, building collaborative partnerships through teaming.

Time One: Charismatic Hero

Time Two: Transformational

Time Three: Inspirational but Graceful Exit

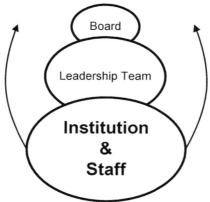

<u>Figure 13.3</u>. From Charismatic Hero to the Inspirational Agenda: Understanding the Difference.

In time two, the inspirational leader begins to transition him/herself out of the prominent position, empowering more staff and creating an atmosphere and structure where emergent leaders can develop and flourish. In the final stage (time three), the inspirational leader is present and is coaching the process, but plays no greater role than ensuring a vision, cross-institutional communication, and that the reduction in bureaucracy and hierarchy continues.

The inspirational leader rises in an organization, transitions change (i.e., implements the triadic heterarchical planning process), acquires inspiration from the followers, and has the character and courage to empower others to lead. As more organizations employ the inspirational leaders they will begin to realize the value of the followers, the need for leadership development activities, and a general belief that all people should be called upon to lead some component of the successful organization. Inspirational leaders realize that all of the success of the modern organization emerges from the success derived from a collective visionary effort. Thus, the role of the inspirational leader is only to lead briefly, not to seek glory, but to seek a common purpose of success. The inspirational leader knows that only through working toward a common purpose can real success be achieved.

Reaping the Bounty of Success

The ultimate success objective of inspirational leadership is to set new standards by listening to the needs, hopes and desires of others and by making informed decisions that will advance the organization. Success can only be found in the ability to assist others in achieving their goals. Once others have accomplished and achieved their goals, they will realize the rewards of following.

Prior to any fruitful discussion of planning execution success, it is essential to understand the real and valid nature of failure. Most leaders mistakenly view their failures in terms of failed projects, a declining bottom line or the lack of implementation of their ideas. These are the effects of failure not the causes or origins. In reality, I can name each of my failures personally; each has a unique and distinct name. At the core of each of my failings (which are manifested in failed outcomes) is a person or small group of people, each of whom has a name, a face and a spirit that I have impaired by my inability to lead him or her to success. Ideas and projects never fail—people do. To fail at leading is to provide no inspiration, motivation, support, information or communication and/or to not manifest a realization of the ability of each and every individual person.

The best and most fruitful rewards come in the awareness that we have provided a unique service to each individual that has followed us. The essence of inspirational leaders is that they serve, and their benefit is realized not by aspiration or goal attainment but by their ability to remember and follow their conscience, values and humanity. These leaders leave a legacy that endures because of their character, integrity and conscience. All other constructed leaders develop a set of skills and practices that work, but they fail to endure.

The final reaping of success in leadership is the legacy left to the organization, the followers and the collective memory. The true test of a leader's impact is a study of what happens when they are no longer the leader of the group. If that group sustains momentum, continues to grow and improve, continues to move forward, and remains successful, the leader has gloriously succeeded and known a triumph few individuals ever know. Legacy will naturally emerge from the character and conscience of the followers. Conscience should navigate the leadership journey, as it is well-formed and universal, set in the values of respect, honesty, humanity, equality of contribution and reward, and is in the presence and desire for a life that succeeds within a world that is fair.

Inspirational leaders are those people who can think to create a better workplace and more success, can act to achieve positive results and can succeed while maintaining the momentum of success. The inspirational leader realizes that risk is warranted since the phenomenon of eternal recurrence (see Chapter 15) constantly provides new and more generous opportunities to succeed. These leaders value human existence and serve the person found within each of their followers, they release the limitations of their egos, and they set new expectations of excellence for themselves and for their followers to achieve.

Never tell people how to do things. Tell them what to do and they will surprise you with their ingenuity. – General George S. Patton Jr.

Rewarding Success

Thanks is sometimes a mask for ingratitude. True gratitude is expressed in deeds rather than words. -- Anonymous

Rewarding employees is one of the most difficult and time consuming tasks performed by leaders in contemporary organizations. As organizations continuously seek to change and modify the strategic direction, the best employees look for better environments, working conditions, and rewards for their efforts. Advocates of organizational change express the need to transform traditional reward structures to match the emergent demands, responsibilities, and expectations of successful companies in the new economy. This will become even more paramount as we enter unprecedented economic conditions with the failure of Wall Street.

Heterarchical organizations will need to develop complex reward structures to match the high execution demands required for outstanding employee performance. These revised reward structures will require more regulated and authentic accountability structures to ensure that rewards are going to those that deserve them. Organizational leaders should create conditions and circumstances that enhance their competitive advantage by enabling all employees to increase their value and reap the rewards of professional success.

A Simple Truth

Prior to any fruitful discussion on reward structures or reward practices, it is important to suggest that one form of reward will always remain more meaningful than any other. Monetary compensation (whether you call it cash, money, greenbacks, the gift that keeps on giving, loot, or booty) is what most employees consider a real reward. As a consultant and CEO, I have heard countless numbers of leaders and managers talk about the value of performance, the value of work, the importance of the workplace environment, and numerous other examples of what is important other than money. They often refer to how money no longer means as much to them, or how they once worked for money and that it was a mistake. Of course in my experience these same people were, one hundred percent of the time, the highest paid employees of the organization.

The simple truth is that there is no form of reward that can replace money in those parts of life where money is used. For example, a young single mother may indeed select a place of employment based on proximity to childcare or on family friendly policies; but if the compensation rate will not cover the cost of diapers, formula, baby food, and shelter, the woman will seek employment elsewhere. Or a young male executive may choose to work at your location for the ability to excel in management quickly or to have a better title. If after a time, the high performer notices large numbers of lesser performing executives making the same or more money, the youthful high performer will choose to work for your competitor (and you will likely live to regret it). If your compensation rates are not competitive or fail to reward star performers, any other system of rewards will be ineffective in either motivating or gratifying these valued employees.

Money matters most; all other rewards are the "icing on the cake." The simple truth is that for most employees money is the essential motivation, all other forms of rewards are important but not essential. Or as I have often heard, "I could be treated this badly anywhere, I might as well have the money too." Employees that are motivated by something other than money are known as statistical anomalies. I offer this not as a point of philosophical debate, or a suggestion of what is "right," I merely state it to frame your perception and strategy in a capitalist economy. Money is the fruit of one's labor in American society; your organizational reward structure should materialize from this social fact.

Risks Create Rewards

The successful organization is composed of risk takers who calculate the likelihood of success and then take strategic actions to realize that success. These risk takers can only emerge in an organization that practices empowerment across all levels of the organization.

Most leader/managers will fear the empowerment process at first. Therefore, the first risk takers will be those leaders who fully empower their respective staff members. For organizations to develop a learning organization culture of increasing empowerment and continuous improvement, the senior leadership should practice empowerment by rewarding all employees who empower others or take advantage of the empowerment afforded to them.

Empowered organizations have a greater likelihood of success. However, unlike the command-and-control hierarchies of the past, empowered heterarchies succeed because of the strategic efforts of many employees and teams. In the past, a leader would direct staff, develop strategic plans, and manage people and processes to produce more effective results. Thus, the successful executive would receive the majority of the rewards of success.

In a heterarchy, the leader empowers many employees and coaches them to success. Many more people are responsible for the strategic success of the organization. Therefore, the rewards should be more evenly distributed, and systems of rewarding should be developed to ensure that the level of each reward is directly related to the level of performance (i.e., the level of risk undertaken by the employee). Rewards evenly distributed do not improve performance; rather they stifle the aspiration to take risks, to take on more responsibility, and the desire for success[1]. Rewards should be stratified to reflect the level of effort or risk, and of personal, team, or departmental accomplishment.

Creating the Ideal Workplace

To develop an organizational culture and environment where differential rewards are implemented (in either a collective bargaining or non-union culture), leaders will need to create systems of trust and trustworthiness by creating the ideal workplace. The ideal workplace is one where territorial games and fiefdoms are abolished, and the value of work-life balance is deemed important and essential for organizational success.

Many organizations without a clear strategic direction are composed of employees engaged in territorial games designed to control the access to power and information. Simmons (1998) has demonstrated that these territorial impulses have stripped many rational human beings from their ability to make good decisions. Organizations that lack open and honest communication patterns are full of rumors, information manipulation, and power games. Political maneuvering becomes the central focus of employees; the work thus becomes a secondary factor.

Inspirational leaders need to seize control of the contemporary organization by blasting open the door to empowerment, by communicating constantly, and by demonstrating the values of trust and trustworthiness. The inspirational leader will challenge territorial games and the fatal illusions of the current power structures. Far too many contemporary leaders gained authority based on their ability to manipulate others and the political structures of the command-and-control hierarchies. Inspirational leaders should be prepared to reward those employees that join the

---

[1] This is the point where most readers will determine that this sounds appropriate in theory, but cannot possibly work in a collective bargaining environment. If leaders develop trust, principles of the learning organization, and empowerment, they can negotiate systems of differential rewards. In the late 1990's, I served as an executive at a community college where we negotiated incentive pay increases, discretionary pay increases, incentive bonuses, incentive stipends, and merit bonuses in faculty, professional, and support union contracts. If it can be done in a Northeastern community college environment, it can be negotiated at your firm. As CEO, I later negotiated this again in a faculty contract. The incentives once enacted became very popular. In the second contract negotiated as CEO, the total time to negotiate was less than 90 minutes.

quest for transformation and the goal of vanquishing fiefdoms and the internal political saboteurs.

When rewards are provided to those who value and practice trust and trustworthiness, the silent majority will ally themselves with the inspirational leaders. In this effort, the inspirational leader will demonstrate the value of creating an ideal working environment. The inspirational leader will create visions of a better working environment and will publicly declare mechanisms for achieving his/her vision. Internal saboteurs will resist this effort. Rewarding the stars and high performers over the politically savvy will lead the majority to the new culture of learning and success.

Inspirational leaders want to create a context of openness and honesty in the working environment on every level. They believe that honesty, open communication, and the freedom to do your best work are the essential components of a trustworthy and healthy working environment. To create this context, they offer employees the ability to discuss ideas and not be afraid of negative value judgments because of disagreements on intellectual ideals.

Inspirational leaders demonstrate that if people communicate openly, honestly, and often with one another, they will develop the best ideas and thoughts, the best actions and strategies, and the best results. They teach the staff to learn, to disagree, and to be proactively discontent on an intellectual level, never allowing disagreements to become personalized, politicized, or part of a territorial destructive strategy.

The Integration of Fun & Games

The development of an ideal working environment necessitates the creation of a learning centered environment that is fun and comprised mainly of work centered games. Recently, the value integrating work and fun has been described as a worthy goal (Lundin, Paul, & Christensen, 2000; & Yerkes, 2001). I would argue that rather than making this a management strategy, organizations would be better served by integrating fun and games directly and indirectly into their reward structures and systems.

When fun is integrated with work as a reality rather than as a means to something better, the result can be the creation of a more desired workplace and a diminishment of political and territorial games. Employees becoming imaginative about how to improve the workplace are more essential than those using their creative energy to develop destructive practices to embarrass other departments or management. The energy emergent from a fun-based learning centered workplace will improve relationships between co-workers, teams, and departments. When fun is appropriately linked to the workplace, energy and creativity designed to improve work become normal practice. The improvement of work leads to the performance enhancement of all employees.

Lundin et al, have demonstrated that fun filled workplaces contain employees who choose an attitude of fun and play, who then act out their playfulness, engage others in the fun, and who are focused on their work (2000). Fun requires a leader that creates an atmosphere of play, and who encourages the staff to play with each other, with customers, and with staff members throughout the organization. Leaders need to create a culture where employees can choose to play, to have fun, and to succeed. Fun centered workplaces will be found in successful organizations and not within the unsuccessful ones. Triadic planning linked to the learning organization can create an environment of success conducive to fun and games, however, it will take an inspirational leader to engage the staff and demonstrate the creativity found in a fun and balanced workplace.

Creating Incentives & Rewarding Results Appropriately

The strategy of creating the ideal workplace of success, fun, and learning centeredness comes from a reward structure that provides positive reinforcement to star performers while encouraging less than star performers to either change their behavior or to fully accept and excel in their current positions. Figure 14.1 demonstrates a typology for reward distribution that can serve as the best method of motivation for behavioral change and reinforcement. It is important to realize that people (i.e., leaders) can inspire others to engage in proactive action, while rewards can motivate for future success.

The distribution of rewards is one of the most overcomplicated and overanalyzed processes of management. Most employees can be placed into one of four dominant types of performers. There is the poor performer who routinely fails to accomplish any assigned or generally expected task. This individual adds little value to the firm, while pilfering a great deal of the organization's resources. The most significant problem of poor performers is not only that they fail to complete their work, but that they also demand a great deal of time and energy from management and leadership. In essence, the poor performer is expensive both financially and in terms of the morale of fellow employees.

Leaders should spend little time with poor performers; no more than 10% of the total time manager/leaders spend in employee motivation should be wasted on the poor performers. Traditionally, managers spend hours with poor performers, giving them chance after chance, while hoping for better results. The inspirational leader will realize the costs associated with these employees, and begin the termination paperwork process. Poor performers should receive an initial talent assessment to determine if the work-talent match is the cause of their lack of performance. If so, the employee should be transferred or demoted. If the problem is not a work-talent mismatch, the only time the leader should spend with a poor performer is to give the necessary sanctions to ensure a quick and effective termination of employment.

Leaders should also not spend a great deal of time with an average performer. Normally, leaders will attempt to change and motivate the average employee hoping again for better results. However, inspirational leaders will spend no more than 15% of their time with average performers. Leader "face" time is a form of reward for appropriately compensated employees; it should be withheld in an effort to motivate a change of behavior among these employees. The average employee fulfills the minimum requirements of their respective role; therefore, the leaders should again conduct a work-talent assessment to determine fit. If employee fit is not the issue, the leader should attempt to motivate the employee with encouragement and with

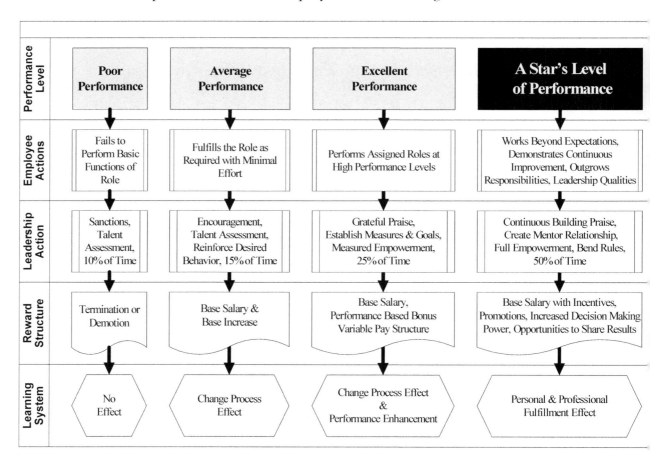

Figure 14.1. Triadic Heterarchical Strategic Reward System Typology.

reward strategies (which in this case can exist as either positive or negative reinforcement), designed to specifically address particular behaviors. The average employee should receive a base salary and no more than the negotiated base annual increase. Finally, the leader might attempt to use the learning process to change the behavior of this type of employee.

Excellent performers, a group where leaders also tend to spend a good deal of time, should be treated well and have their positive behavior praised as a model for other employees to emulate. The excellent performers excel at their given role. They perform at high levels constantly. The leader should consistently offer excellent performers a level of grateful praise for their efforts and their excellence. Leaders should use public accountability and goal mechanisms to celebrate their accomplishments. Excellent performers should receive high levels of empowerment directly linked to the accountability system and preset goals. Leaders should spend at least 25% of their time with these performers.

Leaders often are tempted to promote excellent performers (this is usually a mistake). Excellent performers are excellent because they have a talent for the work they are currently performing. Promotions do not always lead to continued excellence, and quite often they can lead to situations of future failure. Excellent performers should be left in the positions they are excelling at, they should be rewarded with a good base salary, performance based bonuses, and variable pay increases linked to the achievement of the preset goals. Leaders should use learning organization processes to enhance the performance of these employees, and/or to encourage them to develop other talents that may later lead to a promotion.

Finally, there exists one other type of performer (often confused with the excellent performers). I refer to this employee type as the star performer. Star performers differ from excellent performers because they not only perform at an excellent level in their current position, but they also work beyond leader expectations. They demonstrate a public desire for continuous learning and improvement, they constantly outgrow their current level of responsibility, and they display many of the qualities needed to produce an inspirational leader (as described in Chapter 13).

Leaders should spend the majority of their time with their star performers (at least 50%). They should mentor star performers and should view the stars as their legacy to the organization. Leaders should use continuously building praise as a motivational and inspirational tool. Leaders might offer stars full empowerment to accomplish goals, and they should let stars set their own development goals, marveling at the star's level of accomplishment. Additionally, leaders might view stars as their favorite employees, bending rules to accommodate the needs of these stars, and publicly acknowledging their accomplishments to motivate all other employees.

Star level employees are the organization's best employees (its future leaders) and they should receive a base salary with pay incentives linked to accomplishments. The star employee, unlike the excellent performer, should be considered for promotion and increased decision-making authority. Star employees should be given the opportunity to share in the success results of the team, department, and firm. The star employee will embrace the learning organization concept to fulfill their goals for personal and professional fulfillment.

The personal planning process (Chapter 12) can allow leaders to understand where individual employees fall within the reward typology (Figure 14.1). This typology is designed to provide a framework for reward delivery and reward system development. Individual organizations should develop the specific reward structures and systems that fit within both their existing traditional culture and their desired ideal culture.

The traditional strategic thinking about rewards is that they are about retaining good people, or attracting the best people, or raising employee morale. This work is about transforming your organization, and creating an empowered workforce that moves the organization toward increasing levels of quality and success. The successful organizations of the future will develop reward systems designed to both motivate employees to change, and to link rewards to strategic plans and strategic goals. The basic premise of any effective reward system should be that it can motivate people to take actions that are in accord with the overall strategy of the firm (Wilson, 1995, p. 361). Rewards are applied best when they lead the organization toward the vision and the fulfillment of its mission. The most successful organizations link rewards directly to progression toward worthy strategic goals and values.

Success is the progressive realization of a worthy goal. – Earl Nightingale

Chapter 15

Executing the Strategic Plan

Written with assistance of Barbara A. Pratt

> *We faced great obstacles, yet we did not give up; we felt great resistance, yet*
> *we did not give in; we grew weary from the long fight, yet we did not lie down*
> – Barack Obama

Outcomes of Execution-The Author's Experience

At the time that this book was first published, I was actively consulting a number of organizations in my strategic planning system. Yet I was becoming increasingly frustrated with the lack of follow through and completion of the planning process. I knew this system would benefit an organization, but in many instances the entity would begin to see some successes and then back away from proper execution. The worst enemy of accomplishment is often success. People invariably become complacent with minor successes and then pull back from the risks that will bring them exceptional performance.

By 2003, I was so completely frustrated that I left consulting work behind. I also left the organization I was professionally associated with due to its utter lack of leadership, candor, moral rectitude, and integrity. Instead, I began a search for the best organization to lead to test the theories and systems of my approach to strategic planning.

At the age of thirty-three I assumed the presidency of a small community college in Northwest New Jersey on the precipice of extinction. It was the perfect sandbox to put planning principles to the ultimate test. The local community despised the college as a result of years of litigation that culminated with local legislators actually suing the college in the state supreme court to challenge its existence. The institutional culture was one of distrust and/or apathy. The college was fiscally suffering, had little market share, and employee morale was so low I was not certain why many people even came to work. Employees were routinely watched on surveillance cameras by management as a leadership style. Extensive paperwork and endless approvals were required for even the smallest transaction. The college didn't have email with a calendar or scheduling system, so no one would have the power to arrange a meeting to discuss issues. Had it not been for public funding the college would have been bankrupt. It was therefore the perfect testing ground for these strategic planning processes.

Five years later as I write this chapter, we have transformed this college using the principles of triadic heterarchical strategic planning. Today, the public is enamored with the institution; we enjoy unprecedented public support in funding, private gifts, and in market share. The same legislators that once sued to close the college have initiated the largest facility expansion since its founding. It is an organization that enjoys no debt and maintains a significant annual surplus. Students now choose the college because of its academic reputation. Total enrollment market share has increased 83%, with full-time student enrollment increasing by 149%. More students graduate than at any time in the college's history and students return each fall at a higher rate than at any time in its history of the institution. There has been significant employee turnover, but of those who remain, nearly all have been trained and upgraded their professional skills with most enjoying promotions and advancement. Employee morale has not only improved significantly internally but it now outscores nationally normed figures at a statistically significant level. All employees are empowered to make decisions to ensure that the college is successful in its vision, mission, values & goals.

This move from a culture of failure to a climate of entitled success was the result of hard work and dedication of both management and employees. It is the result of great planning, executed precisely, rewarded appropriately, and celebrated unceasingly. The key to success has been the successful implementation of the plan.

Leading the Implementation Process

Once you have your plan in place, the work has just begun to transform your organization. Your leadership will be the essential element in the implementation and realization of organizational, departmental, and employee goals. You must lead by example, make the hard decisions, and be the model of change that can propel the organization into greatness.

The leader is the person empowered to change the social elements of the business. In a rare circumstance that requires a top to bottom implementation, only the leader can raise the organization's morale. The leader must engage and change the values, beliefs and behaviors that often stifle plan execution. The leader's beliefs and behaviors will then spread throughout the organization.

The best means to reach this advantage is to engage each employee in robust dialog about information, accountability and the results that are expected. Other managers and staff in the organization will then emulate the dialogue of the leader. To execute the plan the best people must be empowered to implement the plan. People are the key to planning. Not all employees are "doers." Where choices need to be made, chose the "doers" over the "talkers." Those who choose inertia and debate over candid dialog and forward progress must be replaced.

As a leader, you also must celebrate the organization's success in implementing the plan. Nothing motivates employees more than recognition of their efforts. While individual recognition is helpful, an institution-wide celebration can help your employees to realize that they are part of a team effort.

Once you realize that you must change the culture toward unprecedented success, that you must engage in a candor-based robust dialogue of change, that people are the key to implementation, and that you need to reward performers over storytellers, you are ready to engage in the hardest work to date. You are ready to make the changes that will leave a legacy that can outlast your time as leader.

Realism, Candor & Authenticity

In the past five years, I have come to the conclusion that one of the fundamental elements missing in organizations today is a sense of realism. People just do not comprehend the reality and context in which they are working. I have sat in meetings, where countless people made recommendations for strategies, goals, and actions that made no logical sense.

One needs look no further than at the contemporary American auto industry to see examples of failure. This industry has focused on short-term profits rather than making long-term investments in energy-efficient vehicles. They pay executives extraordinary salaries for ignoring the environment. They compensate dealerships at levels that mean huge losses for the parent company. They pay workers at rates so far above national averages that they cannot possibly sustain their market share for the quality of the product versus the price they charge. These are seemingly intelligent people at every level, but they have no sense of reality.

In weak moments, when I have been presented with such requests that remind me of the auto industry's failures, I am often reminded of the Rodney Dangerfield line in *Back to School*. When the professor asks Rodney's character where the factory should be built, he responds, "Try Fantasyland." Of course, I do not recommend stating this line out loud, but thinking it is fine. Why are so many people lacking any sense of reality?

The lack of reality may come from the utter lack of candor found in most business dialog today. In my profession of higher education we call this collegiality. Now this concept of collegiality started as a model ideal; intellectuals would debate great philosophical ideas of the time with great passion and intensity. But, all would agree regardless of opinion that everyone would be heard and that consensus should be an ideal type of outcome of such discussions. Collegiality has been so distorted that it now means we shall define complex problems out of existence by both ignoring them and never deciding that any one point has more merit than another. Collegiality today means "lets all just get along," it means it is "wrong" to challenge the ideas of another, that it is rude to ask tough questions, and above all else the ideal type goal is to be sweet and nice.

In New Jersey, the community colleges had achieved two major milestones by 2007. First, the legislature had finally agreed to create a system of seamless transfer of credits between community and state colleges in the system. Secondly, a merit based scholarship program was enacted that promised the top 20% of high school graduates a college degree by paying for them to attend the community colleges for two years then the state colleges for the remaining two years. The four-year public college leaders challenged these programs and they fought to dilute both initiatives to benefit their institutions.

In the year-long process that arguably destroyed these two great initiatives, the real damage was done in the back room discourse. The majority of community college presidents decided that obtaining the admiration of their four-year public counterparts was more desirable than the fight to defend initiatives that would benefit their students. The basis for compromise by the community colleges presidents was civility. Candor was absent and viewed as unseemly or rude. Heaps of praise were given to my colleague negotiators who at each meeting gave up more and more ground only to return to meeting as triumphant victors of the students. When questioned, the need to diminish their cognitive dissonance required them to recall versions of reality that resembled the highest levels of revisionism. These were some truly naked emperors[1].

Now, I am certain that some of my colleagues would deny my version of the events above and vigorously claim that I have simplified the facts and distorted the reality. The fact is simple, an utter lack of candor is, as Jack Welch, put it the "dirty little secret of business." It is ripping apart American institutions, it is tearing down corporate American, and it is destroying the fabrics of our daily lives.

Lack of candor blocks the best ideas, the best results. It stops the best people from getting results. Real debate and dialog disappears. Bad news is hidden, information is horded, and it has led this nation to the brink in the collapse of Wall Street. It is only when it is too late do anything that people ask the tough questions, not to make things better but to place blame.

It is your tough role as leader to return candor to a place of distinction. You must ask the tough questions, you must use candor in performance appraisals, and you must engage more people in candid conversations to ensure that an abundance of better ideas rise to the top. Be candid with your people, but by all means be candid and honest with yourself about your leadership. Candor will make you competitive, it will

---

[1] Not that all presidents acted this way, but the tyranny of the majority ruled out in the end to ensure the inevitable mediocrity predicted by Nietzsche's philosophy. In the end, the most common game of American adulthood emerged, follow the follower. A leader leads, regardless of opinion, by their conscience. Examples of leaders in my life are found in the Acknowledgements.

get the best results, it will diminish boring speeches and replace them with engaged meaningful conversation.

To those who think that candor only hurts people, please remember candor avoidance erodes trust, it leads to situations like Detroit where too many good people will lose their livelihood because they spent years swelling in fake praise that had no business in reality. Or it leads to a young person who has worked hard academically for years only to learn that the promise of a higher education has been denied to them so that some college presidents could hear meaningless praise and feel liked. Candor is hard, it can be unpopular, but like all things of value, you will learn it is worth any price you will pay in popularity if you desire results and outcomes that matter.

To become a leader capable of candor, you must become authentic in your vales and beliefs. You must ask the tough questions of yourself, you must realize your worth internally and stop seeking praise from people who don't matter. Legacy and praise most often do not go hand-in-hand. Authentic leaders know themselves, their shortcomings and their talents. They work to find the authenticity in others and they remember that all glory is fleeting and not worth the effort of piling it on themselves.

To this point I have another great example from my last five years of work. Being an avid motorcyclist, I look forward to each spring season, when I find the fresh air both rejuvenating and rewarding. I often have some of my best ideas while riding. Now, as an all boys preparatory school graduate, I ride a Harley Davidson in the tradition of Malcolm Forbes, not in the tradition of Marlon Brando in *The Wild Ones*.

However, I once made the mistake of riding the bike to a meeting of college presidents. Several months later in the midst of my injecting candor into a regular meeting of college presidents, I was asked to attend a private lunch with another president. Now, I do not tell this story with malice, as I know in his heart he really had the best of intentions. At this lunch, the president proceeded to tell me that I need to tone it down. He asks me how I could have ridden that motorcycle to a meeting of college presidents and embarrass my fellow colleagues. He commented, "I mean you wore blue jeans, I don't ever leave my house in blue jeans, someone might see me, how could they ever take me seriously?"

I have never ridden the motorcycle to the meeting again as I do not want to negatively affect my colleagues. However, I have often mused about how inauthentic a leader can become when clothing choices are the great policy decisions of a life? How far from reality has one gone? When the authenticity is absent, your leadership will suffer and so will your organization. Be yourself, be true to you, and only then you can be true to others. You will find your voice and the candor to bring people back to reality. Everyone may not listen and few may appreciate it, but you will find yourself surrounded by winners who choose action over talk, substance over stories, and real success over the self-congratulatory praise of mediocrity.

Reward Performance Outcomes

To implement any plans performance must be linked to outcomes. If you do not reward the best performers, they will leave your organization. To avoid this problem, five years ago, I challenged my organization to reach for a new idea of success:

> *The programs and services in the circles are most essential to our business, we will become and be recognized as the 1st, 2nd or 3rd best in practice in each of these mission critical, mission support, and mission service areas. The college and these programs and services are more important than any one person, office, or agenda. Those who are trustworthy, constantly improving, are dedicated first to these areas, and who lead toward best practice will be rewarded and create a legacy. The remainder will assist other organizations in the achievement of mediocrity."*

After five years, only forty percent of the non-faculty staff that had heard this message were still with the College. Most of the others had self-selected themselves into different career opportunities. However, for those who remained, the results were unprecedented. Each and every one of these employees had been financially rewarded in some way for our progress and success. Many were promoted and act today as the legacy leaders of the organization. Always reward those who achieve the performance standards set before them. Provide incentives for achievement.

Goals & Follow-up

To execute a plan effectively not only will you need candor in conversations and rewards for performance, but you will also need to set goals to achieve. In any plan you should have three to four macro level goals. Do not make them so vague that only you can declare whether they are successful or not. Make the doable and incrementally measurable for your employees. Ensure that they are within your budget, realistic, that you have the people power to implement them and that your people can see the finish line for each goal. Establish benchmarks and intended outcomes to allow employees to understand the performance goals that they are to reach.

Throughout the implementation process you will need to meet with your employees and follow-up on each goal to set benchmarks and milestones that are measurable. Too many plans are so big that people feel as if they are trying to eat and elephant in a single bite. Establish a follow-up schedule that enables employees to achieve the goals in small sequential steps. You are the leader; your adherence and preference for a follow-up schedule will filter throughout the organization.

The Seven Pitfalls of Implementation

There are seven common pitfalls that stall or diminish plan implementation. I urge you to always be on the lookout for these difficulties.

1. <u>Bad Planning</u>

   Ensure that your plans are conducted cross-institutionally and that you set goals that are realistic and achievable. Do not fall into the trap of establishing a plan that is too broad in order to please all stakeholders. The plan must be achievable and must have firm priorities and measurable objectives.

2. <u>Micromanagement</u>

   Micromanagement is the bane of all planning. Spend time working on the accountability and follow-up systems rather than minute details. Do not sit and tell employees what they should be doing. If you micromanage the process, you will both fail and go crazy by the number of times people will fail to act waiting for you to tell them what to do.

3. <u>Abandon the Plan</u>

   Do not exhaust your employees with an intricate planning process so that they do not have the energy for the implementation phase. Complete your plan with the intent to implement its goals and objectives, not to satisfy some planning requirement. A plan is a failure if it just sits on the shelf. Your plan must be available to assist you during times of crisis.

4. <u>Failure to Communicate</u>

   Develop your authentic leadership self, lead your way, speak with candor and spend your time communicating the plan, its goals, and your vision for the future. A failure to communicate can doom the most effective plan.

5. <u>Relying on the Wrong Players</u>

   Hire people who are results oriented. Rid your organization of the untrustworthy. Develop others, and help those who cannot perform to find jobs or careers that are better for them personally and professionally.

6. Talk Vision, Forget Action

Think and take action. Look for the big talkers in your organization, determine if they produce results; if not help them find an organization that values talk over action. Rely on those who are willing to implement rather than just discuss.

7. Ignore Context

Examine your organization's time and place. Get in touch with and embrace your reality. Realize how the external world and your internal culture are interrelated and take action to understand and to exploit your current context for maximum results.

Expected Outcomes of Plan Execution

The triadic heterarchical strategic planning model is designed to give the leaders the ability to provide substantive continuous improvement results at the level of the organization, department, and the individual. If implemented fully, and embraced by the staff, the following organizational success indicators should be expected:

1. The development of an effective and substantial information database.
2. The improvement of communication and company wide participation across levels, functions, and departments.
3. The synergy and unification of vision, mission, values, beliefs, and goals.
4. Increased cross-institutional decision-making ability.
5. The development of effective success tactics through strategic thinking.
6. The development of a coherent and defensible decision making strategy that corresponds with the future direction of the organization.
7. The development of a success culture that proactively avoids problems when possible and solves them when necessary.
8. An improvement of overall organizational level performance.
9. Increases in teamwork and cross-functional expertise.
10. The ability to deal effectively with emergent complex circumstances through the development of a heterarchical strategic culture of success.

Once the culture of continuous improvement and success is realized, the departmental planning outcomes will also have been realized. The anticipated departmental outcomes expected include:

1. A synergy between the organizational vision, mission, and values with those of each department and the firm.
2. Diminished bureaucracy and the command-and-control based hierarchy.

3. Increased levels of empowerment for the employees.
4. The emergence of a departmental culture of individual accountability, shared responsibility, and candor based communication.
5. The full implementation of the strategic organizational plan through the acknowledgement and "buy-in" of the departmental objectives, specifically designed to implement the organization's strategic goals.
6. The definition and realization of the core business functions of the department.
7. The emergence of authentic leaders that can change the institutional culture, empower employees, inspire action, and create mechanisms of accountability and responsibility.
8. The development and implementation of an employee talent inventory.
9. The establishment of realistic and concrete objectives that each department can be held accountable to achieve
10. The realization of the need to publicly pledge support to the institution and other departments, and the responsibility to keep all cross-functional promises.

As the departmental culture of quality and excellence is developed and implemented the leaders of individual departments work with all employees to implement a personal planning system to ensure that staff members can reap the benefits of the learning organization. The anticipated personal outcomes that should be expected include:

1. A fully realized cross-organizational synergy of vision, mission, values, and goals that encompasses the global (organizational), local (departmental), and individual (personal) levels of each employee's professional life.
2. Employees that realize the importance of their professional life and goals, while balancing them effectively with their personal life priorities and obligations.
3. The development of the organization's guiding principles for the successful employee.
4. The professional development of employees at every level of the organization, who come to view themselves as professionals in need of continuous improvement.
5. Employees who consider their beliefs and values as important and who develop a set of ideals from which emerges a culture of trust and trustworthiness.
6. Employees who develop and embrace personal missions that work to fulfill the organizational and departmental missions.
7. Employees, who regardless of level or educational attainment, have developed a plan for the improvement of themselves, their departments, and the organization.
8. Employees who candidly view their respective roles as part of a larger process, who hold their peers accountable, and who feel responsible for organizational success.

9. Employees that embrace change and organizational transformation as the natural order of the business environment.
10. Employees that view their work with hope for a endlessly better future.

Planning for Tomorrow: No End to Your Organization's Potential

Above all else, implementing triadic heterarchical planning will teach your leaders and staff that there is no limit to their growth potential. As you begin the process you will start from the global (organizational) and proceed to the level of the individual (personal). Once you have reversed the process and begin planning from the level of empowered learned employees, your organization will realize its true potential. Employees will grow with their respective level of responsibility. Leaders will grow as they lead a continuously increasing intelligent and talented staff. The organization will prosper as it becomes a outcomes-centered organization. There are no limits to your productivity and ideas, when you are setting the best agendas through effective triadic planning.

Ultimately, no one can predict the future, but an organization that has the best, most empowered employees, coupled with the best management and leadership system is more likely to succeed. Teach your people to plan, and both you and they will reap rewards for a lifetime.

Make no little plans; they have no magic to stir men's blood . . . Make big plans, aim high in hope and work. – Daniel H. Burnham

Comprehensive Bibliography

Only some of the many excellent books on leadership, management, planning, research, philosophy, and learning can be mentioned here. Many of these works have guided the development of the ideas and leadership philosophy found within this work. Selection criteria include recency of the work to either the first or second edition of this book, worthiness of the author, readability, usefulness to non-experts, and my own belief that an educated person who leads a contemporary organization should be familiar with the listed work. Certain classical works are also included, as well as a few others I often recommend to those managing under my leadership.

Adams, R. N. (1975). Energy and structure: A theory of social power. Austin, TX: University of Texas Press.

Adams, S. (1996). The Dilbert principle: A cubicle's eye view of bosses, meetings, management fads & and other workplace afflictions. New York, NY: Harperbusiness.

Alfred, R. L. (1996). Competition for limited resources: Realities, prospects, and strategies. In D. S. Honeyman, J. L. Wattenbarger, & K. C. Westbrook (Eds.), A struggle to survive: Funding higher education in the next century (pp. 209-228). Thousand Oaks, CA: Corwin Press, Inc.

Alfred, R. & Carter, P. (1998). Staying competitive: New tactics for organizational development. Community College Journal, 68(3), 30-34.

Alfred, R, & Kreider, P. (1991). Creating a culture for institutional effectiveness. Community, Technical, and Junior College Journal, 61(5), 34-40.

American Association of Community and Junior Colleges. (1988). Building communities: A vision for a new century. Washington, DC: National Center for Higher Education.

American Association of Community Colleges. (1994). Community colleges: Core indicators of effectiveness. Washington D.C.: A Report of the Community College Roundtable.

American Association of Community Colleges, Association of Community College Trustees, & W. K. Kellogg Foundation Initiative. (2000). The knowledge net: A report of the new expeditions initiative: Connective communities, learners, and colleges. Washington, D.C.: Author.

Amey, M. Dirkx, J., Flaga, C., & Ward, R. (1998). Becoming a learning college: The building blocks of change. Lansing, Michigan: Lansing Community College.

Anderson, K., & Zemke, R. (1998). Delivering knock you socks off service. New York, NY: AMACOM.

Angelo, T.A. (1991). New directions for teaching and learning: Classroom research: Early lessons from success. San Francisco, CA: Jossey Bass.

Argyris, C. (1991, May-June). Teaching smart people how to learn. Harvard Business Review, 99-109.

Argyris, C. (1998, May-June). Empowerment: The emperor's new clothes. Harvard Business Review, 98-105.

Astin, H. S., & Leland, C. (1991). Women of influence, women of vision: A cross-generational study of leaders and social change. San Francisco, CA: Jossey-Bass.

Aurelius, M. (2002). The emperor's handbook. New York: Scribner.

Austin, W. (1999a). A strategic planning workbook: Salem Community College. Carneys Point, New Jersey: Salem Community College. (ERIC Document Reproduction Service No. ED 425 791).

Austin, W. (1999b). Salem Community College's 1999-2002 strategic plan authoring & implementation strategy. Carneys Point, New Jersey: Salem Community College. (ERIC Document Reproduction Service No. ED 431 461).

Austin, W. (1999c). The Salem Community College unit (departmental) planning workbook. Carneys Point, New Jersey: Salem Community College. (ERIC Document Reproduction Service No. ED 431 462).

Austin, W. (2001). A heterarchical systems thinking approach to the development of individual planning and evaluation to synergize strategic planning in higher education practice. Ann Arbor, MI: UMI Dissertation Services, A Bell & Howell Company.

Austin, W. (2002). Strategic planning for smart leadership: Rethinking your organization's collective future through a work-book based, three level model. Stillwater, OK: New Forums Press.

Austin, W. (2004). Super leaders think, act, and achieve their way to success. In Real World Leadership Strategies that Work. Sevierville, TN: Insight Publishing Company.

Balderston, F. (1995). Managing toady's university. San Francisco, CA: Jossey-Bass Publishers.

Baldridge, J. V., & Okimi, P. H. (1982, October) Strategic planning in higher education. AAHE Bulletin, 6, 15-18.

Banathy, B. (1968). Instructional systems. Belmont, CA: Fearon.

Bannister, D. R. (1999). Chapter 1. In A. Vlamis (Ed.), <u>Smart leadership.</u> (pp. 1-9). New York, New York: AMA Management Briefing Publication.

Bardwick, J. (1998). <u>In praise of good business: How optimizing risk rewards both your bottom line and your people.</u> New York, New York: John Wiley & Sons, Inc.

Barker, J. A. (1992a). <u>Paradigms: The business of discovering the future.</u> New York, NY: Harper Business.

Barker, J. A. (1992b). <u>Future edge: Discovering the new paradigms of success.</u> New York, NY: William Morrow.

Baskett, H. K. M., (1994, March). Advice to the learnlorn. <u>Training & Development,</u> 61-64.

Bass, B. M. (1990). <u>Bass & Stogdill's handbook of leadership: Theory, research, & managerial applications.</u> New York, NY: The Free Press.

Bass, B. M. (1995). <u>Leadership and performance beyond expectations.</u> New York, NY: The Free Press.

Bass, B. M. (1998). <u>Transformational leadership: Industrial, military, and educational impact.</u> Mahwah, NJ: Erlbaum Associates.

Bear, M., Cooper, L., & Ebner, F. F. (1987). A physiological basis for a theory of synapse modification. <u>Science,</u> 237:42-48.

Belasco, J. A. (1990). <u>Teaching the elephant to dance: Empowering change in your organization</u> (Cassette Recording). Beverly Hills, CA: Dove Audio.

Belasco, J. A., & Stayer, R. C. (1993). <u>Flight of the buffalo: Soaring to excellence, learning to let employees lead.</u> New York, NY: Warner Books.

Belasco, J. A., & Stead, J. L. (1999). <u>Soaring with the phoenix: Renewing the vision, reviving the spirit, and re-creating the success of your company.</u> New York, NY: Warner Books.

Belasco, J. A. (2001). <u>The ten commandments of success.</u> Beverly Hills, CA: New Millennium Press.

Bellah, R., Madsen, R., Sullivan, W., Swindler, A. & Tinton, S. (1992). <u>The good society.</u> New York, NY: Vintage Books.

Bendell, T., Boulter, L., & Gatford, K. (1997). <u>The benchmarking workout: A tool kit to help you construct would class organizations.</u> Boston, MA: Pitman Publishing, Ltd.

Bennis, W. (1982, May). Leadership transforms vision into action. <u>Industry Week,</u> 54-56.

Bennis, W., & Biederman, P. W. (1997). <u>Organizing genius: The secrets of creative collaboration.</u> Reading, MA: Addison-Wesley.

Bennis, W., & Goldsmith, J. (1994). <u>Learning to lead: A workbook on becoming a leader.</u> New York, NY: Addison-Wesley.

Bensimon, E. M., & Neumann, A. (1993). <u>Redesigning collegiate leadership: Teams and teamwork in higher education.</u> Baltimore, MD: The Johns Hopkins University Press.

Blanchard, K. (1996). Turning the organizational pyramid upside down. In F. Hesselbien, M. Goldsmith, & R. Beckhard (Eds.), <u>The leader of the future.</u> (pp. 81-88). San Francisco, CA: Jossey-Bass Publishers.

Blanchard, K, & Bowles, S. (1997). <u>Gung-ho: Turn on the people in any organization.</u> New York, NY: William Morrow & Company.

Blanchard, K., Edington, D. W., & Blanchard, M. (1999). <u>The one minute manager balances work and life.</u> New York, NY: William Morrow & Co.

Blanchard, K., Carew, D., & Parisi-Carew, E. (2000). <u>The one minute manager builds high performing teams.</u> New York, NY: William Morrow and Company, Inc.

Blanchard, K., Carlos, J. P., & Randolph, A. (1996). <u>Empowerment takes more than a minute.</u> San Francisco, CA: Berrett-Koehler Publishers.

Blanchard, K., O'Connor, M., & Ballard, J. (1994). <u>Managing by values.</u> San Francisco, CA: Berrett-Koehler Publishers.

Block, P. (1987). <u>The empowered manager: Positive political skills at work.</u> San Francisco, CA: Jossey-Bass, A Wiley Company.

Block, P. (1993). <u>Stewardship choosing service over self-interest.</u> San Francisco, CA: Berrett-Koehler Publishers Inc.

Bolman, L. G., & Deal, T.E. (1995). <u>Leading with soul: an uncommon journey of spirit.</u> San Francisco, CA: Jossey-Bass Publishers.

Bolman, L. G., & Deal, T. E. (1997). <u>Reframing organizations: Artistry, choice, and leadership.</u> San Francisco, CA: Jossey-Bass Publishers.

Bormann, E.G., & Bormann, N.C. (1992). <u>Effective small group communication (5th ed.).</u> Edina, MN: Burgess.

Bossidy, L., & Charan, R. (2002). <u>Execution: The discipline of getting things done.</u> New York: Crown Business.

Bottomore, T., Harris, L., Kiernan, V. G., & Miliband, R. (Eds.). (1988). <u>A dictionary of Marxist thought.</u> Cambridge, MA: Basil Blackwell, Inc.

Boudon, R. (1981). The undesired consequences and types of structures of systems of interdependence. In Peter Blau (ed.). <u>Continuities in social inquiry.</u> Beverly Hills, CA: Sage.

Boulding, K. (1978). <u>Ecodynamics: A new theory of societal evolution.</u> Beverly Hills, CA: Sage.

Bourdieu, P. (1990). <u>In other words.</u> Stanford, CA: Stanford University Press.

Bourdieu, P. (1991). <u>Language & Symbolic Power.</u> (G. Raymond & M. Adamson, Trans.). Cambridge, MA: Harvard University Press. (Original work published 1982).

Bouton, C., & Garth, R. (1983). <u>New directions for teaching and learning: Learning in groups</u>. San Francisco, CA: Jossey-Bass.

Bowles, S., & Gintis, H. (1976). <u>Schooling in capitalist America: Educational reform and the contradictions of economic life.</u> New York, NY: Basic Books, Inc., Publishers.

Bowsher, J.E. (1998). <u>Revolutionizing workforce performance.</u> San Francisco, CA: Jossey-Bass Pfeiffer.

Bradford, D., & Cohen, A. (1998). <u>Power up: Transforming organizations through shared leadership.</u> New York, New York: John Wiley & Sons, Inc.

Bradford, R. W., Duncan, J. P., & Tracy, B. (2000). <u>Simplified strategic planning: A no-nonsense guide for busy people who want results fast!</u> Worcester, MA: Chandler House Press.

Brassard, M., & Ritter, D. (1994). <u>The memory jogger II: A pocket guide for continuous improvement & effective planning.</u> Methuen, MA: GOAL/QPC.

Breitman, G. (Ed.). (1965). <u>Malcolm X speaks.</u> New York, NY: Grove Weidenfeld.

Breslau, K. (2001, April 30). Looking beyond the dot bomb. <u>Newsweek,</u> 62-64.

Brill, P. L. & Worth, R. (1997). <u>The four levers of corporate change.</u> New York, NY: American Management Association.

Brinckerhoff, P. C. (1997). <u>Mission-based marketing: How your not-for-profit can succeed in a more competitive world.</u> Dillon, Colorado: Alpine Guild.

Brooks, V., Sikes, P., Husbands, C. (1997). <u>The good mentor guide: Initial teacher education in secondary schools.</u> Buckingham, UK: Open University Press.

Brown, J.S., Collins, A., & Duguid, P. (1989). Situated cognition and the culture of learning. <u>Educational Researcher, 18,</u> 32-42.

Brown, R., Kohles, R., Podoloske, D., & Sonnenberg, R. (1992). Becoming a reflective practitioner: Barriers and facilitators. <u>NASPA Journal.</u>

Bruno, R. R. (1995). What's it worth? Field of training and economic status: 1993. Current population reports. Household economic studies. Washington D.C.: Bureau of the Census. (ERIC Document Reproduction Service No. ED 391 947).

Bryan, W. A. (1996). What is total quality management? In W. A. Bryan (Ed.), Total quality management: Applying its principles to student affairs (pp. 3-16). San Francisco, CA: Jossey-Bass Publishers.

Bryson, J. (1995). Strategic planning for public and non-profit organizations. San Francisco, CA: Jossey-Bass Publishers.

Buckingham M., & Coffman, C. (1999). First break all the rules: What the world's greatest managers do differently. New York, NY: Simon & Schuster, Inc.

Buckingham M., & Clifton, D. (2001). Now, discover your strengths. New York, NY: Simon & Schuster, Inc.

Bumphus, W. (1997). Developing an institutional effectiveness model: Continuous quality improvement at work. In J. E. Roueche, L. F. Johnson, S. D. Roueche, & Associates (Eds.), Embracing the tiger: The effectiveness debate & the community college (pp. 101-118). Washington, D.C.: Community College Press.

Burgoyne, J., Pedler, M., & Boydell, T. (1994). Towards the learning company: Concepts and practices. New York, NY: McGraw-Hill.

Burns, S. (1990). Social movements of the 1960s: Searching for democracy. Boston, MA: Twayne Publishers.

Butcher, D., & Atkinson, S. (2000, January). The bottom-up principle. Management Review, 48-53.

Butler, T., & Waldroop, J. (1999, September-October). Job sculpting: The art of retraining your best people. Harvard Business Review, 77(5), 144-152.

Callinicos, A. (1989). Against postmodernism. New York, NY: St. Martin's Press.

Cameron, K. S., & Ulrich, D. O. (1986). Transformational leadership in colleges and universities. In C. J. Smart (Ed.). Higher education: Handbook of theory & research. New York, NY: Agathon Press.

Campbell, A. (1999, March-April). Tailored, not benchmarked: A fresh look at corporate planning. Harvard Business Review, 77(2), 41-50.

Campbell, D. F., & Leverty, L. H. (1999, August/September). Future concerns: Key values for community colleges. Community College Journal, 70(1) 18-23.

Carla, P., & Deming, V. K. (1999). The big book of customer service training games. New York, NY: McGraw-Hill.

Carlson Learning Company. (1994). <u>DISC: Personal profile system: A plan to understand yourself & others.</u> Minneapolis, MN: Author.

Carnegie, D. (1981). <u>How to win friends and influence people.</u> New York: NY: Pocket Books.

Carr, D. K., Hard, K. J. and Trahant, W. J. (1996). <u>Managing the change process. A field book for change agents, consultants, team leaders and reengineering managers.</u> New York, NY: McGraw-Hill.

Carter, P., & Alfred, R. (1997). <u>Reaching for the future: 1997 critical issues paper.</u> Ann Arbor, MI: Consortium for Community College Development.

Carter, P., & Alfred, R. (1998). <u>Making change happen: 1998 Critical issues paper.</u> Ann Arbor, MI: Consortium for Community College Development.

Carver, J. (1990). <u>Boards that make a difference: A new design for leadership in non-profit and public organizations.</u> San Francisco, CA: Jossey-Bass Publishers.

Carver, J., & Mayhew, M. (1994). <u>A new vision of board leadership: Governing the community college.</u> Washington, D.C.: Association of Community College Trustees.

Chair Academy of Leadership Training for Chairs, Deans, and Other Organizational Leaders. (2000, April). <u>Organizational leadership development: A participant handbook for organizational leaders.</u> Mesa, AZ: Author.

Champy, J. (1995). <u>Reengineering management: The mandate for new leadership.</u> New York, NY: Harper Collins.

Chang, R.Y. (1996). <u>Building a dynamic team.</u> Irvine, CA: Richard Chang Associates.

Clark, K. E., & Clark, M. B. (1996). <u>Choosing to lead.</u> Charlotte, NC: Iron Gate Press.

Cloven, D. H., & Roloff, M. E. (1991). Sense-making activities and interpersonal conflict: Communicative cures for the mulling blues. <u>Western Journal of Speech Communication, 55</u>(2), 134-158.

Cohen, A. M. (1994). <u>Indicators of institutional effectiveness.</u> Washington D.C.: Office of Educational Research and Improvement. (ERIC Document Reproduction Service No. ED 385 310).

Collins, J. (2001). <u>Good to great: Why some companies make the leap . . . and others don't.</u> New York: HarperBusiness.

Collins, R. (1983). Micro-methods as a basis for macro-sociology. <u>Urban Life, </u>12:184-202.

Collins, R. (1988). <u>Theoretical sociology.</u> New York, NY: Harcourt Brace Jovanovich, Publishers.

Conger, J. A. (1992). <u>Learning to lead: The art of transforming managers into leaders.</u> San Francisco, CA: Jossey-Bass.

Connelly, O. (2002). <u>On ware and leadership: The words of combat commanders: From Frederick the Great to Norman Schwarzkopf.</u> Princeton, NJ: Princeton University Press.

Conner, D. R. (1992). <u>Managing at the speed of change.</u> New York, NY: Villard Books, A Division of Random House.

Copa, G. H., & Ammentorp, W. (1998). <u>Benchmarking: New designs for the two-year institution of higher education.</u> Berkeley, CA: National Center for Research in Vocational Education. (ERIC Document Reproduction Service No. ED 416 398).

Corrigan, P. (1999). <u>Shakespeare on management: Leadership lessons for today's managers.</u> London: Kogan Page Limited.

Cornish, E. (2004). <u>Futuring: The exploration of the future.</u> Bethesda, MD: World Future Society.

Covey, S. (1989). <u>The 7 habits of highly effective people: Powerful lessons in personal change.</u> New York, NY: Simon & Schuster.

Covey, S. (1992). <u>Principle-centered leadership</u> [CD]. New York, NY: Simon & Schuster, Inc.

Covey, S. (1996). Three roles of the leader in the new paradigm. In F. Hesselbien, M. Goldsmith, & R. Beckhard (Eds.), <u>The leader of the future.</u> (pp. 149-160). San Francisco, CA: Jossey-Bass Publishers.

Crandall, R. (Ed.). (1997). <u>Thriving on change in organizations.</u> Corte Maders, CA: Select Press.

Crook, S., Pakulski, J., & Waters, M. (1992). <u>Postmodernization: Change in advanced society.</u> London: Sage Publications.

Cross, K. P. (2000). <u>Collaborative learning 101.</u> Mission Viejo, CA: League for Innovation in the Community College.

Crumpton, D.J. (2003). <u>Mastering change through conscious choice: Twelve secrets for surviving and thriving in the new world of work.</u> Elk Grove, CA: DCA Publishing.

Damelio, R. (1996). <u>The basics of process mapping.</u> Portland, OR: Productivity, Inc.

D'Aprix, R. (1996). <u>Communicating for change: Connecting the workplace with the marketplace.</u> San Francisco, CA: Jossey-Bass Publishers.

Davenport, T. H. & Prusak, L. (1998). <u>Working knowledge.</u> Boston, MA: Harvard Business School Press.

Davis, S., & Botking, J. (1994). <u>The monster under my bed: How business is mastering the opportunity of knowledge for profit.</u> New York, NY: Simon & Schuster, Inc.

Dauten, D.A., (1999). <u>The gifted boss: how to find, create and keep great employees.</u> New York, NY: William Morrow & Co.

DeCharms, R. (1968). <u>Personal causation.</u> New York, NY: Academic Press.

Deegan, W., & Tillery, D. (1985). <u>Renewing the American community college.</u> San Francisco, CA: Jossey-Bass Publishers.

Derrida, J. (1984). <u>Margins of philosophy.</u> Chicago, IL: University of Chicago Press.

Desjardins, C. & Huff, S. (2001). <u>The leading edge: Competencies for community college leadership in the new millennium.</u> Mission Viejo, CA: League for Innovation in the Community College.

Dessler, G. (2000). <u>Human resource management.</u> Upper Saddle River, NJ: Prentice Hall.

Didsbury, H. F. (ed.). (2003). <u>21st Century opportunities and challenges: An age of destruction or an age of transformation.</u> Bethesda, MD: World Future Society.

Dover, K. (1999, January). Avoiding empowerment traps. <u>Management Review,</u> 51-55.

Downton, J.V. (1973). <u>Rebel leadership: Commitment and charisma in the revolutionary process.</u> New York, NY: The Free Press.

Doyle, J. S. (1999). <u>The business coach: A game plan for the new work environment.</u> New York, NY: John Wiley & Sons, Inc.

Drake, J. D. (1997). <u>Performance appraisal.</u> Menlo Park, CA: Crisp Publications.

Drucker, P. F. (1963). Managing for business effectiveness. In <u>Harvard Business Review: Business classics: Fifteen key concepts for managerial success.</u> (pp. 58-65). Boston, MA: Harvard Business School Publishing Corporation.

Drucker, P. F. (1973). <u>The practice of management.</u> New York, New York: Harper & Row.

Drucker, P. F. (1992). <u>Managing for the future: The 1990's and beyond.</u> New York, NY: Penguin Books.

Drucker, P. F. (1998, November). The future that has already happened. <u>The Futurist,</u> 16-18.

Drucker, P. F. (2001). <u>The essential Drucker: Selections from the management works of Peter F. Drucker.</u> New York, NY: Harperbusiness.

Dumaine, B. (1994, December 26). Why do we work? <u>Fortune,</u> 196.

Dyer, W. (1995). <u>Team building: Current issues and new alternatives.</u> Addison-Wesley Publishing Co.

Eberhardt, B. J., & Shani, A. B. (1984). The effects of full-time versus part-time employment status on attitudes toward specific organizational characteristics and overall job satisfaction. <u>Academy of Management Journal, 27,</u> 893-900.

Eckel, P., Hill, B., & Green, M. (1998). <u>On change I: En route to transformation.</u> Washington, D.C.: American Council on Education.

Eckel, P., Hill, B., Green, M., & Mallon, B. (1999). <u>On change II: Reports from the road: Insights on institutional change.</u> Washington, D.C.: American Council on Education.

Eckel, P., Hill, B., Green, M., & Mallon, B. (2000). <u>On change III: Taking charge of change: A primer for colleges and universities.</u> Washington, D.C.: American Council on Education.

Edwards, M. R. & Ewen, A. J. (1996). <u>360° feedback.</u> New York, NY: AMACOM.

Evans, J. R., & Lindsay, W. M. (1989). <u>The management and control of quality.</u> New York, NY: West Publishing Company.

Evans, N.J., Forney, D. S., & Guido-Dibrito, F. (1998). <u>Student development in college: Theory, research, and practice.</u> San Francisco, CA: Jossey-Bass Publishers.

Fairholm, G. W. (1994). <u>Leadership and the culture of trust.</u> Westport, CT: Praeger Publishers.

Fairhurst, G. T., & Sarr, R. A. (1996). <u>The art of framing.</u> San Francisco, CA: Jossey-Bass Publishers.

Farrington, J., & Fuller, J. (1999). <u>From training to performance improvement.</u> New York, NY: Pfeiffer & Co.

Fogg, C. D. (1999). <u>Implementing your strategic plan: How to turn intent into effective action for sustainable change.</u> New York, New York: American Management Association.

Foucault, M. (1972). <u>The archeology of knowledge.</u> New York, NY: Pantheon.

Foucault, M. (1988). <u>Politics, philosophy, culture: Interviews and other writings 1977-1984.</u> New York, NY: Routledge.

Friedman, S. D., Christensen, P., & DeGroot, J. (1998, November-December). Work and life: The end of the zero-sum game. <u>Harvard Business Review,</u> 119-129.

Galagan, P. A. (1998, September). Peter Drucker. <u>Training & Development,</u> pp. 23-27.

Gallen, D. (1992). <u>Malcolm X: As they knew him.</u> New York, NY: Carroll & Graf Publishers, Inc.

Galpin, T. (1995). Pruning the grapevine. <u>Training & Development, 49</u>(2), 28, 30-33.

Garfinkel, H. (1986). <u>Ethnomethodological studies of work.</u> New York, NY: Routledge & Kegan Paul.

Garvin, D. A. (1993, July-August). Building a learning organization. <u>Harvard Business Review, 71</u>(4), 78-91.

Gerber, L. G. (1997, September-October). Reaffirming the value of shared governance. <u>Academe: Bulletin of the American Association of University Professors, 83</u>(5), 14-19.

Giroux, H. A. (1981). <u>Ideology, culture, and the process of schooling.</u> Philadelphia, PA: Temple University Press.

Goffman, E. (1959). <u>The presentation of self in everyday life.</u> New York, NY: Doubleday.

Goold, M., & Campbell, A. (1998, September-October). Desperately seeking synergy. <u>Harvard Business Review,</u> 130-143.

Gordon, T. (1997). <u>Leader effectiveness training: The no-lose way to release the productive potential of people.</u> Ridgefield, CT: Wyden.

Graham, P., & Hudson-Ross, S. (1999). <u>Teacher/mentor: a dialogue for collaborative learning.</u> New York: Teacher's College Press.

Green, K. C., & Gilbert, S. W. (1995, March-April). Great expectations: Content, communications, productivity, and the role of information technology in higher education. <u>Change,</u> 8-18.

Greene, R. (1998). <u>The 48 laws of power.</u> New York: Viking Press.

Greene, R. (2006). <u>The 33 strategies of war.</u> New York: Penguin Group.

Greenleaf, R. K. (1977). Servant leadership a journey into the nature of legitimate power and greatness. New York, NY: Paulist Press.

Guided by faith: Cluster pastoral planning process. (1995). Philadelphia, Pennsylvania: Archdiocese of Philadelphia.

Habermas, J. (1984). The theory of communicative action: Volume 1: Reason and the rationalization of society. (T. McCarthy, Trans.). Boston, MA: Beacon Press. (Original work published 1981).

Hackman, M. Z., & Johnson, C. E. (1991). Leadership: A communication perspective. Prospect Heights, IL: Waveland Press.

Hakim, C. (1994). We are all self-employed. San Francisco, CA; Berrett-Koehler Publishers Inc.

Hammer, M. (1996). Beyond reengineering: How the process-centered organization is changing our work and our lives [Cassette Recording] New York, NY: Harper Audio.

Harris, Z. M. (1995, April-May). A journey worth taking: Transformational quality and leadership. Community College Journal, 32-36.

Hawk, E. J., Sheridan, G. J. (1999, June). The right staff. Management Review, 43-48.

Hawley, J. (1993). Reawakening the spirit in work. New York, NY: Simon & Schuster.

Helgesen, S. (1995). The web of inclusion: A new architecture for building great organizations. New York, NY: Doubleday Books.

Helgesen, S. (1996). Leading from the grass roots. In F. Hesselbien, M. Goldsmith, & R. Beckhard (Eds.), The leader of the future. (pp. 19-24). San Francisco, CA: Jossey-Bass Publishers.

Henderson, H. (1991). Paradigms in progress. Indianapolis, IN: Knowledge Systems, Inc.

Herzberg, F. (1968). One more time: How do you motivate employees? In Harvard Business Review: Business classics: Fifteen key concepts for managerial success. (pp. 13-22). Boston, MA: Harvard Business School Publishing Corporation.

Heskett, J., & Schlesinger, L. (1996). Leaders who shape and keep performance-oriented culture. In F. Hesselbien, M. Goldsmith, & R. Beckhard (Eds.), The leader of the future. (pp. 111-120). San Francisco, CA: Jossey-Bass Publishers.

Hesselbien, F., Goldsmith, M., & Beckhard, R. (Eds.). (1996). The leader of the future. San Francisco, CA: Jossey-Bass Publishers.

Hilgendorf, E. J. (1998). <u>Assessment designs among community colleges. Revisited.</u> Neosho, MO: Crowder College. (ERIC Document Reproduction Service No. ED 423 938).

Hill, B., Green, M., & Eckel, P. (2001). <u>On change IV: What governing boards need to know and do about institutional change.</u> Washington, D.C.: American Council on Education.

Hines, A. (1995, November-December). A checklist for evaluating forecasts. <u>The Futurist.</u> pp. 20-24.

Hitt, W. D. (1988). <u>The leader-manager: Guidelines for action.</u> Columbus, OH: Battelle Memorial Institute Press.

How a teacher exposed New Era: He returns to a quiet life after seeing through the huge charity scam. (1997, September 24). <u>The Philadelphia Inquirer.</u> p. A12.

Howell, E. (2000, August). Strategic planning for a new century: Process over product. <u>ERIC Digest.</u> Los Angeles, CA: ERIC Clearinghouse for Community Colleges.

Hoyle, J. R. (1995). <u>Leadership and futuring: Making visions happen.</u> Thousand Oaks, CA: Corwin.

Hubbard, B. M. (1998, May). Seeking our future potentials. <u>The Futurist.</u> 29-32.

Hudgins, J. L., & Mahaffey, C. J. (1998). When institutional effectiveness and performance funding co-exist. <u>Journal of Applied Research in the Community College. 5</u>(1), 21-28.

Immerwahr, J. (1999). <u>Taking responsibility: Leader's expectations of higher education.</u> Washington, D.C.: The National Center for Public Policy and Higher Education.

Jacobs, R. W. (1994). <u>Real time strategic change.</u> San Francisco, CA: Berrett-Koehler Publishers, Inc.

Jacobs, R. W. (1994). <u>Strategic change: How to involve an entire organization in fast and far-reaching change.</u> San Francisco, CA: Berrett-Koehler Publishers, Inc.

Jaworski, J. (1996). <u>Synchronicity: The inner path of leadership.</u> San Francisco, CA: Berrett-Koehler Publishers.

Johansson, F. (2006). <u>The Medici effect: What elephants & epidemics can teach us about innovation.</u> Boston: Harvard Business School Press.

Johnson, N. J. (1998, April-May). Study reveals surprising perceptions of community college leadership. <u>Community College Journal.</u> 37-38.

Johnson, S. (1998). <u>Who moved my cheese?: An amazing way to deal with change in your life and work.</u> New York, NY: Putnam Publishing Group.

Johnston, W. B., & Packer, A. H. (1987). <u>Workforce 2000: Work and workers for the 21st Century.</u> Indianapolis, IN: Hudson Institute.

Jones, G. R., George, J. M., & Hill, C. W. L. (2000). <u>Contemporary management.</u> Boston, MA: Irwin McGraw Hill.

Judy, R., & D'Amico, C. (1997). <u>Workforce 2020: Work and workers in the 21st Century.</u> Indianapolis, IN: Hudson Institute.

Jurinski, J. (1993). <u>Strategic planning.</u> New York, New York: American Management Association.

Kanter, R. M., Stein, B., & Todd, J. (1992). <u>The challenge of organizational change: How companies experience it and leaders guide it.</u> New York, NY: The Free Press.

Karre, I. (1994). <u>Busy noisy, and powerfully effective.</u> Greeley, CO: Pioneer Press.

Katezenbach, J. R., & Smith, D. K. (1999). <u>The wisdom of teams: Creating the high-performance organization.</u> New York, NY: Harper Business.

Kaye, B., & Jordan-Evans, S., (1999). <u>Love 'em or lose 'em: getting good people to stay.</u> San Francisco, CA: Berrett-Koehler Publications.

Kearns, K. (1996). <u>Managing for accountability.</u> San Francisco, Jossey-Bass Publishers.

Kennedy, P. (1993). <u>Preparing for the twenty-first century.</u> New York, NY: Vintage Books.

Kinlaw, D.C., (1999). <u>Coaching for commitment: Interpersonal strategies for obtaining superior performance from individuals and teams.</u> San Francisco, CA: Jossey-Bass.

Knoke, W. (1996). <u>Bold new world: The essential road map to the twenty-first century.</u> New York, NY: Kodansha International.

Knowdell, R. L. (1998, June-July). The 10 new rules for strategizing your career. <u>The Futurist.</u> 19-24.

Kochner, C., & McMahon, T. R. (1996). What TQM does not address. In W. A. Bryan (Ed.), <u>Total quality management: Applying its principles to student affairs</u> (pp. 81-96). San Francisco, CA: Jossey-Bass Publishers.

Kontopoulos, K. (1993). <u>The logics of social structure.</u> New York, New York: Cambridge University Press.

Kotter, J. P. (1990). <u>A force for change: How leadership differs from management.</u> New York, NY: The Free Press.

Kotter, J. P., & Heskett, J. L. (1992). <u>Corporate culture and performance.</u> New York, NY: The Free Press.

Kouzes, J. M., & Posner, B. Z. (1987). <u>The leadership challenge: How to get extraordinary things done in organizations.</u> San Francisco, CA: Jossey-Bass.

Kouzes, J. M., & Posner, B. Z. (1990). <u>Leadership practices inventory (LPI): A self-assessment and analysis.</u> San Diego, CA: Pfeiffer & Company.

Kouzes, J., M., & Posner, B. Z. (1996). Seven lessons for leading the voyage of the future. In F. Hesselbein, M. Goldsmith, & R. Beckhard (Eds.), <u>The leader of the future.</u> (pp. 99-110). San Francisco, CA: Jossey-Bass Publishers.

Kragness, M. E. (1993). <u>Dimensions of leadership profile: An approach to understanding and developing effective leaders.</u> Minneapolis, MN: Carlson Learning Company.

Kram, K. (1998). <u>Mentoring at work: developmental relationships in organizational life.</u> Lunham: University Press of America.

Kranitz, G., & Hart, K. R. (1998, June). <u>Linking strategic planning, institutional assessment, and resource allocation: Paradise Valley Community College's model.</u> Paper presented at the Annual Summer Institute of Institutional Effectiveness and Student Success in the Community College (ERIC Document Reproduction Service No. ED 421 195).

Kriegel, R., & Brandt, D. (1996). <u>Sacred cows make the best burgers: Paradigm-busting strategies for developing change-ready people and organizations.</u> New York, NY: Warner Books.

Kuhn, T. S. (1970). <u>The structure of scientific revolutions.</u> Chicago, IL: The University of Chicago Press.

Lacey, K. (2000). <u>Making mentoring happen: a simple and effective guide to implementing a successful mentoring program.</u> Middlesex: Business and Professional Publishing.

Lawler, E. E. (1996). <u>From the ground up: Six principles for building the new logic corporation.</u> San Francisco, CA: Jossey-Bass Publishers.

Lawler, E. E. (2003). <u>Treat people right: How organizations and individuals can propel each other into a virtuous spiral of success.</u> San Francisco, CA: Jossey Bass, Inc.

Leanne, S. (2008). <u>Say it like Obama: The power of speaking with purpose and vision.</u> New York: McGraw-Hill.

Leatherman, D. (1992). <u>Quality leadership through empowerment: Standards of leadership behavior.</u> Amherst, MA: HRD Press, Inc.

Lencioni, P. (1998). <u>The five temptations of a CEO: A leadership fable.</u> San Francisco, CA: Jossey-Bass.

Lencioni, P. (2002). <u>The five dysfunctions of a team: A leadership fable.</u> San Francisco, CA: Jossey-Bass.

Lencioni, P. (2006). <u>Silos, politics, and turf wars: A leadership fable about destroying the barriers that turn colleagues into competitors.</u> San Francisco, CA: Jossey-Bass.

Lepsinger, R. & Lucia, A. D. (1997). <u>The art and science of 360° feedback.</u> San Francisco, CA: Jossey-Bass.

Levinson, H. (1984). Management by guilt. In M. F. R. Kets de Vries (Ed.), <u>The irrational executive. Psychoanalytic explorations in management.</u> New York, NY: International Universities Press.

Lieberman, D. J. (2000). <u>Get anyone to do anything: Never feel powerless again – with psychological secrets to control and influence every situation.</u> New York: St. Martin's Griffin.

Lieberman, D. J. (2007). <u>You can read anyone: Never be fooled, lied to, or taken advantage of again.</u> Lakewood, NJ: Viter Press.

Lineberry, C., & Carleton, J. R. (1992). Culture change. In H. D. Stolovitch & E. J. Keeps (Eds.), <u>Handbook of human performance technology</u> (pp. 233-246). San Francisco, CA: Jossey-Bass Publishers.

Lippitt, R. (1981). Humanizing planned change. In H. Meltzer & W. R. Nord (Eds.), <u>Making organizations humane and productive, a handbook for practitioners</u> (pp. 463-474). New York, NY: Wiley.

Lombardi, J. V., & Capaldi, E. D. (1996). Accountability and quality evaluation in higher education. In D. S. Honeyman, J. L. Wattenbarger, & K. C. Westbrook (Eds.), <u>A struggle to survive: Funding higher education in the next century</u> (pp. 86-106). Thousand Oaks, CA: Corwin Press, Inc.

London, M. (1960). <u>Change agents: New roles and innovation strategies for human resource professionals.</u> San Francisco, CA: Jossey-Bass Publishers, Inc.

Losyk, B. (1997, March-April). Generation X: What they think and what they plan to do. <u>The Futurist,</u> pp. 39-44.

Lucamado, L., & Cheney, S. (1997, July). Learning from the best. <u>Training & Development,</u> 25-28.

Lucas, C. J. (1994). <u>American higher education: A history.</u> New York, NY: St. Martin's Griffin.

Lundin, S. C. Paul, H, & Christensen, J. (2000). <u>Fish: A remarkable way to boost morale and improve results.</u> New York, NY: Hyperion.

Lucas, J. (1997). <u>Fatal illusions.</u> New York, New York: American Management Association.

Machiavelli, N. (1966). <u>The prince.</u> New York, NY: Bantam Books.

Mack, T.C. (Ed.). (2006). <u>Creating global strategies for humanity's future.</u> Bethesda, MD: World Future Society.

Mack, T.C. (Ed.). (2007). <u>Hopes and visions for the 21st Century.</u> Bethesda, MD: World Future Society.

Maddux, R. B. (1993). <u>Effective performance appraisals.</u> Menlo Park, CA: Crisp Publications.

Martino, J. (1993, July-August). Technological forecasting. <u>The Futurist.</u> pp.13-16.

Marx, K. (1990a). Capital. In D. McLellan (Ed.), <u>Karl Marx: Selected writings</u> (pp. 415-507). New York, NY: Oxford university Press.

Marx, K. (1990b). On Money. In D. McLellan (Ed.), <u>Karl Marx: Selected writings</u> (pp. 109-110). New York, NY: Oxford university Press.

Marx, K. (1990c). Theses on Feuerbach. In D. McLellan (Ed.), <u>Karl Marx: Selected writings</u> (pp. 156-158). New York, NY: Oxford university Press.

Maurer, R. (1996). <u>Beyond the wall of resistance: Unconventional strategies that build support for change.</u> Austin, TX: Bard Books, Inc.

Maxwell, J. C. (1998). <u>The 21 irrefutable laws of leadership.</u> Nashville, TN: Thomas Nelson.

McClelland, D. C. (1975). <u>Power: The inner experience.</u> New York, NY: Irvington Publishers.

McClenney, B. (1997). Productivity and effectiveness at the Community College of Denver. In J. E. Roueche, L. F. Johnson, S. D. Roueche, & Associates (Eds.), <u>Embracing the tiger: The effectiveness debate & the community college</u> (pp. 71-82). Washington, D.C.: Community College Press.

McLaughlin, G., Howard, R., Balkan, L., & Blythe, E. (1998). <u>People, processes, and managing data.</u> Tallahassee, FL: Association for Institutional Research.

McRae, H. (1994). <u>The world in 2020: Power, culture, and perspective.</u> Boston, MA: Harvard Business School Press.

Mendell, J. S., & Gerjuoy, H. G. (1984). Anticipatory management or visionary leadership: A debate. <u>Managed Planning.</u> 33(3), 28-31, 63.

Meyer, H. H., Kay, E., & French, J. R. P. (1964). Split roles in performance appraisal. In <u>Harvard Business Review: Business classics: Fifteen key concepts for managerial success.</u> (pp. 134-140). Boston, MA: Harvard Business School Publishing Corporation.

Michigan State University. (1998, January). <u>Becoming a learning college: The building blocks of change: A report of the strategic thinking task force.</u> Lansing, MI: Author.

Middle States Commission on Higher Education. (2000). <u>Public opinion on higher education and accreditation: A research report prepared by Strategic Communications.</u> Philadelphia, PA: Author.

Miller, W. (1999, January). Building the ultimate resource: Today's competitive edge comes from intellectual capital. <u>Management Review,</u> 42-45.

Mintzberg, H., Ahlstrand, B., & Lampel, J. (1998). <u>Strategy safari: A guided tour of the wilds of strategic management.</u> New York, NY: The Free Press.

Mintzberg, H., & Van der Heyden, L. (1999, September-October). Organigraphs: Drawing how companies really work. <u>Harvard Business Review,</u> 77(5), 87-94.

Mohrman, S. A., & Mohrman Jr., A. M. (1997). <u>Designing and leading team-based organizations : A workbook for organizational self-design.</u> San Francisco, CA: Jossey-Bass.

Mondros, J. B., & Wilson, S. (1994). <u>Organizing for power and empowerment.</u> New York, NY: Columbia University Press.

Morrison, A.M. (1992). <u>The new leaders: Guidelines on leadership diversity in America.</u> San Francisco, CA: Jossey-Bass Publishers.

Morrison, J. L., Renfro, W. L., & Boucher, W. I. (1984). <u>Futures research and the strategic planning process: Implications for higher education.</u> Washington, D.C.: American Association for the Study of Higher Education.

Moses, B. (1999, August-September). Career intelligence: The 12 new rules for success. <u>The Futurist,</u> 28-35.

Mosley, J. (1998). <u>When I go to work I feel guilty: A working mother's guide to sanity and survival.</u> New York, NY: Thorsons Publishing.

Mulder, A. (1999, October-December). <u>A systems approach to management.</u> Fort Lauderdale, FL: Nova Southeastern University.

Mullendore, R. H., & Wang, L. (1996). Tying resource allocation and TQM into planning and assessment efforts. In W. A. Bryan (Ed.), <u>Total quality management: Applying its principles to student affairs</u> (pp. 45-56). San Francisco, CA: Jossey-Bass Publishers.

Murray, J. P., & Murray, J. I. (1998). Job satisfaction and the propensity to leave an institution among two-year college division chairpersons. <u>Community College Review, 25</u>(4), 45-60.

Nedwick, B. P. (1996). <u>Doing academic planning: Effective tools for decision making.</u> Ann Arbor, MI: The Society of College and University Planning.

Newstrom, J. W., & Bittel, L. R. (1990). <u>Supervision: Managing for results.</u> New York, NY: Glencoe McGraw-Hill.

Niebrand, C., Holmes, R., & Horn, E. (1999). <u>Pocket mentor: a handbook for teachers.</u> New York: Allyn & Bacon.

Nightingale, E. (1990). <u>Lead the field.</u> Niles, IL: Nightingale-Conant Corporation.

Noe, R. A. (1999). <u>Employee training and development.</u> Boston, MA: Irwin McGraw-Hill.

Norris, D. M., & Ooulton, N. L. (1991). <u>A guide for planners.</u> Ann Arbor, MI: The Society for College & University Planning.

Obama, B. (2008). <u>The audacity of hope: Thoughts on reclaiming the American Dream.</u> New York: Vintage.

O'Banion, T. (1999). <u>Launching a learning-centered college.</u> Mission Viejo, CA: League for Innovation in the Community College.

O'Reilly, W. J. (2000, October). How to get employees to buy into your mission. <u>Harvard Management Communication Letter, 8.</u>

Ornstein, R. F. (1972). <u>The Psychology of consciousness.</u> New York, NY: Viking Press.

O'Toole, J. (1995). <u>Leading change: Overcoming the ideology of comfort and the tyranny of custom.</u> San Francisco, CA: Jossey-Bass Publishers, Inc.

O'toole, J. (1995). <u>Leading change: The argument for values-based leadership.</u> San Francisco, CA: Jossey-Bass.

Parker, M. (1990). <u>Creating a shared vision.</u> Clarendon Hills, IL: Dialog International, Ltd.

Paul, W. J., Robertson, K. B., & Herzberg, F. (1969). Job enrichment pays off. In <u>Harvard Business Review: Business classics: Fifteen key concepts for managerial success.</u> (pp. 141-158). Boston, MA: Harvard Business School Publishing Corporation.

Peddy, S. (1999). <u>The art of mentoring: lead, follow and get out of the way.</u> Los Angeles, CA: Learning Connections.

Pennebaker, J.W. (1990). <u>Opening up: The healing power of confiding in others.</u> New York: William Morrow and Company.

Pinchot, G. & Pinchot, E. (1994). <u>The end of bureaucracy & the rise of the intelligent organization.</u> San Francisco, CA: Berrett-Koehler Publishers, Inc.

Pine II, B. J., & Gilmore, J. H. (1998, July-August). Welcome to the experience economy. <u>Harvard Business Review,</u> 97-105.

Pirenne, H. (1952). <u>Medieval cities: Their origins and the revival of trade.</u> Princeton, NJ: Princeton University Press.

Porter, M. (1998). <u>Competitive strategy: Techniques for analyzing industries and competitors.</u> New York, NY: Free Press.

Portillo, J. (1997). <u>A step by step approach to strategic personal planning.</u> Lake Quivira, Kansas: Terrace Trail Press.

Potter, E. D., & Youngman, J. A. (1995). <u>Employment policy for the twenty-first century.</u> Lakewood, CO: Glenbridge Publishing, Ltd.

Quinn, R. E., & Hall, R. H. (1983). Environments, organizations, and policy makers: Towards an integrative framework. In R. H. Hall and R. E. Quinn (Eds.), <u>Organization theory and public policy: Contributions and limitations.</u> Beverly Hills, CA: Sage.

Randolph, W. A., & Blackburn, R. S. (1989). <u>Managing organizational behavior.</u> Homewood, IL: Irwin.

Ray, D. (1994). <u>Teaming up: making the transition to a self-directed, team-based organization.</u> New York: McGraw-Hill.

Ringle, M. D., & Updegrove, D. Is strategic planning for technology an oxymoron? <u>CAUSE/EFFECT (21),</u> 1, 18-23.

Roberts, W. (1991). <u>Leadership secrets of Attila the Hun.</u> New York, NY: Warner Books.

Romney, M. (2004). <u>Turnaround: Crisis, leadership and the Olympic games.</u>Washington, DC: Regnery Publishing, Inc.

Rooney, C. (1999). <u>Los Angeles Pierce College planning guide.</u> Woodland Hills, CA: Pierce College. (ERIC Document Reproduction Service No. ED 429 626).

Rosen, R. H. (1996). <u>Leading people: Transforming business from the inside out.</u> New York, NY: Penguin Books.

Rosner, B., Halcrow, A., & Levins, A. (2001). <u>The boss's survival guide: Everything you need to know about getting through (and getting the most out of) every day.</u> New York, NY: McGraw-Hill.

Rost, J. C. (1993). Leadership for the twenty-first century. New York, NY: Praeger.

Rothwell, W. (1996). Beyond training and development: State-of-the-art strategies for enhancing human performance. New York, New York: AMACOM.

Roueche, J. E., Baker III, G. A., & Rose, R. R. (1989). Shared vision: Transformational leadership in American community colleges. Washington, D.C.: Community College Press.

Roueche, J. E., & Roueche, S. D. (1998, April-May). Dancing as fast as they can: Community colleges facing tomorrow's challenges today. Community College Journal. 31-35.

Rowley, D. J., Lujan, H. D., & Dolence, M. G. (1998). Strategic choices for the academy. San Francisco, CA: Jossey-Bass.

Rummler, G. (1995). Improving performance. San Francisco, CA: Jossey-Bass Publishers.

Ryan, G. J. (2001, June). The practical politics of leadership building in learning colleges. Paper presented at the 13th Annual Summer Institute. Annapolis, MD: The Consortium for Community College Development.

Sanderson, S. K. (1988). Macrosociology. New York, NY: Harper & Row Publishers.

Schein, E. H. (1992). Organizational culture and leadership. San Francisco, CA: Jossey-Bass.

Schlenger, S., & Roesch, R. (1989). How to be organized in spite of yourself: Time and space management that works with your personal style. New York, NY: Nal Books, A Division of Penguin Books USA, Inc.

Schlenker, B. R. (1980). Impression management: The self-concept, social identity, and interpersonal relations. Monterey, CA: Brooks/Cole.

Scholtes, P. R. (1995). The team handbook: How to use teams to improve quality. Madison, WI: Joiner.

Scholtes, P. R. (1998). The leader's handbook: Making things happen, getting things done. New York, NY: McGraw-Hill, Inc.

Scot, G. G. (1994). The empowered mind: How to harness the creative force within you. Englewood Cliffs, NJ: Prentice-Hall.

Senge, P. (1990). The fifth discipline: The art and practice of the learning organization. New York, New York: Doubleday.

Senge, P. (1996). Leading learning organizations: The bold, the powerful, and the invisible. In F. Hesselbien, M. Goldsmith, & R. Beckhard (Eds.), The leader of the future. (pp. 41-58). San Francisco, CA: Jossey-Bass Publishers.

Senge, P., Kleimer, A., Roberts, C., Ross, R. B., and Smith, B. J. (1994). The fifth discipline fieldbook: Strategies and tools for building a learning organization. New York, NY: Currency Doubleday.

Senge, P. M., Kleiner, A., Roberts, C., Ross, R., Roth, G., & Smith, B. (Eds.). (1999). A fifth discipline resource: The dance of change: The challenges to sustaining momentum in learning organizations. New York, New York: Doubleday.

Segil, L., Goldsmith, M., & Belasco, J. (eds.). (2003). Partnering: The new face of leadership. New York: AMACOM.

Seymour, D. (1996, April). The Baldridge in education: Why it is needed and what the first year produced. AAHE Bulletin. 9-14.

Shaw, G., Brown, R., Bromiley, P. (1998, May-June). Strategic stories: How 3M is rewriting business planning. Harvard Business Review. 41-50.

Sheehy, G. (1995). New passages: Mapping you life across time. New York, NY: Random House.

Sherr, L., & Teeter, D. (Eds.). (1991). Total quality management in higher education: New directions for institutional research. San Francisco, CA: Jossey-Bass Publishers.

Simmons, A. (1998). Territorial games: Understanding & ending turf wars at work. New York, NY: AMACOM.

Slater, R. (1999). Jack Welch and the GE way: management insights and leadership secrets of the legendary CEO. New York, NY: McGraw Hill.

Smircich, L., & Morgan, G. (1982). Leadership: The management of meaning. Journal of Applied Behavioral Science. 18, 257-273.

Smith D. (1996). Taking charge of change: 10 principles for managing people and performance. Reading, MA: Addison-Wesley Publishing Co.

Smith, H. (1995). Rethinking America: A new game plan from the American innovators: Schools, business, people, work. New York, NY: Random House.

Sogunro, O. A. (1998). Leadership effectiveness and personality characteristics of group members. The Journal of Leadership Studies. 5(3), 26-39.

Spence, C. C., & Campbell, D. F. (1996, October-November). Learning communities: Indicators for a new vision for community colleges. Community College Journal. 25-27.

Spybey, T. (1992). <u>Social change, development, and dependency.</u> Cambridge, MA: Polity Press.

Stewart, J. (1991). <u>Managing change through training and development.</u> San Diego, CA: Pfeiffer.

Strauss, W. & Howe, N. (1991). <u>Generations: The history of America's future, 1584 to 2069.</u> New York, NY: Quill, William Morrow & Company, Inc.

Sun Tzu. (1971). <u>The art of war.</u> New York: NY: Oxford University Press.

Swenson, C. R. (1988). The professional log: Techniques for self-directed learning. <u>Journal of Contemporary Social Work,</u> 307-311.

Tannen, D. (1986). <u>That's not what I meant: How conversation style makes or breaks relationships.</u> New York, NY: Ballantine Books.

Tapscott, D. (1996). <u>The digital economy: Promise and peril in the age of networked intelligence.</u> New York, NY: McGraw-Hill.

Tapscott, D. & Caston, A. (1992). <u>Paradigm shift: The new promise of information technology.</u> New York, NY: McGraw-Hill.

Taylor, B., Meyerson, J., Morrell, L., & Park, D. (1990). <u>Strategic analysis: Using comparative data to understand your institution.</u> Washington, D.C.: Association of Governing Boards of Universities & Colleges.

Thies-Sprinthall, L., & Reiman, A. (1997). <u>Mentoring and supervision for teacher development.</u> New York, NY: Addison-Wesley Publishing Company.

Tierney, W. G. (Ed.). (1998). <u>The responsive university: Restructuring for high performance.</u> Baltimore, MD: The Johns Hopkins University Press.

Todd, T. S., & Baker III, G. A. (1998). Institutional effectiveness in two-year colleges: The southern region of the United States. <u>Community College Review, 26</u>(3), 57-76.

Toffler, A. (1970). <u>Future shock.</u> New York, NY: Bantam Books.

Toffler, A. (1980). <u>The third wave.</u> New York, NY: Morrow.

Tompkins, P. K., & Cheney, G. (1985). Communication and unobtrusive control. In R. McPhee & P. Tompkins (Eds.), <u>Organizational communication: Traditional themes and new directions.</u> Beverly Hills, CA: Sage.

Townsend, P. L., & Gebhardt, J. (1997). <u>Recognition, gratitude and celebration.</u> New York, NY: J. Wiley.

Tzu S. (1963). <u>The art of war.</u> New York, NY: Oxford University Press.

Ulrich, D. (1998, January-February). A new mandate for human resources. <u>Harvard Business Review,</u> 124-134.

Underwood, J. C., & Hammons, J. O. (1999). Past, present, and future variations in the community college organizational structure. <u>Community College Review, 26</u>(4), 39-60.

United Nations. (1990). <u>Global outlook 2000.</u> New York, NY: United Nations Publications.

Vaill, P. B. (1978). Toward a behavior description of high performing systems. In M. W. McCall, & M. M. Lombardo (Eds.), <u>Leadership: Where else can we go?</u> Durham, NC: Duke University Press.

Van Ekeren, G. (2001). <u>12 simple secrets of happiness at work: Finding fulfillment, reaping rewards.</u> Paramus, NJ: Prentice Hall Press.

Varcoe, K.E. (1987, March). Organization change principles applied to building a sense of student involvement in the educational community. Paper presented at the ACPA/NASPA Convention.

Varcoe, K.E. (1993). Strategic planning and the quality movement. <u>Book of readings: Societal factors affecting education.</u> Fort Lauderdale, Fl: Programs for Higher Education, Nova Southeastern University.

Vlamis, A. (Ed.). (1999). <u>Smart leadership.</u> New York, NY: AMA Publications Division.

Vogt, J. F., & Murrell, K. L. (1990). <u>Empowerment in organizations: How to spark exceptional performance.</u> San Diego, CA: University Associates, Inc.

Von Clausewitz, C. (1982). <u>On war.</u> New York: NY: Penguin Classics.

Wagner, C. G. (ed.). (2008). <u>Seeing the future through new eyes.</u> Bethesda, MD: World Future Society.

Wah, L. (2000, January). The emotional tightrope. <u>Management Review,</u> 38-43.

Waitley, D. (1995). <u>Empires of the mind: Lessons to lead and succeed in a knowledge-based world.</u> New York, NY: William Morrow & Company.

Walker, J. W. (1992). <u>Human resource strategy.</u> New York, NY: McGraw-Hill, Inc.

Watkins, K. E., & Marsick, V. J. (1993). <u>Sculpting the learning organization: Lessons in the art and science of systemic change.</u> San Francisco, CA: Jossey-Bass.

Weisbord, M. R. (1992). <u>Discovering common ground.</u> San Francisco, CA: Berrett Koehler Publishers.

Weisborg, M. & Janoff, S. (1995). <u>Future search: an action guide to finding common ground in organizations and communities.</u> San Francisco, CA: Barrett-Koehler Publishers.

Wetlaufer, S. (1999, January-February). Organizing for empowerment: An interview with AES's Roger Sant and Dennis Bakke. <u>Harvard Business Review, 77</u>(1), 111-123.

Whalen, E. L. (1996). Responsibility-centered management: An approach to decentralized financial operations. In D. S. Honeyman, J. L. Wattenbarger, & K. C. Westbrook (Eds.), <u>A struggle to survive: Funding higher education in the next century</u> (pp. 127-154). Thousand Oaks, CA: Corwin Press, Inc.

Wheatley, M. J. (1996). <u>Leadership and the new science: Learning about organization from an orderly universe</u> [Cassette Recording]. San Bruno, CA: Audio Literature.

Whitney, J. O., & Packer, T. (2000). <u>Power plays: Shakespeare's lessons in leadership and management.</u> New York: Simon & Schuster.

Wickman, F., & Sjodin, T. (1996). <u>Mentoring: the most obvious yet overlooked key to achieving more in life than you ever dreamed possible: a success guide for mentors and protégés.</u> New York: Irwin Professional Publishing.

Wilkins, W. (1999, May). Take risks when there's no danger. <u>The Futurist.</u> 60.

Wilson, C. D., Miles, C. L., Baker, R. L., & Schoenberger, R. L. (2000). <u>Learning outcomes: For the 21st century: report of a community college study.</u> Mission Viejo, CA: League for Innovation in the Community College.

Wilson, T. B. (1994). <u>Innovative reward systems for the changing workplace.</u> New York, NY: McGraw-Hill.

Witt, A. A., Wattenbarger, J. L., Gollattscheck, J. F., & Suppiger, J. E. (1994). <u>America's community colleges: The first century.</u> Washington, D.C.: Community College Press.

Woodward, H. & Buchholz, S. (1987). <u>Aftershock: Helping people through corporate change.</u> (Hess, K. Ed.). New York, NY: John Wiley and Sons, Inc.

Wren, D. A. (1994). <u>The evolution of management thought.</u> New York, NY: John Wiley & Sons, Inc.

Yankelovich, D. (1981, April). New rules in American life: Searching for self-fulfillment in a world turned upside down. <u>Psychology Today, 15</u>(4), 35-91.

Yate, M. (1991). <u>Keeping the beast and other thoughts on building a super competitive workforce.</u> Holbrook, MA: Bob Adams, Inc.

Yerkes, L. (2001). <u>Fun works: Creating places where people love to work.</u> San Francisco, CA: Berrett-Koehler Publishers, Inc.

Young, D. (1996). <u>Building your company's good name: How to create and protect the reputation your organization wants and deserves.</u> New York, New York: AMACOM.

Zachary, L. (2000). <u>The mentor's guide: facilitating effective learning relationships.</u> San Francisco, CA: Jossey-Bass.

Zachary, L. J. (2005) <u>Creating a mentoring culture: The organization's guide.</u> San Francisco, CA: Jossey-Bass.

Zand, D. E. (1997). <u>The leadership triad: Knowledge, trust, and power.</u> New York, NY: Oxford University Press.

Zeichner, K.M. & Liston, D.P. (1987). Teaching student teachers to reflect. <u>Harvard Educational Review, 57</u> (1), 23-48.

Zeiss, T. (1997). <u>Developing the world's best workforce.</u> Washington, DC: American Association of Community Colleges.

Printed in Great Britain
by Amazon